Lectures on
Advanced Econometric Theory

Lectures on Advanced Econometric Theory

Denis Sargan

Edited and
with an Introduction by
Meghnad Desai

Basil Blackwell

First published 1988

Basil Blackwell Ltd
108 Cowley Road, Oxford, OX4 1JF, UK

Basil Blackwell Inc.
432 Park Avenue South, Suite 1503
New York, NY 10016, USA

British Library Cataloguing in Publication Data

Sargan, Denis
Lectures on advanced econometric theory
1. Econometrics
I. Title II. Desai, Meghnad
330′.028

ISBN 0-631-14956-2

Library of Congress Cataloging-in-Publication Data

Sargan, John Denis.
Lectures on advanced econometric theory / Denis Sargan: edited and with an introduction by Meghnad Desai.
p. cm.
Lectures delivered in a course at the London School of Economics in 1983–1984.
Bibliography: p.
Includes index.
ISBN 0-631-14956-2
1. Econometrics. I. Desai, Meghnad. II. Title.
HB139.S26 1988
330′.028–dc 19 88-5093
CIP

Typeset in 10½ on 12 pt Times by Unicus Graphics Ltd, Horsham
Printed in Great Britain by Bookcraft Ltd, Bath, Avon

Contents

Introduction

When Denis Sargan decided to take the early retirement option at sixty, many of his students and colleagues realized that an era in econometrics teaching and research was about to end. Denis arrived at LSE from Leeds in 1964 as Reader in Statistics and became Professor of Econometrics in 1965. He went on to teach and research in econometrics at LSE for the next twenty years setting new standards of rigour and innovativeness. The MSc Econometrics and Mathematical Economics course which he taught at first with Bill Phillips and later with Frank Hahn, Terence Gorman and Amartya Sen trained a score of students each year, all carefully selected and put through a most demanding regime. The fame of the LSE course in econometrics spread as did that of Denis. His presidency of the Econometric Society in 1980 and the ranking in 1987 of LSE's department as the best in theoretical econometrics in the world are but two pieces of evidence. Denis was also made the Tooke Professor of Economic Science and Statistics in 1982.

These lectures were recorded in 1983–4 – Denis's last active year as a teacher of the course Advanced Econometric Theory. Two students, Franco Peracchi and Pedro Gonzalez, recorded them. The idea at first was to have them typed up and given to Denis as a surprise present on his retirement. The temptation to have them published was however too great for his associates so we decided to show Denis the typescript; he has gone over it and made various amendments. The normal delays of having technical manuscripts typed and checked, not to mention my own commitments, have delayed publication up to now. But I am happy to have been associated in a small way with bringing these lectures, at last, to a larger public. I must thank David Hendry and Peter Phillips, both former students of Denis, for their encouragement for this project.

Reading these lectures with their terse style and very compact presentation of advanced material will give some idea of what it must have been like to be a student. Some econometrics textbooks make the going so easy that one feels as if one is travelling at a slow stately pace in a luxury liner. Others offer speed with comfort, much like flying in a 747. There are some which add speed to glamour as in a Concorde. But the highly professional approach with speed and sparse comfort is best compared to the Blackbird which flies at Mach 2. You only ride it when you want no frills, fast travel from here to there, but you have to be well prepared to take it.

Meghnad Desai

Preface

In 1983–4 when I was about to retire, Meghnad Desai arranged that two of the MSc students taking my course on econometric theory at LSE should produce transcripts of the lectures so that these might form the basis of a book. When it was accepted for publication I revised it so that it now more closely resembles the course as I gave it, both in intention and motivation. The course was originally conceived to allow the student to derive most of the asymptotic theory of the linear simultaneous equation model from a few clearly stated theorems of asymptotic theory.

I am thankful to Franco Peracchi and Pedro Gonzalez for providing the original material and to Jonathan Thomas for his work on a later draft, and also to Christine Wills, Pandora Geddes and Jean Canfield who were responsible for the typing. Finally I am grateful to Meghnad Desai for initiating and organizing this work.

Denis Sargan

1

Foundations of Asymptotic Theory

1.1 Results on Convergence and on Orders of Magnitude

1.1.1 Convergence of a Sequence of Random Variables (r.v.s)

Let $\{X_T\}$ be a sequence of *random variables* (r.v.s) indexed by T and let $F_T(x) = \Pr\{X_T < x\}$ be the cumulative distribution function of X_T. $F_T(x)$ is assumed to satisfy all the usual properties (see Rao, 1973), pp. 84–7), in particular the only discontinuities that $F_T(\cdot)$ can have are upward jumps, and

$$\lim_{\substack{h \to 0 \\ h>0}} F_T(x + h) = F_T(x).$$

Definition 1: The definition of r.v.s $\{X_T\}$ is said to converge in distribution to a r.v. X with cumulative distribution function F_∞, written $X_T \xrightarrow{D} X$, if $\lim_{T \to \infty} F_T(x) = F_\infty(x)$ at all continuity points of F_∞.

Consider the special case when the limiting probability density function is a unit step function at some value x^*. As $T \to \infty$ the median of the distribution of X_T tends to x^* and the horizontal scale of the distribution, measured in terms of any central percentile tends to zero. In this case Definition 1 is equivalent to the following:

Definition 2: The sequence of r.v.s $\{X_T\}$ is said to converge in probability to the constant x^*, written $\operatorname{plim} X_T = x^*$, if for every given $\delta > 0$

$$\lim_{T\to\infty} \Pr\{|X_T - x^*| \geq \delta\} = 0.$$

Theorem 1 (Slutsky Theorem): Let X_T be a sequence of r.v.s with plim $X_T = x^*$. If $Y_T = f(X_T)$ and $f(\ )$ is continuous at x^* then

$$\text{plim } Y_T = f(\text{plim } X_T) = f(x^*).$$

Definition 2 and Theorem 1 can be generalized to the case in which X_T is a vector r.v. or a matrix whose elements are r.v.s (see Fuller, 1976, p. 188).

Example 1: Consider the matrix of 2nd moments $\mathbf{X}_T'\mathbf{X}_T/T$ and assume that

$$\text{plim } (\mathbf{X}_T'\mathbf{X}_T/T) = \mathbf{M}$$

the matrix $\mathbf{M}$ is a finite, positive definite matrix.

Since $\mathbf{M}$ is non-singular, $\mathbf{M}^{-1}$ exists. Since the inverse transformation is a continuous function of the elements of a matrix at any point where the matrix is non-singular, one can apply the Slutsky Theorem to obtain

$$\text{plim}\left(\frac{\mathbf{X}_T'\mathbf{X}_T}{T}\right)^{-1} = \left[\text{plim}\left(\frac{\mathbf{X}_T'\mathbf{X}_T}{T}\right)\right]^{-1} = \mathbf{M}^{-1}.$$

Example 2: Consider the latent roots of the matrix $(\mathbf{X}_T'\mathbf{X}_T/T)$. These are the solution of the determinantal equation

$$\det\left(\frac{\mathbf{X}_T'\mathbf{X}_T}{T} - \lambda\mathbf{I}\right) = 0.$$

Since the latent roots are continuous functions of the elements of $(\mathbf{X}_T'\mathbf{X}_T/T)$, applying the Slutsky Theorem gives

$$\text{plim } \lambda = \bar{\lambda}$$

where $\det(\mathbf{M} - \bar{\lambda}\mathbf{I}) = 0$.

A stronger definition of convergence is the following:

Definition 3: The sequence of r.v.s $\{X_T\}$ is said to converge in mean square to the constant x^* if

$$\lim_{T\to\infty} \mathrm{E}\,(X_T - x^*)^2 = 0.$$

(Convergence in mean square implies convergence in probability, and hence in distribution). This is a straightforward consequence of Chebyshev's Inequality.

(Thus, when x^* is a constant, one has the following relations between the various definitions of convergence

convergence in mean square → convergence in probability
→ convergence in distribution.)

1.1.2 Orders of Magnitude

In a non-stochastic set-up, one has the following definitions:

Definition 4: Given two sequences of real numbers $\{a_T\}$ and $\{\phi_T\}$ we say that a_T is of order ϕ_T written $a_T = \mathrm{O}(\phi_T)$, if there exists a constant $\mathrm{M} > 0$ such that $|a_T/\phi_T| < \mathrm{M}$ for all T. Clearly $a_T = \mathrm{O}(1)$ if the sequence $\{a_T\}$ is bounded.

Definition 5: Given two sequences of real numbers $\{a_T\}$ and $\{\phi_T\}$ we say that a_T is of lower order than ϕ_T, written $a_T = \mathrm{o}(\phi_T)$ if

$$\lim_{T\to\infty}\left|\frac{a_T}{\phi_T}\right| = 0.$$

Clearly $a_T = \mathrm{o}(\phi_T)$ implies that $a_T = \mathrm{O}(\phi_T)$.

The definitions of order of magnitude can be extended to sequences of r.v.s by replacing the notion of boundedness by boundedness in probability and that of limit by the notion of convergence in probability.

Definition 6: Given a sequence $\{X_T\}$ of real r.v.s and a sequence $\{\phi_T\}$ of real numbers, we say that X_T is of the order in probability ϕ_T written $X_T = \mathrm{O_p}(\phi_T)$ if for any $\varepsilon > \mathrm{o}$ there exists M_ε such that for all T

$$\Pr\left\{\left|\frac{X_T}{\phi_T}\right| > \mathrm{M}_\varepsilon\right\} \leq \varepsilon.$$

Definition 7: Given a sequence $\{X_T\}$ of real r.v.s and a sequence $\{\phi_T\}$ of real numbers we can say that X_T is of smaller order in probability than $\phi_T = \mathrm{o_p}(\phi_T)$ if

$$\operatorname{plim}\left|\frac{X_T}{\phi_T}\right| = 0.$$

The algebra of non-stochastic orders of magnitude holds for orders in probability (see Fuller, 1976, pp. 180, 189–91). So one has the following:

Theorem 2: Let $\{X_T\}$ and $\{Y_T\}$ be sequences of real r.v.s and $\{\phi_T\}$ and $\{\psi_T\}$ be sequences of (positive) real numbers.

(i) If $X_T = O_p(\phi_T)$ and $Y_T = O_p(\psi_T)$ then

$$X_T Y_T = O_p(\phi_T \psi_T)$$
$$|X_T|^s = O_p(\phi_T^s) \qquad s \geq 0$$
$$X_T + Y_T = O_p[\max(\phi_T, \psi_T)].$$

(ii) If $X_T = o_p(\phi_T)$ and $Y_T = o_p(\psi_T)$ then

$$X_T Y_T = o_p(\phi_T \psi_T)$$
$$|X_T|^s = o_p(\phi_T^s) \qquad s \geq 0$$
$$X_T + Y_T = o_p[\max(\phi_T, \psi_T)].$$

(iii) If $X_T = o_p(\phi_T)$ and $Y_T = O_p(\psi_T)$ then

$$X_T Y_T = o_p(\phi_T \psi_T).$$

A sufficient condition for $X_T = O_p(\phi_T)$ is that $E(X_T^2) = O(\phi_T^2)$ (notice that the latter is a non-stochastic order of magnitude). The converse is however not true, i.e., $X_T = O_p(\phi_T)$ does not imply that $E(X_T^2) = O(\phi_T^2)$.

1.1.3 Mann and Wald Approximation Theorem

The definition of convergence in probability can be generalized to the case in which x^* is not a constant but is itself a r.v. whose distribution does not depend on T.

Definition 8: The sequence of r.v.s $\{X_T\}$ is said to converge in probability to the r.v. X, written $X_T \underset{\rightarrow}{p} X$, if plim $|X_T - X| = 0$. Convergence in probability implies convergence in distribution (notice however that the converse is not true):

Theorem 3 (Mann and Wald Approximation Theorem): Let $\{X_T, Y_T\}$ be a sequence of pairs of r.v.s such that plim $|X_T - Y_T| = 0$. Then

$$X_T \underset{\rightarrow}{D} X \Rightarrow Y_T \underset{\rightarrow}{D} X.$$

1.1.4 Transformation Theorems

Suppose that $X_T \underset{\rightarrow}{D} X$. What is the limiting distribution of a r.v. Y_T

which is a function of X_T?

First consider the case in which Y_T is a linear function of X_T, say, $Y_T = A_T X_T$.

Theorem 4 (Cramer Linear Transformation Theorem): Let $\{\mathbf{X}_T\}$ be a sequence of random vectors and let $\{\mathbf{A}_T\}$ be a sequence of random rectangular or square matrices of appropriate order. Then

$$\mathbf{X}_T \underset{\rightarrow}{\mathrm{D}} \mathbf{X} \text{ and } \operatorname{plim} \mathbf{A}_T = \mathbf{A} \rightarrow \mathbf{A}_T X_T \underset{\rightarrow}{\mathrm{D}} \mathbf{AX}.$$

It follows from Theorem 4 that if $\mathbf{X}_T \underset{\rightarrow}{\mathrm{D}} \mathbf{X}$, where $\mathbf{X} \sim N(\boldsymbol{\mu}, \boldsymbol{\Omega})$ and $\operatorname{plim} \mathbf{A}_T = \mathbf{A}$, then $\mathbf{Y}_T$ is asymptotically normally distributed with mean $\mathbf{A}\boldsymbol{\mu}$ and variance $\mathbf{A\Omega A}'$, in short $\mathbf{Y}_T \mathrel{\widetilde{a}} N(\mathbf{A}\mu, \mathbf{A\Omega A}')$. (Note the notation $\widetilde{a}$ means that the left-hand stochastic variable has the asymptotic distribution specified on the right-hand side.)

Example 3: Consider the linear regression model

$$\mathbf{y}_t = \underset{(1 \times n)}{\mathbf{x}_t'} \underset{(n \times 1)}{\beta} + u_t, \qquad u_t \sim \mathrm{IID}(0, \sigma^2), \tag{1.1}$$

where the vector $\mathbf{x}_t$ also contains lagged dependent variables.

In matrix notation (1.1) can be written as

$$\underset{(T \times 1)}{\mathbf{y}} = \underset{(T \times n)}{\mathbf{X}} \underset{(n \times 1)}{\beta} + \underset{(T \times 1)}{\mathbf{u}},$$

$$\mathrm{E}(\mathbf{u}) = 0, \ \mathrm{E}(\mathbf{uu}') = \sigma^2 \mathbf{I}_T. \tag{1.2}$$

The least squares equations lead to

$$\mathbf{X}'\mathbf{X}\,(\hat{\boldsymbol{\beta}} - \boldsymbol{\beta}) = \mathbf{X}'\mathbf{u} \tag{1.3}$$

where $\hat{\boldsymbol{\beta}}$ denotes the OLS estimator.

Assume that

(i) $\operatorname{plim} (\mathbf{X}'\mathbf{X}/T) = \mathbf{M}$.

(ii) $\mathbf{M}$ is a finite, positive definite matrix ('no multicollinearity' assumption).

(iii) $\mathbf{w} = \dfrac{\mathbf{X}'\mathbf{u}}{\sqrt{T}} \mathrel{\widetilde{a}} \mathrm{N}(0, \sigma^2\mathbf{M})$.

Notice that $\mathbf{w} = \mathrm{O_p}(1)$. This suggests that the proper rescaling for (1.3) is obtained by dividing both sides by $\sqrt{T}$:

$$\frac{\mathbf{X}'\mathbf{X}}{T}\sqrt{T}\,(\hat{\boldsymbol{\beta}} - \boldsymbol{\beta}) = \frac{\mathbf{X}'\mathbf{u}}{\sqrt{T}}.$$

By the Slutsky Theorem,

$$\text{plim}\,\frac{\mathbf{X}'\mathbf{X}^{-1}}{T} = \left[\text{plim}\,\frac{\mathbf{X}'\mathbf{X}}{T}\right]^{-1} = \mathbf{M}^{-1}.$$

Then, by applying the Cramer Linear Transformation Theorem

$$\sqrt{T}(\hat{\boldsymbol{\beta}} - \boldsymbol{\beta}) = \frac{\mathbf{X}'\mathbf{X}^{-1}}{T}\,\mathbf{w} \;\tilde{a}\; \mathrm{N}(0, \sigma^2\mathbf{M}^{-1}\mathbf{M}\mathbf{M}^{-1})$$

i.e.

$$\sqrt{T}(\hat{\boldsymbol{\beta}} - \boldsymbol{\beta}) \;\tilde{a}\; \mathrm{N}(0, \sigma^2\mathbf{M}^{-1}).^{(1)}$$

When Y_T is a general function of X_T, say $Y_T = f(X_T)$, one has the following result.

Theorem 5 (General Transformation Theorem): Let $\{X_T\}$ be a sequence of r.v.s and let the function $f: X_T \rightarrow f(X_T)$ be continuous almost everywhere[(2)] and independent of T. Then if

$$X_T \underset{\rightarrow}{\mathrm{D}} X \qquad f(X_T) \underset{\rightarrow}{\mathrm{D}} f(X).$$

Theorem 5 can be generalized to the case in which X_T is a vector r.v. and f is a vector valued function (see Fuller, 1976, p. 196).

Example 4: Consider the $(T \times n)$ stochastic matrix $\mathbf{X}$ introduced in Example 3. Let $\mathbf{M}_T = \mathbf{X}'\mathbf{X}/T$ and assume that $\text{plim}\,\mathbf{M}_T = \mathbf{M}$, a finite, positive definite matrix. Define the vector

$$\mathbf{e}_T := \text{vec}\,[\sqrt{T}(\mathbf{M}_T - \mathbf{M})].$$

This is an $[n(n+1)/2 \times 1]$ vector, since $\mathbf{X}'\mathbf{X}$ is an $(n \times n)$ symmetric matrix. Assume that

$$\mathbf{e}_T \;\tilde{a}\; \mathrm{N}(0, \boldsymbol{\Omega}_e)$$

where $\boldsymbol{\Omega}_e = \lim_{T\to\infty} \mathrm{E}(\mathbf{e}_T\mathbf{e}'_T)$, provided that the expectations exist for all T. We want to test whether the $\mathbf{M}$ satisfies some set of constraints, e.g. $\mathbf{M}$ is diagonal. First notice that if $\mathbf{e} \sim \mathrm{N}(0, \boldsymbol{\Omega}_e)$, then

[1]The variance matrix of the asymptotic normal distribution is called the asymptotic variance matrix and may be abbreviated to be called the AVM. Thus in this case the AVM is $\sigma^2\mathbf{M}^{-1}$.

[2]Almost everywhere with respect to the asymptotic distribution, i.e. the probability of the X_T being contained in the set of discontinuities tends to zero as $T\rightarrow\infty$.

$$\mathbf{e}'_T\, \boldsymbol{\Omega}_e^{-1}\, \mathbf{e}_T \ \tilde{a}\ \chi^2\left[\frac{n(n+1)}{2}\right].$$

Since $\mathbf{e}_T \underset{\rightarrow}{D} \mathbf{e}$, it then follows from Theorem 5 that

$$\mathbf{e}'_T\, \hat{\boldsymbol{\Omega}}_e^{-1}\, \mathbf{e}_T \ \tilde{a}\ \chi^2\left[\frac{n(n+1)}{2}\right].$$

In practice, however, the matrices $\boldsymbol{\Omega}_e$ and $\mathbf{M}$ are unknown. Suppose first that $\mathbf{M}$ is diagonal and $\boldsymbol{\Omega}_e$ is a continuous function of a set of parameters $\boldsymbol{\theta}$ say $\boldsymbol{\Omega}_e = \boldsymbol{\Omega}_e(\boldsymbol{\theta})$ and suppose that $\boldsymbol{\theta}$ is unknown but can be estimated consistently by $\hat{\boldsymbol{\theta}}$, i.e., plim $\hat{\boldsymbol{\theta}} = \boldsymbol{\theta}$. Let $\hat{\boldsymbol{\Omega}}_e = \boldsymbol{\Omega}_e(\hat{\boldsymbol{\theta}})$. Then by the Slutsky Theorem

$$\text{plim}\ \hat{\boldsymbol{\Omega}}_e = \boldsymbol{\Omega}_e.$$

This result can be applied to the above problem. Let

$$\mathbf{e}'_T\hat{\boldsymbol{\Omega}}_e^{-1}\mathbf{e}_T = f(\mathbf{e}_T, \hat{\boldsymbol{\Omega}}_e).$$

Since $\mathbf{e}_T \underset{\rightarrow}{D} \mathbf{e}$ and plim $\hat{\boldsymbol{\Omega}}_e = \boldsymbol{\Omega}_e$, it follows from the General Transformation Theorem that $f(\mathbf{e}_T, \boldsymbol{\Omega}_e) \underset{\rightarrow}{D} f(\mathbf{e}, \boldsymbol{\Omega}_e)$, i.e.

$$\mathbf{e}'_T\, \hat{\boldsymbol{\Omega}}_e^{-1}\, \mathbf{e}_T \ \tilde{a}\ \chi^2\left[\frac{n(n+1)}{2}\right].$$

Of course in practice, $\mathbf{M}$ is also unknown, and we would have to consider an alternative criterion, but in the case where we are testing for diagonality we can simply reduce e_T to a $\frac{1}{2}[n(n-1)]$ vector by omitting diagonal elements, and test in the same way.

Example 5: Write model (1.2) as

$$\mathbf{y} = \underset{(T\times n_1)}{\mathbf{X}_1}\ \underset{(n_1\times 1)}{\boldsymbol{\beta}_1} + \underset{(T\times n_2)}{\mathbf{X}_2}\ \underset{(n_1\times 1)}{\boldsymbol{\beta}_2} + \mathbf{u}$$

where $n_1 + n_2 = n$ and consider testing the null hypothesis that $\boldsymbol{\beta}_1 = \bar{\boldsymbol{\beta}}_1$ against the alternative that $\boldsymbol{\beta}_1 \neq \bar{\boldsymbol{\beta}}_1$.

Partition the matrix $(\mathbf{X}'\mathbf{X}/T)^{-1}$ as

$$\left(\frac{\mathbf{X}'\mathbf{X}}{\mathrm{T}}\right)^{-1} = \begin{pmatrix} \mathbf{K}_{11} & \mathbf{K}_{12} \\ \mathbf{K}_{21} & \mathbf{K}_{22} \end{pmatrix}.$$

and let

$$\text{plim}\left(\frac{\mathbf{X}'\mathbf{X}}{T}\right)^{-1} = \mathbf{M}^{-1} = \begin{pmatrix} \bar{\mathbf{K}}_{11} & \bar{\mathbf{K}}_{12} \\ \bar{\mathbf{K}}_{21} & \bar{\mathbf{K}}_{22} \end{pmatrix}.$$

Since $\mathbf{M}^{-1}$ is a positive definite matrix both $\bar{\mathbf{K}}_{11}$ and $\bar{\mathbf{K}}_{22}$ are positive definite matrices.

As a test statistic consider

$$\xi_T = \frac{T(\hat{\boldsymbol{\beta}}_1 - \bar{\boldsymbol{\beta}}_1)'\mathbf{K}_{11}^{-1}(\hat{\boldsymbol{\beta}}_1 - \bar{\boldsymbol{\beta}}_1)}{s^2}$$

$$= \frac{[\sqrt{T}(\hat{\boldsymbol{\beta}}_1 - \bar{\boldsymbol{\beta}}_1)]'\mathbf{K}_{11}^{-1}[\sqrt{T}(\hat{\boldsymbol{\beta}}_1 - \bar{\boldsymbol{\beta}}_1)]}{s^2}$$

where $s^2 = (\mathbf{y} - \mathbf{X}\hat{\boldsymbol{\beta}})'(\mathbf{y} - \mathbf{X}\hat{\boldsymbol{\beta}})/(T - n)$ and $\hat{\boldsymbol{\beta}}$ is the OLS estimator of $\boldsymbol{\beta}$. Notice that ξ_T/n_1 is the usual F-test statistic for testing the null hypothesis that $\boldsymbol{\beta}_1 = \bar{\boldsymbol{\beta}}_1$. The test criterion may also be written as

$$\xi_T = f[\sqrt{T}(\hat{\boldsymbol{\beta}}_1 - \bar{\boldsymbol{\beta}}_1), \mathbf{K}_{11}, s^2].$$

Assume that

$$\sqrt{T}(\hat{\boldsymbol{\beta}} - \boldsymbol{\beta}) \mathrel{\tilde{a}} \mathrm{N}(0, \sigma^2\mathbf{M}^{-1})$$

from which

$$\sqrt{T}(\hat{\boldsymbol{\beta}}_1 - \boldsymbol{\beta}_1) \mathrel{\tilde{a}} \mathrm{N}(0, \sigma^2\bar{\mathbf{K}}_{11}).$$

Thus, if the null hypothesis is true, $\sqrt{T}(\hat{\boldsymbol{\beta}}_1 - \bar{\boldsymbol{\beta}}_1) \xrightarrow{D} \mathbf{e}_1$, where

$$\mathbf{e}_1 \sim N(0, \sigma^2\bar{\mathbf{K}}_{11}).$$

One can also show that plim $s^2 = \sigma^2$.

Since the test criterion is continuous almost everywhere in all its arguments, it then follows from the General Transformation Theorem that

$$\xi_T \xrightarrow{D} f(\mathbf{e}_1, \bar{\mathbf{K}}_{11}, \sigma^2)$$

But

$$f(\mathbf{e}_1, \bar{\mathbf{K}}_{11}, \sigma^2) = \tfrac{1}{2}\mathbf{e}_1'\,\bar{\mathbf{K}}_{11}^{-1}\mathbf{e}_1 \sim \chi^2(n_1)$$

and so, under the null hypothesis

$$\xi_T \xrightarrow{D} \chi^2(n_1).$$

This shows that the usual test based on the F-distribution is asymptotically equivalent to a test based on the χ^2-distribution and is a valid approximation in large samples.

1.2 Central Limit Theorems (CLTs)

1.2.1 The Case of Non-Stochastic Regressors

Consider the linear regression model (1.2)

$$\underset{(T \times n)}{\mathbf{y} = \mathbf{X}} \underset{(n \times 1)}{\boldsymbol{\beta}} + \mathbf{u}, \qquad \mathrm{E}(\mathbf{u}) = 0, \qquad \mathrm{E}(\mathbf{uu}') = \sigma^2\mathbf{I}.$$

In the previous section it has been assumed that

$$\mathbf{w} = \frac{\mathbf{X}'\mathbf{u}}{\sqrt{T}} \;\tilde{a}\; \mathrm{N}(0, \sigma^2\mathbf{M})$$

where $\mathbf{M} = \text{plim}\,(\mathbf{X}'\mathbf{X}/T)$.

If the regressors are non-stochastic, the ith element of the vector $\mathbf{w}$

$$w_i = \frac{\Sigma_t^{T=1} x_{it}\, u_t}{\sqrt{T}}, \qquad i = 1, \ldots, n$$

is a weighted sum, with non-stochastic weights, of iid errors.

Suppose that:

Assumption 1.1(A1.1):
$\lim_{T\to\infty} (\mathbf{X}'\mathbf{X}/T) = \mathbf{M}$, a finite, positive definite (p.d.) matrix. With some further assumptions,[3] standard CLTs can be used to show that

$$\mathbf{w} \;\tilde{a}\; \mathrm{N}(0, \sigma^2\mathbf{M}).$$

First consider the implications of the condition A1.1. A convergence condition on the 2nd moment matrix of the type of A1.1 is required whenever the model contains exogenous variables. Notice that A1.1 is not an innocuous assumption since it may not be satisfied in important cases, e.g. in the case of time trends.

If A1.1 is not satisfied, the usual procedure is to introduce a non-stochastic square matrix $\mathbf{D}_T$ such that

$$\lim_{T\to\infty} \mathbf{D}_T \mathbf{X}'\mathbf{X}\, \mathbf{D}'_T = \mathbf{M}^*$$

where $\mathbf{M}^*$ is a finite, positive definite matrix.

Consider the least squares equations

$$\mathbf{X}'\mathbf{X}\,(\hat{\boldsymbol{\beta}} - \boldsymbol{\beta}) = \mathbf{X}'\mathbf{u}.$$

Pre-multiplying by $\mathbf{D}_T$ gives the rescaled expression

$$\mathbf{D}_T(\mathbf{X}'\mathbf{X})\mathbf{D}'_T(\mathbf{D}'_T)^{-1}\,(\hat{\boldsymbol{\beta}} - \boldsymbol{\beta}) = \mathbf{D}_T\, \mathbf{X}'\mathbf{u}.$$

Let $\mathbf{e}_T = (\mathbf{D}'_T)^{-1}\,(\hat{\boldsymbol{\beta}} - \boldsymbol{\beta})$ and $\mathbf{w}^* = \mathbf{D}_T\mathbf{X}'\mathbf{u}$. Then

$$\mathrm{E}(\mathbf{w}^*\mathbf{w}^{*\prime}) = \sigma^2\, \mathbf{D}_T(\mathbf{X}'\mathbf{X})\mathbf{D}'_T$$

[3]Examples of such assumptions are that (a) $|x_{it}| < b$, for some $b > 0$ and all i and t, or that (b) $\lim_{T\to\infty}\Sigma_{t,i}|x_{it}|^3/T^3 = 0$ for all i.

and so the variance of $\mathbf{w}^*$ tends to a constant as $T \to \infty$, i.e.

$$\lim_{T\to\infty} \mathrm{E}(\mathbf{w}^*\mathbf{w}^{*\prime}) = \sigma^2\mathbf{M}^*.$$

Notice that the case where the convergence condition A1.1 is satisfied is just a special case where $\mathbf{D}_T = \mathbf{I}_T/\sqrt{T}$.

Since $\mathbf{w}^*$ is a non-stochastic weighted sum of identically and independently distributed r.v.s u_ts, one can apply standard CLT (again subject to further conditions) to show that

$$\mathbf{w}^* \;\widetilde{a}\; \mathrm{N}(0, \sigma^2\mathbf{M}^*).$$

It then follows from the Cramer Linear Transformation Theorem that

$$\mathbf{e}_T = (\mathbf{D}_T)^{-1}(\hat{\boldsymbol{\beta}} - \boldsymbol{\beta}) \;\widetilde{a}\; \mathrm{N}(0, \sigma^2\mathbf{M}^{*-1}).$$

Example 6: Consider the linear trend regression

$$y_t = \beta_0 + \beta_1 t + u_t.$$

The $\mathbf{X}'\mathbf{X}$ matrix is

$$\begin{pmatrix} T & \dfrac{T(T-1)}{2} \\ \dfrac{T(T-1)}{2} & \dfrac{T(T+1)(2T+1)}{6} \end{pmatrix}$$

The appropriate rescaling is in this case

$$\mathbf{D}_T = \begin{pmatrix} 1/\sqrt{T} & 0 \\ 0 & 1/\sqrt{T^3} \end{pmatrix}$$

Thus

$$\mathbf{D}_T(\mathbf{X}'\mathbf{X})\mathbf{D}_T' = \begin{pmatrix} 1 & \dfrac{1}{2}\left(1+\dfrac{1}{T}\right) \\ \dfrac{1}{2}\left(1+\dfrac{1}{T}\right) & \dfrac{1}{6}\left(1+\dfrac{1}{T}\right)\left(2+\dfrac{1}{T}\right) \end{pmatrix}$$

and so

$$\lim_T \mathbf{D}_T(\mathbf{X}'\mathbf{X})\mathbf{D}_T' = \begin{pmatrix} 1 & 1/2 \\ 1/2 & 1/3 \end{pmatrix}$$

which is non-singular.

Note that in this case $\mathbf{D}_T$ can be taken to be diagonal.

1.2.2 CLTs for the Model Containing Stochastic Regressors

Consider the case where a vector of observations at time t, $\mathbf{x}(t)$ is generated by some strictly stationary stochastic process satisfying the following conditions:

(i) The process $\mathbf{x}(t)$ has absolutely continuous spectrum with continuous spectral density.

(ii) The process $\mathbf{x}(t)$ has fourth moments and its fourth-cumulant function $K_{ijks}(0, n, p, q)$ satisfies

$$\sum\sum\sum_{n,p,q=0}^{\infty} |K_{ijks}(0, n, p, q)| < \infty, \quad \text{all } i, j, k, s$$

where $K_{ijks}(0, n, p, q)$ is the cumulant for x_{it}, $x_j(t+n)$, $x_k(t+p)$, $x_s(t+q)$.

(iii) The process $x(t)$ is uniformly mixing.

Condition (ii) essentially means that the fourth-cumulants must become small as the lags become large, and can be regarded as a form of uniform mixing requirement. (For a definition of the uniform mixing condition see Hannan, 1970, p. 202.)

Let

$$c_{ij(k)} = \frac{\Sigma_{t=1}^{T} x_i(t)\, x_j(t+k)}{T}$$

be the sample 2nd moment for the kth lag of x, and let $\mathbf{c}_T$ be the vector whose elements are moments for different values of k, $c_{ij}(k_s)$ for some finite set of integers. Then an important result proved by Hannan is that

$$\sqrt{T}[\mathbf{c}_T - \mathrm{E}(\mathbf{c}_T)] \mathrel{\widetilde{a}} \mathrm{N}(0, \mathbf{V})$$

where

$$V = \lim_{T\to\infty} \{\mathrm{T}[\mathbf{c}_T - \mathrm{E}(\mathbf{c}_T)][\mathbf{c}_T - \mathrm{E}(\mathbf{c}_T)]'\}.$$

(For the formal statement of the theorem, see Hannan 1970, Theorem 14, p. 228.)

An analogous result is obtained if the $x(t)$ are generated by a linear process:

$$\mathbf{x}(t) = \sum_{l=0}^{\infty} \mathbf{A}(l)\, \mathbf{u}(t-l) \text{ with } \sum_{l=0}^{\infty} \|\mathbf{A}(l)\|^2 < \infty,$$

where the errors $u(t)$ are serially independent, having a finite fourth-cumulant. This condition is much easier to verify than the mixing condition (iii) and is sufficient for regular ARMA models.

A problem with the Hannan Theorem is that it did not deal directly with non-stochastic exogeneous variables. One way of dealing with this is to assume that the exogenous variables are generated by a suitable stochastic process. Consider two vector stochastic processes $\{\mathbf{y}_t\}$ and $\{\mathbf{z}_t\}$. Assume that $\mathbf{y}_t$ is linearly related to $\mathbf{z}_t$ through

$$\mathbf{B}(L)\mathbf{y}_t + \mathbf{C}(L)\mathbf{z}_t = \mathbf{u}_t,$$

where $\mathbf{B}(L)$ and $\mathbf{C}(L)$ are matrix lag polynomials, and $\mathbf{B}(L)$ has stable latent roots. If the $\mathbf{u}_t$s are generated by some stochastic process which is independent of $\mathbf{z}_t$ then the Hannan Theorem can be applied to show that all the 2nd moments have appropriate asymptotic normal distribution and that in particular $\Sigma_t \mathbf{z}_t \mathbf{u}'_{t-k}/\sqrt{T}$ for different k are asymptotically jointly normal. This is usually sufficient to derive the asymptotic properties of the estimators of the parameters of the model.

1.3 Consistency

1.3.1 Consistency of the Maximum Likelihood (ML) Estimates

Consider the linear regression model

$$\mathbf{y} = \mathbf{X}\boldsymbol{\beta} + \mathbf{u}, \quad \mathbf{u} \sim \mathrm{N}(0, \sigma^2\mathbf{I}). \tag{1.4}$$

The log likelihood function for this model is

$$L = -\frac{T}{2}\log 2\pi - \frac{T}{2}\log \sigma^2 - \frac{1}{2\sigma^2}\mathbf{u}'\mathbf{u}.$$

Since the log likelihood function is of the order T it may be rescaled by dividing by T to obtain an expression of order 1:

$$\begin{aligned}\frac{L}{T} &= -\tfrac{1}{2}\log 2\pi - \tfrac{1}{2}\log \sigma^2 - \frac{1}{2\sigma^2}\left(\frac{\mathbf{u}'\mathbf{u}}{T}\right)\\ &= -\tfrac{1}{2}\log 2\pi - \tfrac{1}{2}\log \sigma^2 - \frac{1}{2\sigma^2}\left(\frac{\mathbf{y}'\mathbf{y}}{T} - 2\,\frac{\mathbf{y}'\mathbf{X}}{T}\boldsymbol{\beta} + \boldsymbol{\beta}'\,\frac{\mathbf{X}'\mathbf{X}}{T}\boldsymbol{\beta}\right).\end{aligned}$$

Notice that the rescaled log likelihood function is independent of T and is a constant function of the data 2nd moments $(\mathbf{y}'\mathbf{y}/T)$, $(\mathbf{y}'\mathbf{X}/T)$ and $(\mathbf{X}'\mathbf{X}/T)$. Thus it may be written as

$$\frac{L}{T} = f(\mathbf{z}_T, \boldsymbol{\theta})$$

where $\boldsymbol{\theta}{:} = (\boldsymbol{\beta}', \sigma^2)$ is a vector of unknown parameters and

$$\mathbf{z}_T = \left(\frac{\mathbf{y}'\mathbf{y}}{T}, \frac{\mathbf{y}'\mathbf{X}}{T}, \frac{\mathbf{X}'\mathbf{X}}{T}\right)$$

is a set of sufficient statistics for the likelihood function.

Under the usual conditions on the linear regression model the plim of z_T exists, say, plim $\mathbf{z}_T = \mathbf{z}^*$. Since the rescaled log likelihood function is a continuous function of $\mathbf{z}_T$ and $\boldsymbol{\theta}$ and is independent of T, then by the Slutsky Theorem

$$\text{plim}\, f(\mathbf{z}_T, \boldsymbol{\theta}) = f(\mathbf{z}^*, \boldsymbol{\theta})$$

i.e. the (rescaled) likelihood function for model (1.4) converges in probability to a well-defined limiting function.

For more general models one must ensure that the plim of the likelihood function exists and is some function of $\boldsymbol{\theta}$ and of the true value $\bar{\boldsymbol{\theta}}$ of the parameter vector, say $F(\bar{\boldsymbol{\theta}}, \boldsymbol{\theta})$. In some cases the plim of the likelihood function may also depend on the non-stochastic variables of the model.

If the following conditions are satisfied:

(i) plim $L(\mathbf{z}_T, \boldsymbol{\theta})/T = F(\bar{\boldsymbol{\theta}}, \boldsymbol{\theta})$,
(ii) $F(\bar{\boldsymbol{\theta}}, \bar{\boldsymbol{\theta}}) > F(\bar{\boldsymbol{\theta}}, \boldsymbol{\theta})$ for all θ in the parameter space, i.e. the limiting function F achieves a unique global maximum at the true value $\bar{\theta}$,
(iii) the plim converges uniformly (which is automatically satisfied in the special case where sufficient statistics exist, and the rescaled likelihood function is a continuous function of the sufficient statistics),

then the ML estimates of $\boldsymbol{\theta}$ will have the consistency property, i.e.

$$\text{plim}\ \widetilde{\boldsymbol{\theta}} = \bar{\boldsymbol{\theta}}.$$

Notice that conditions (i) and (ii) are conditions for global identification since they enable us to derive consistent estimates by ML methods. (For a full treatment see Jennrich, 1969, and Frydman, 1980.)

What happens if the limiting function $F(\bar{\boldsymbol{\theta}}, \boldsymbol{\theta})$ has more than one maximum, say, a finite number of them? This clearly implies some lack of identifiability in the sense that we cannot discriminate between a finite number of alternative models on the basis of the data available. This is often the case with autoregression models. But more frequently the set of global maxima is an infinite set as in simultaneous equations models with linear constraints on the coefficients. However condition (ii) does give a suitable criterion for identifiability in both cases.

1.3.2 Consistency of the Least Squares Estimator

The results in Section 1.3.1 can be extended to ensure consistency of any econometric estimator derived by maximizing (or minimizing) a criterion function which converges in probability to a well-defined limiting function with a unique global maximum (or minimum) at the true parameter value.

As an illustration consider the non-linear-in-parameter regression model

$$\underset{(T\times 1)}{\mathbf{y}} = \underset{(T\times k)}{\mathbf{X}}\ \underset{(k\times 1)}{\boldsymbol{\beta}(\boldsymbol{\theta})} + \underset{(T\times 1)}{\mathbf{u}}, \qquad \mathrm{E}(\mathbf{u}) = 0 \tag{1.5}$$

where $\boldsymbol{\theta}$ is a $(p \times 1)$ vector of unknown parameters with $p < k$, and $\boldsymbol{\beta} : \boldsymbol{\theta} \rightarrow \boldsymbol{\beta}(\boldsymbol{\theta})$ is continuous in the neighbourhood of the true value $\bar{\boldsymbol{\theta}}$.

We will not assume that the errors are white noise or normally distributed. They may be autocorrelated, e.g. because of mis-specification of the structural part of the model. We will, however, assume that plim $(\mathbf{X}'\mathbf{u}/T) = 0$, i.e. that the errors and the regressors are completely uncorrelated in large samples.

The non-linear least squares estimator is the solution to the problem

$$\mathrm{Min}_{\theta}\, S(\theta) = \mathbf{u}'\mathbf{u} = \mathbf{y}'\mathbf{y} - 2\mathbf{y}'\mathbf{X}\boldsymbol{\beta}(\boldsymbol{\theta}) + \boldsymbol{\beta}'(\boldsymbol{\theta})\mathbf{X}'\mathbf{X}\boldsymbol{\beta}(\boldsymbol{\theta}). \tag{1.6}$$

Consider the plim of the rescaled criterion function (1.6):

$$\begin{aligned}\mathrm{plim}\,\frac{S(\theta)}{T} &= \mathrm{plim}\,\frac{\mathbf{y}'\mathbf{y}}{T} - 2\,\mathrm{plim}\,\frac{\mathbf{y}'\mathbf{X}}{T}\,\boldsymbol{\beta}(\boldsymbol{\theta})\\ &\quad + \boldsymbol{\beta}'(\boldsymbol{\theta})\,\mathrm{plim}\,\frac{\mathbf{X}'\mathbf{X}}{T}\,\boldsymbol{\beta}(\bar{\boldsymbol{\theta}}).\end{aligned}$$

Assume that plim $(\mathbf{X}'\mathbf{X}/T) = \mathbf{M}$, a finite, positive definite matrix, and that plim $(\mathbf{y}'\mathbf{y}/T) = \mathrm{m}$, a positive constant. Also

$$\mathrm{plim}\,\frac{\mathbf{y}'\mathbf{X}}{T} = \mathrm{plim}\,\frac{\mathbf{u}'\mathbf{X}}{T} + \boldsymbol{\beta}'(\bar{\boldsymbol{\theta}})\,\mathrm{plim}\,\frac{\mathbf{X}'\mathbf{X}}{T}$$

where $\bar{\boldsymbol{\theta}}$ denotes the true value of $\boldsymbol{\theta}$. Under the assumption that plim $(\mathbf{X}'\mathbf{u}/T) = 0$, the plim of the criterion function becomes

$$\begin{aligned}\mathrm{plim}\,\frac{S(\theta)}{T} &= F(\bar{\theta}, \theta)\\ &= \mathrm{m} - 2\boldsymbol{\beta}'(\bar{\boldsymbol{\theta}})\mathbf{M}\boldsymbol{\beta}(\boldsymbol{\theta}) + \boldsymbol{\beta}'(\boldsymbol{\theta})\,\mathbf{M}\boldsymbol{\beta}(\boldsymbol{\theta})\\ &= \mathrm{m} - \boldsymbol{\beta}'(\bar{\boldsymbol{\theta}})\mathbf{M}\boldsymbol{\beta}(\bar{\boldsymbol{\theta}}) + [\boldsymbol{\beta}(\boldsymbol{\theta}) - \boldsymbol{\beta}(\bar{\boldsymbol{\theta}})]'\mathbf{M}[\boldsymbol{\beta}(\boldsymbol{\theta}) - \boldsymbol{\beta}(\bar{\boldsymbol{\theta}})]\end{aligned}$$

which achieves a global minimum at $\boldsymbol{\beta}(\boldsymbol{\theta}) = \boldsymbol{\beta}(\bar{\boldsymbol{\theta}})$. If $\theta = \bar{\theta}$ is the unique global minimum, i.e. $F(\bar{\boldsymbol{\theta}}, \bar{\boldsymbol{\theta}}) > F(\bar{\boldsymbol{\theta}}, \boldsymbol{\theta})$ for all $\boldsymbol{\theta}$ in the parameter space, then the non-linear least squares estimates of $\boldsymbol{\theta}$ is consistent. This condition is satisfied if $\boldsymbol{\beta}(\boldsymbol{\theta}) = \boldsymbol{\beta}(\bar{\boldsymbol{\theta}})$ has the unique solution $\boldsymbol{\theta} = \bar{\boldsymbol{\theta}}$.

If there is more than one global minimum then we may expect more than one local minimum of the sample criterion function.

1.4 Asymptotic Distribution of the Maximum Likelihood (ML) Estimator for Regression Equations

1.4.1 The Case of Independent Observations

Consider the linear regression model

$$y_t = \boldsymbol{\beta}'\mathbf{x}_t + u_t, \qquad u_t \sim \mathrm{NID}(0, \sigma_u^2), \qquad t = 1, \ldots, T. \tag{1.7}$$

Let $\bar{\boldsymbol{\theta}}$ be the true value of $\boldsymbol{\theta}: = (\boldsymbol{\beta}', \sigma^2)'$ and let $L_T(\boldsymbol{\theta})$ be the (log) likelihood function.

The ML estimator $\tilde{\boldsymbol{\theta}}$ is the solution to the system of equations emerging from the first-order conditions for a maximum of the likelihood function

$$\frac{\partial L_T(\boldsymbol{\theta})}{\partial \boldsymbol{\theta}} = 0.$$

If the model is globally identified, i.e. the conditions of Section 1.3.1 are satisfied, then the ML estimator $\tilde{\boldsymbol{\theta}}$ is consistent. We want to establish the asymptotic distribution of $\tilde{\boldsymbol{\theta}}$.

Assume that the likelihood function has continuous 2nd derivatives. Then expanding around $\bar{\boldsymbol{\theta}}$ by using the Mean Value Theorem gives

$$\left(\frac{\partial L_T}{\partial \boldsymbol{\theta}}\right)_{\tilde{\boldsymbol{\theta}}} = 0 = \left(\frac{\partial L_T}{\partial \boldsymbol{\theta}}\right)_{\bar{\boldsymbol{\theta}}} + \left(\frac{\partial^2 L}{\partial \boldsymbol{\theta} \partial \boldsymbol{\theta}'}\right)_{\boldsymbol{\theta}^*} (\tilde{\boldsymbol{\theta}} - \bar{\boldsymbol{\theta}})$$

where $\boldsymbol{\theta}^*$ is some point between $\bar{\boldsymbol{\theta}}$ and $\tilde{\boldsymbol{\theta}}$.

After rescaling by dividing by $1/\sqrt{T}$, we obtain

$$\sqrt{T}(\tilde{\boldsymbol{\theta}} - \bar{\boldsymbol{\theta}}) = \left[-\frac{1}{T}\left(\frac{\partial^2 L_T}{\partial \boldsymbol{\theta} \partial \boldsymbol{\theta}'}\right)_{\boldsymbol{\theta}^*}\right]^{-1} \left[\frac{1}{\sqrt{T}}\left(\frac{\partial L_T}{\partial \boldsymbol{\theta}}\right)_{\bar{\boldsymbol{\theta}}}\right]. \tag{1.8}$$

If the model is globally identified, the plim of the rescaled likelihood function is strictly concave in a neighbourhood of the true value $\bar{\boldsymbol{\theta}}$, and so

$$\text{plim}\left[\frac{1}{T}\left(\frac{\partial^2 L}{\partial\boldsymbol{\theta}\partial\boldsymbol{\theta}'}\right)_{\boldsymbol{\theta}^*}\right] = \mathbf{H} = \text{plim}\left[\frac{1}{T}\left(\frac{\partial^2 L}{\partial\boldsymbol{\theta}\partial\boldsymbol{\theta}'}\right)_{\bar{\boldsymbol{\theta}}}\right]$$

is a finite, symmetric, negative definite matrix. Notice that the sufficient condition for consistency is also a sufficient condition for the existence of an asymptotic distribution of the ML estimator. But in this case the limiting function F is a quadratic in $\boldsymbol{\theta}$, the uniqueness condition implies that **H** is non-singular. This in turn is a necessary condition for the asymptotic distribution of the ML estimator to exist. (This is not always the case, but is true for the model of this section. In general a model may be consistent but not have an asymptotic normal distribution.) Thus, to determine the asymptotic distribution of the ML estimator it remains to determine the asymptotic distribution of the 'score vector'

$$\frac{1}{\sqrt{T}}\left(\frac{\partial L_T}{\partial\boldsymbol{\theta}}\right)_{\bar{\boldsymbol{\theta}}}.$$

Suppose that the observations in (1.7) are independently distributed with conditional probability density function (pdf) $f(y_t|\mathbf{x}_t, \theta)$. Then the (conditional) joint pdf of the sample $\mathbf{y}: = (y_1, \ldots, y_T)$ is given by

$$f_T(\theta) = \Pi_{t=1}^T f_t(y_t|\mathbf{x}_t, \theta) = \Pi_{t=1}^T f_t(u_t|\theta)$$

and the (log) likelihood function is therefore

$$L_T(\theta) = \log f_T(\theta) = \sum_{t=1}^T l_t(\theta|u_t)$$

where

$$l_t: = \log f_t.$$

Theorem 6: If regularity conditions ensuring that it is possible to differentiate under the integral sign are satisfied then

$$\mathrm{E}\left(\frac{\partial L_T}{\partial\boldsymbol{\theta}}\right) = 0$$

and

$$\text{Var}\left(\frac{\partial L_T}{\partial\boldsymbol{\theta}}\right) = \underset{\theta}{\mathbf{V}} = \mathrm{E}\left[\left(\frac{\partial L_T}{\partial\boldsymbol{\theta}}\right)\left(\frac{\partial L_T}{\partial\boldsymbol{\theta}}\right)'\right] = -\mathrm{E}\left(\frac{\partial^2 L_T}{\partial\boldsymbol{\theta}\partial\boldsymbol{\theta}'}\right).$$

Proof: Integrating the conditional density of y over the whole sample space gives

$$\int f_T(\mathbf{y}|\boldsymbol{\theta})\,\mathrm{d}\mathbf{y} = 1,$$

for all values of $\boldsymbol{\theta}$.

Under regularity conditions, we can differentiate this expression with relation to $\boldsymbol{\theta}$ to obtain

$$\int \frac{\partial f_T}{\partial \boldsymbol{\theta}}\,\mathrm{d}y = 0, \text{ again for all values of } \boldsymbol{\theta}. \tag{1.9}$$

Since $L_T = \operatorname{Log} f_T$ one has

$$\frac{\partial L_T}{\partial \boldsymbol{\theta}} = \frac{1}{f_T}\frac{\partial f_T}{\partial \boldsymbol{\theta}}$$

from which

$$\frac{\partial f_T}{\partial \boldsymbol{\theta}} = f_T\frac{\partial L_T}{\partial \boldsymbol{\theta}}.$$

Therefore, by susbstituting in (1.9) one obtains

$$\int \frac{\partial L_T}{\partial \boldsymbol{\theta}} f_T\,\mathrm{d}\mathbf{y} = \mathrm{E}\left(\frac{\partial L_T}{\partial \boldsymbol{\theta}}\right) = 0.$$

Now differentiate this with respect to $\boldsymbol{\theta}$. Under regularity conditions one has

$$\int \left(\frac{\partial^2 L_T}{\partial \boldsymbol{\theta}\partial \boldsymbol{\theta}'}\right) f_T\,\mathrm{d}\mathbf{y} + \int \left(\frac{\partial L_T}{\partial \boldsymbol{\theta}}\right)\left(\frac{\partial f_T}{\partial \boldsymbol{\theta}}\right)'\mathrm{d}\mathbf{y} = 0$$

from which proceeding as before gives

$$-\int \left(\frac{\partial^2 L_T}{\partial \boldsymbol{\theta}\partial \boldsymbol{\theta}'}\right) f_T\,\mathrm{d}\mathbf{y} = \int_{\mathbf{y}} \left(\frac{\partial L_T}{\partial \boldsymbol{\theta}}\right)\left(\frac{\partial L_T}{\partial \boldsymbol{\theta}}\right)' f_T\,\mathrm{d}\mathbf{y}$$

i.e.

$$-\mathrm{E}\left(\frac{\partial^2 L_T}{\partial \boldsymbol{\theta}\partial \boldsymbol{\theta}'}\right) = \mathrm{E}\left[\left(\frac{\partial L_T}{\partial \boldsymbol{\theta}}\right)\left(\frac{\partial L_T}{\partial \boldsymbol{\theta}}\right)'\right].$$

When the observations are independent the $L_T(\boldsymbol{\theta}|u_t)$ are independent, and if there are no exogenous variables, they are identically distributed, so that it follows from standard CLTs that

$$\frac{1}{\sqrt{T}}\frac{\partial L_T}{\partial \tilde{\boldsymbol{\theta}}}\bigg|_{\boldsymbol{\theta}} \mathrel{\tilde{a}} \mathrm{N}(0, \bar{\mathbf{V}}_\theta)$$

where

$$\bar{\mathbf{V}}_\theta: = \lim_{T\to\infty} \frac{\mathbf{V}_\theta}{T} = \lim_{T\to\infty}\mathrm{E}\left[\frac{1}{T}\left(\frac{\partial L_T}{\partial \boldsymbol{\theta}}\right)\left(\frac{\partial L_T}{\partial \boldsymbol{\theta}}\right)\right]$$

is a positive definite matrix. If there are non-stochastic exogenous variables a similar result can be proved on suitable fairly simple assumptions.

Assume that

$$\operatorname{plim}\left[\frac{1}{T}\left(\frac{\partial^2 L_T}{\partial\boldsymbol{\theta}\partial\boldsymbol{\theta}'}\right)_{\bar{\boldsymbol{\theta}}}\right] = \mathbf{H} = \lim_{T\to\infty}\mathrm{E}\left[\frac{1}{T}\left(\frac{\partial^2 L_T}{\partial\boldsymbol{\theta}\partial\boldsymbol{\theta}'}\right)\right].$$

Then Theorem 1 implies that

$$\bar{\mathbf{V}}_\theta = -\mathbf{H}.$$

Finally, by applying the Cramer Linear Transformation Theorem to (1.8) we obtain the asymptotic distribution of the ML estimator

$$\sqrt{T}(\tilde{\boldsymbol{\theta}} - \bar{\boldsymbol{\theta}}) \mathrel{\tilde{a}} \mathrm{N}(0, \mathbf{H}^{-1}\bar{\mathbf{V}}_\theta\mathbf{H}^{-1})$$

or

$$\sqrt{T}(\tilde{\boldsymbol{\theta}} - \bar{\boldsymbol{\theta}}) \mathrel{\tilde{a}} \mathrm{N}(0, \bar{\mathbf{V}}_\theta^{-1}).$$

(End of proof)

1.4.2 The Case of Dependent Observations

Consider the case where the observations in (1.7) are not independently distributed.

Let $\mathbf{y}_t^*$ and $\mathbf{x}_t^*$ denote past values of y_t and x_t. Then the density of y_t conditional on past observations can be written as

$$f_t(y_t|\mathbf{y}_t^*, \mathbf{x}_t, \mathbf{x}_t^*, \boldsymbol{\theta}).$$

Proceeding as in Section 1.4.1 we obtain the log likelihood function

$$L_T(\boldsymbol{\theta}) = \sum_{t=1}^{T} l_t(\boldsymbol{\theta}|u_t)$$

where

$$l_t(\boldsymbol{\theta}|u_t) = \log f_t(u_t|\mathbf{y}_t^*, \mathbf{x}_t^*, \boldsymbol{\theta}).$$

Since the observations are not independently distributed the simple kind of CLT used in Section 1.4.1 cannot be applied. A CLT can however still be derived by using the following important property of the score vector:

Theorem 7: Under regularity conditions the score vector has the Martingale property, i.e.

$$\mathrm{E}\left[\frac{\partial L_T}{\partial \boldsymbol{\theta}}\middle|\Phi_{T-1}\right] = \frac{\partial L_{T-1}}{\partial \boldsymbol{\theta}}$$

where Φ_{T-1} denotes the information available at time $T-1$.

Proof: The likelihood function (1.5) can be written as

$$L_T(\boldsymbol{\theta}) = l_T(\boldsymbol{\theta}) + \sum_{t=1}^{T-1} l_t(\boldsymbol{\theta})$$

from which

$$\mathrm{E}\left[\frac{\partial L_T}{\partial \theta}\middle|\Phi_{T-1}\right] = \mathrm{E}\left[\frac{\partial l_T}{\partial \theta}\middle|\Phi_{T-1}\right] + \sum_{t=1}^{T-1} \frac{\partial[l_T(\theta)]}{\partial \theta}. \tag{1.10}$$

We want to show that the first term on the right-hand side of (1.10) is equal to zero. Integrating the conditional density of y_t over the whole sample space gives

$$\int f_t(y_t|\mathbf{y}_t^*, \mathbf{x}_t, \mathbf{x}_t^*, \boldsymbol{\theta})\, \mathrm{d}y_t = 1$$

from which one obtains, under regularity conditions

$$\int \frac{\partial f_t}{\partial \boldsymbol{\theta}}\, \mathrm{d}y_t = 0. \tag{1.11}$$

Since $l_t = \log f_t$ one has that

$$\frac{\partial f_t}{\partial \theta} = \frac{\partial l_t}{\partial \theta} f_t$$

so that (1.7) becomes

$$\int \frac{\partial l_t}{\partial \boldsymbol{\theta}} f_t\, (y_t|\mathbf{y}_t^*, \mathbf{x}_t, \mathbf{x}_t^*, \boldsymbol{\theta})\, \mathrm{d}y_t = 0$$

i.e.

$$\mathrm{E}\left[\frac{\partial l_t}{\partial \boldsymbol{\theta}}\middle|\Phi_{T-1}\right] = 0.$$

Thus from (1.10)

$$\mathrm{E}\left[\frac{\partial L_T}{\partial \boldsymbol{\theta}}\middle|\Phi_{T-1}\right] = \frac{\partial L_{T-1}}{\partial \boldsymbol{\theta}}.$$

(End of proof)

Theorem 2 is important since it allows the use of a Martingale CLT of the same form as the one obtained in Section 1.4.1

$$\frac{1}{\sqrt{T}}\left(\frac{\partial L_T}{\partial \boldsymbol{\theta}}\right)_{\bar{\boldsymbol{\theta}}} \ \widetilde{a}\ \mathrm{N}(0, \bar{\mathbf{V}}_\theta).$$

Example 7: As an illustration consider the AR(r) model

$$y_t = \beta_1 y_{t-1} + \ldots + \beta_r y_{t-r} + u_t, \qquad u_t \sim \mathrm{NID}(0,\sigma^2)$$
$$t=1, \ldots, T. \quad (1.12)$$

Let $\mathbf{y}^*_{r+1} = (y_1, \ldots, y_r)'$ and assume that

$$\mathrm{E}(\mathbf{y}^*_{r+1}, \mathbf{y}^{*\prime}_{r+1}) = \sigma^2 \mathbf{\Omega}_r.$$

By using the prediction error decomposition the log likelihood function of model (1.12) can be written as

$$L_T(\theta) = -\frac{T}{2}\log 2\pi - \frac{1}{2}\log|\mathbf{\Omega}_r| - \frac{T}{2}\log\sigma^2 - \frac{1}{2\sigma^2}(\mathbf{y}^{*\prime}_{r+1}\,\mathbf{\Omega}_r^{-1}\,\mathbf{y}^*_{r+1}) - \frac{1}{2\sigma^2}\sum_{t=r+1}^{T} u_t^2 \qquad (1.13)$$

where

$$\theta = (\beta_1, \ldots, \beta_r; \sigma^2)'.$$

Notice that since for $t = r+1, \ldots, T$ the dtn of y_t conditional on $\mathbf{y}^*_t$ is normal with mean $\beta_1 y_{t-1} + \ldots + \beta_r y_{t-r}$ and variance σ^2 one has

$$l_t = \log f_t(y_t|\mathbf{y}^*_t, \theta) = -\frac{1}{2}\log 2\pi - \frac{1}{2}\sigma^2 - \frac{u_t^2}{2\sigma^2}$$

so that

$$\frac{\partial l_t}{\partial \beta_s} = -\frac{u_t\, y_{t-s}}{\sigma^2}, \qquad t = r+1, \ldots, T; \qquad s = 1, \ldots, r.$$

As $T \to \infty$ the importance of the second and the fourth terms in (1.13) becomes negligible and so

$$\frac{1}{\sqrt{T}}\frac{\partial L_T}{\partial \beta_s} = \frac{1}{\sqrt{T}}\left(\sum_{t=r+1}^{T}\frac{\partial l_t}{\partial \beta_s} + \sum_{t=1}^{r}\frac{\partial l_t}{\partial \beta_s}\right)$$
$$= \frac{1}{\sqrt{T}}\frac{\Sigma_{t=r+1}^{T} u_t\, y_{t-s}}{\sigma^2} + \mathrm{o}\left(\frac{1}{\sqrt{T}}\right).$$

Thus as $T \to \infty$ we are back to the case of Section 1.4.1 in which the

CLTs of that section can be applied. Therefore in this case one need not invoke a Martingale CLT in order to establish the asymptotic distribution of the score vector and therefore of the ML estimator. This is generally the case in the estimation of ARMA models. Usually the general Martingale CLTs are only needed for qualitative dependent variables and for non-linear models.

2

Simultaneous Equation Models

This chapter introduces the notation used throughout all the next chapters, as well as some useful results on matrix algebra and calculus.

2.1 Notation and the Reduced Form (RF) and Structural Form (SF) Likelihood Functions

Consider a set of n equations at time t,

$$\mathbf{A}\mathbf{x}_t \equiv \mathbf{B}\mathbf{y}_t + \mathbf{C}\mathbf{z}_t = \mathbf{u}_t, \quad t = 1, \ldots, T \tag{2.1}$$

Equation (2.1) is the *structural form* (SF) of the *simultaneous equation model* (SEM) where,

$\mathbf{A}$: = $(\mathbf{B} : \mathbf{C})$ is the matrix of coefficients of order $n \times (n + m)$
$\mathbf{B}$: = square matrix of coefficients of the endogenous variables in the SEM of order $(n \times n)$
$\mathbf{C}$: = matrix of coefficients of the predetermined variables in the SEM of order $(n \times m)$
$\mathbf{x}_t$ = $\begin{pmatrix} \mathbf{y}_t \\ \hline \mathbf{z}_t \end{pmatrix}$
$\mathbf{y}_t$ = $(n \times 1)$ vector of the endogenous variables in the SEM at time t
$\mathbf{z}_t$ = $(m \times 1)$ vector of the predetermined variables in the SEM at time t
$\mathbf{u}_t$ = $(n \times 1)$ vector of disturbances at time t, with $\mathrm{E}(\mathbf{u}_t\mathbf{u}_t') = \Omega_u$ for all $t = 1, \ldots, T$.

Grouping along time we can express (2.1) compactly as

$$\mathbf{AX}' = \mathbf{U}' \tag{2.2}$$

where $\mathbf{X}$ is the $T \times (n + m)$ matrix,

$$\mathbf{X}: = \begin{pmatrix} \mathbf{x}_1' \\ \mathbf{x}_T' \end{pmatrix} \text{ and } \mathbf{U}:_{(T \times n)} = \begin{pmatrix} \mathbf{u}_1' \\ \mathbf{u}_T' \end{pmatrix}$$

with

$$\mathrm{E}\left(\frac{\mathbf{U}'\mathbf{U}}{T}\right) = \mathbf{\Omega}_u. \tag{2.3}$$

The corresponding *reduced form* (RF) of this SEM is

$$\mathbf{y}_t = \mathbf{Pz}_t + \mathbf{v}_t, \qquad t = 1, \ldots, T \tag{2.4}$$

where

$\mathbf{P}: \; = \; -\mathbf{B}^{-1}\mathbf{C} = \; (n \times m)$ matrix of the RF coefficients
$\mathbf{v}_t \; = \; \mathbf{B}^{-1}\mathbf{u}_t = \; (n \times 1)$ vector of the RF disturbances.

Compactly, (2.4) can be expressed as

$$\mathbf{Y}' = \mathbf{PZ}' + \mathbf{V}' \tag{2.5}$$

where

$$\underset{(T \times n)}{\mathbf{Y}:} = \begin{pmatrix} \mathbf{y}_1' \\ \mathbf{y}_T' \end{pmatrix}, \qquad \underset{(T \times m)}{\mathbf{Z}:} = \begin{pmatrix} \mathbf{z}_1' \\ \mathbf{z}'_T \end{pmatrix}$$

$$\text{and} \quad \underset{(T \times n)}{\mathbf{V}} = \begin{pmatrix} \mathbf{v}_1' \\ \mathbf{v}_T' \end{pmatrix} = \begin{pmatrix} \mathbf{B}^{-1}\mathbf{u}_1' \\ \mathbf{B}^{-1}\mathbf{u}_T' \end{pmatrix}$$

with

$$\mathrm{E}\left(\frac{\mathbf{V}'\mathbf{V}}{T}\right) = \mathbf{\Omega}_\mathrm{v} = \mathbf{B}^{-1}\mathbf{\Omega}_\mathrm{u}(\mathbf{B}')^{-1}. \tag{2.6}$$

We have assumed that det $\mathbf{B} \neq 0$ so that $\mathbf{B}$ has an inverse.

If some identities are present, their corresponding $\mathbf{u}_{it}$ will be zero, and their corresponding coefficients in $\mathbf{A}$ will be known. Assuming the disturbances in equation (2.2) are uncorrelated and normally distributed, and assuming that there are no identities present, the RF log likelihood function is derived from

$$L(\mathbf{P}, \mathbf{\Omega}_\mathrm{v}): = -\frac{Tn}{2}\log 2\pi - \frac{T}{2}\log \det \mathbf{\Omega}_\mathrm{v} - \frac{1}{2}\operatorname{tr}(\mathbf{\Omega}_\mathrm{v}^{-1}\mathbf{V}'\mathbf{V}). \tag{2.7}$$

If there exist, say, k lagged endogenous variables, we follow the convention that t still goes from 1 to T, changing only from joint distribution to joint distribution conditional on $\mathbf{y}_0, \mathbf{y}_{-1}, \ldots, \mathbf{y}_{-k}$.

From (2.5) we can see that the Jacobian of the transformation from the joint distribution of $\mathbf{V}$ to that of $\mathbf{Y}$ is unity, thus the RF log likelihood function is, from (2.7)

$$L(\mathbf{P}, \mathbf{\Omega}_v) := -\frac{Tn}{2}\log 2\pi - \frac{T}{2}\log\det\mathbf{\Omega}_v - \frac{1}{2}\operatorname{tr}[\mathbf{\Omega}_v^{-1}(\mathbf{Y}' - \mathbf{PZ}')(\mathbf{Y} - \mathbf{ZP}')]. \tag{2.8}$$

Substituting now

$$\mathbf{P} = -\mathbf{B}^{-1}\mathbf{C}$$

$$\mathbf{\Omega}_v = \mathbf{B}^{-1}\mathbf{\Omega}_u(\mathbf{B}')^{-1}$$

$$\det\mathbf{\Omega}_v = (\det\mathbf{B})^{-2}\det\mathbf{\Omega}_u,\ \log\det\mathbf{\Omega}_v = \log\det\mathbf{\Omega}_u - 2\log|\det\mathbf{B}|$$

into (2.8), and noticing that

$$(\mathbf{Y}' - \mathbf{PZ}') = \mathbf{B}^{-1}(\mathbf{BY}' + \mathbf{CZ}') = \mathbf{B}^{-1}\mathbf{AX}'$$

we obtain from (2.8)

$$\begin{aligned}
L(\mathbf{A}, \mathbf{\Omega}_u) &= -\frac{Tn}{2}\log 2\pi - \frac{T}{2}\log\det\mathbf{\Omega}_u + T\log|\det\mathbf{B}| \\
&\quad - \frac{1}{2}\operatorname{tr}[\mathbf{\Omega}_v^{-1}\mathbf{B}^{-1}\mathbf{AX}'\mathbf{XA}'(\mathbf{B}')^{-1}] \\
&= -\frac{Tn}{2}\log 2\pi - \frac{T}{2}\log\det\mathbf{\Omega}_u + T\log|\det\mathbf{B}| \\
&\quad - \frac{1}{2}\operatorname{tr}[(\mathbf{B}')^{-1}\mathbf{\Omega}_v^{-1}\mathbf{B}^{-1}\mathbf{AX}'\mathbf{XA}'] \\
&= -\frac{Tn}{2}\log 2\pi - \frac{T}{2}\log\det\mathbf{\Omega}_u + T\log|\det\mathbf{B}| \\
&\quad - \frac{1}{2}\operatorname{tr}(\mathbf{\Omega}_u^{-1}\mathbf{AX}'\mathbf{XA}')
\end{aligned} \tag{2.9}$$

which is the structural form log likelihood function. This can also be obtained starting from the joint distribution of the $\mathbf{u}_t$, with $|\det\mathbf{B}|^T$ as the Jacobian of the transformation from $\mathbf{u}_t$ to $\mathbf{y}_t$.

2.2 Appendix: The 'vec' Operator, Kronecker Product and Other Useful Results

Consider an $n \times (n + m)$ matrix $\mathbf{A}$

$$\mathbf{A} = \begin{pmatrix} \mathbf{a}'_1 \\ \mathbf{a}'_n \end{pmatrix} = \begin{pmatrix} a_{11} \ldots a_{1n} a_{1n+1} \ldots a_{1n+m} \\ a_{n1} \ldots a_{nn} a_{nn+1} \ldots a_{nn+m} \end{pmatrix} \tag{2.10}$$

Definition 1: The 'vec' operator is such that, for $\mathbf{A}$ given in (2.10)

$$\text{vec } \mathbf{A} = \begin{pmatrix} \mathbf{a}_1 \\ \mathbf{a}_2 \\ \mathbf{a}_n \end{pmatrix}$$

where $\mathbf{a}_j$, $j = 1, \ldots, n$ is the jth row transposed (i.e. in column form). Since each row of $\mathbf{A}$ is of order $1 \times (n + m)$, vec $\mathbf{A}$ is a column vector of order $n(n + m) \times 1$.

Notice that this definition corresponds to vec $(\mathbf{A}')$ if we follow the usual textbook procedure of stacking the column one below the other, rather than the rows as we did.

Definition 2: Consider two matrices $\mathbf{A}$, $\mathbf{B}$ of order $n \times (n + m)$ and $(p \times q)$ respectively. Then the Kronecker product of $\mathbf{A}$ and $\mathbf{B}$, denoted $A \otimes B$, is defined by the $np \times (n + m)q$ matrix

$$\mathbf{A} \otimes \mathbf{B} = \begin{pmatrix} a_{11}\mathbf{B} \ldots a_{1n+m}\mathbf{B} \\ \ldots\ldots\ldots\ldots \\ \ldots\ldots\ldots\ldots \\ a_{n1}\mathbf{B} \ldots a_{nn+m}\mathbf{B} \end{pmatrix}$$

Properties of 'vec' operator:

(i) $(\text{vec}\,\mathbf{A})'\,(\text{vec}\,\mathbf{B}) = \text{tr}(\mathbf{A}'\mathbf{B})$;

(ii) $\text{vec}(\mathbf{ABC}) = (\mathbf{A} \otimes \mathbf{C}')\,\text{vec}\,\mathbf{B}$;

(iii) $\text{tr}(\mathbf{ABCD}) = (\text{vec}\,\mathbf{A}')'\,(\mathbf{B} \otimes \mathbf{D}')\,\text{vec}\mathbf{C}$ [from (i) and (ii)].

Properties of the Kronecker product:

(i) $(\mathbf{A} \otimes \mathbf{B})' = (\mathbf{A}' \otimes \mathbf{B}')$;

(ii) $\text{tr}\,(\mathbf{A} \otimes \mathbf{B}) = \text{tr}\,(\mathbf{A})\,\text{tr}\,(\mathbf{B})$ (only if $\mathbf{A}$ and $\mathbf{B}$ are square matrices);

(iii) $(\mathbf{A} \otimes \mathbf{B})^{-1} = (\mathbf{A}^{-1} \otimes \mathbf{B}^{-1})$ (provided $\mathbf{A}$ and $\mathbf{B}$ are non-singular);

(iv) $(\mathbf{A} \otimes \mathbf{B})\,(\mathbf{C} \otimes \mathbf{D}) = (\mathbf{AC} \otimes \mathbf{BD})$ (provided $\mathbf{AC}$ and $\mathbf{BD}$ exist);

(v) $|\mathbf{A} \otimes \mathbf{B}| = |\mathbf{A}|^n \, |\mathbf{B}|^m$ for $\mathbf{A}$: = (m, m) matrix and $\mathbf{B}$: = (n, n) matrix;

(vi) rank $(\mathbf{A} \otimes \mathbf{B})$ = rank $\mathbf{A} \cdot$ rank $\mathbf{B}$.

3

Identification and the Treatment of General Linear Restrictions

3.1 Observational Equivalence

A model is the specification of the probability distribution for a set of observations. A structure is the specification of the parameters of that distribution. Therefore a structure is a model in which all the parameters are assigned numerical values. Let $\bar{\boldsymbol{\theta}}$ be the true set of parameters, and $\boldsymbol{\theta}^*$ any other alternative, and let $\mathbf{X}$ be the set of data.

Definition 1: Two structures of a model defined as the (conditional) probability density function $p(\mathbf{x}|\boldsymbol{\Theta})$, $\mathbf{x} \in \mathbf{X}$, $\boldsymbol{\theta} \in \boldsymbol{\Theta}$, are said to be *observationally equivalent* if

$$p(\mathbf{x}|\bar{\boldsymbol{\theta}}) = p(\mathbf{x}|\boldsymbol{\theta}^*) \qquad \forall \mathbf{x} \in \mathbf{X}$$

or equivalently

$$L(\mathbf{x}|\bar{\boldsymbol{\theta}}) = L(\mathbf{x}|\boldsymbol{\theta}^*) \qquad \forall \mathbf{x} \in \mathbf{X}$$

where $L(\cdot)$ is the likelihood function.

Definition 2: A structure $L(\mathbf{x}|\bar{\boldsymbol{\theta}})$ is identifiable if there is no other observationally equivalent structure. If a structure is not identifiable, i.e. if

$$L(\mathbf{x}|\bar{\boldsymbol{\theta}}) = L(\mathbf{x}|\boldsymbol{\theta}^*)$$

for a set of alternatives $\boldsymbol{\theta}^*$, then the structure is said to be unidentifiable (or under-identifiable).

The idea is as follows. There are two sources of information:

(i) sample information, given by the observations matrix $\mathbf{X}$
(ii) prior information given by restriction equations, and the assumed form of the model.

The observational equivalence occurs when we only have sample information, and for any set of data this is insufficient to differentiate between $\bar{\boldsymbol{\theta}}$ and some other $\boldsymbol{\theta}^*$, i.e. by observing $\mathbf{X}$, both $\bar{\boldsymbol{\theta}}$ and $\boldsymbol{\theta}^*$ are equally compatible with the data.

Let us see this more formally for the simple simultaneous equation model. Consider equation (2.8) with $\bar{\mathbf{P}} = -\bar{\mathbf{B}}^{-1}\bar{\mathbf{C}}$ and assume there are no constraints on $\boldsymbol{\Omega}_u$. Then observational equivalence implies

$$\bar{\mathbf{P}} = -\bar{\mathbf{B}}^{-1}\bar{\mathbf{C}} = -\mathbf{B}^{*-1}\mathbf{C}^* \tag{3.1}$$

and

$$\bar{\boldsymbol{\Omega}}_v = \bar{\mathbf{B}}^{-1}\bar{\boldsymbol{\Omega}}_u(\bar{\mathbf{B}}')^{-1} = \mathbf{B}^{*-1}\boldsymbol{\Omega}_u^*(\mathbf{B}^{*\prime})^{-1}.$$

Define $\mathbf{H} = \mathbf{B}^*\bar{\mathbf{B}}^{-1}$, so that $\mathbf{B}^* = \mathbf{H}\bar{\mathbf{B}}$. Since $\mathbf{C}^* = \mathbf{B}^*\bar{\mathbf{B}}^{-1}\bar{\mathbf{C}}$, from (3.1), this implies that, $\mathbf{C}^* = \mathbf{H}\bar{\mathbf{C}}$. Thus

$$\mathbf{A}^* = \mathbf{H}\bar{\mathbf{A}} \text{ and } \boldsymbol{\Omega}_v^* = \mathbf{B}^*\bar{\boldsymbol{\Omega}}_v\mathbf{B}^{*\prime} = \mathbf{H}\bar{\boldsymbol{\Omega}}_u\mathbf{H}'.$$

Hence when the two models are observationally equivalent, i.e. when they have the same reduced form, they differ only by a linear transformation $\mathbf{H}$. Therefore, in order to obtain the identification of the model we must consider the second type of information, i.e. we must introduce constraints on $\mathbf{A}$ and $\boldsymbol{\Omega}_u$. This is done in the next section.

3.2 Rank and Order Conditions for Identification

Consider the linear simultaneous equation model $\mathbf{AX}' = \mathbf{U}'$, where $\mathbf{A}$ is an $n \times (n+m)$ matrix. Consider only the introduction of r linear constraints, expressed by the following non-homogenous equation,

$$\boldsymbol{\Phi} \operatorname{vec} \mathbf{A} = \boldsymbol{\phi} \tag{3.2}$$

where $\boldsymbol{\Phi} = r \times n(n+m)$ matrix and $\boldsymbol{\phi} = (r \times 1)$ vector, both known. This representation allows for cross-equation restrictions.

Suppose that $\mathbf{A}^*: = \mathbf{H}\bar{\mathbf{A}}$ satisfies (3.2), i.e.

$$\boldsymbol{\Phi} \operatorname{vec} \mathbf{A}^* = \boldsymbol{\phi}.$$

If the model is correctly specified, restriction (3.2) must be equally satisfied by the true $\bar{\mathbf{A}}$,

$$\mathbf{\Phi} \text{ vec } \bar{\mathbf{A}} = \boldsymbol{\phi}.$$

Theorem 1 (Rank condition for identification): A necessary and sufficient condition for identification of the structure defined by $\bar{\mathbf{A}}$, in a model

$$\underset{n \times (n+m)}{\mathbf{A}} \quad \underset{(n+m) \times T}{\mathbf{X}'} = \underset{n \times T}{\mathbf{U}'}$$

subject to a set of linear restrictions vec $\mathbf{A} = \boldsymbol{\phi}$, is that

$$\text{rank } [\mathbf{\Phi}(\mathbf{I}_n \otimes \bar{\mathbf{A}}')] = n^2$$

i.e. $\mathbf{\Phi}(\mathbf{I}_n \otimes \bar{\mathbf{A}}')$ must have full column rank.

Proof: Subtracting both sets of equations, we obtain the homogeneous equation

$$\mathbf{\Phi} \text{ vec } (\mathbf{A}^* - \bar{\mathbf{A}}) = 0$$

or

$$\mathbf{\Phi} \text{ vec } [(\mathbf{H} - \mathbf{I}_n)\bar{\mathbf{A}}] = 0.$$

Using the fact vec $(\mathbf{ABC}) = (\mathbf{A} \otimes \mathbf{C}')$ vec $\mathbf{B}$, this can be expressed as

$$\mathbf{\Phi}(\mathbf{I} \otimes \bar{\mathbf{A}}') \text{ vec } (\mathbf{H} - \mathbf{I}_n) = 0.$$

Now if rank $[\mathbf{\Phi}(\mathbf{I} \otimes \bar{\mathbf{A}}')]$ is full, then the only solution to the homogenous equation is that the $(n^2 \times 1)$ vector, vec $(\mathbf{H} - \mathbf{I}_n)$, is zero, which implies $\mathbf{H} = \mathbf{I}$, which implies that $\mathbf{A}^* = \bar{\mathbf{A}}$, i.e. $\bar{\mathbf{A}}$ is the only model and therefore $\bar{\mathbf{A}}$ is identified.

Thus rank $[\mathbf{\Phi}(\mathbf{I} \otimes \bar{\mathbf{A}}')] = n^2$ (full column rank) is a necessary and sufficient condition for identification.
(End of proof)

Corollary (Order condition for identification): Since $\mathbf{\Phi}(\mathbf{I}_n \otimes \mathbf{A}')$ is an $(r \times n^2)$ matrix, to satisfy the condition that rank is greater or equal to n^2, we need the order condition that $r \geq n^2$. The order condition says that the number of restrictions on the model must be greater or equal to the square of the number of equations in the model.

Considering now a case where we have a subset of $N < n$

equations forming a matrix $\mathbf{A}_1$, which satisfy a set of separable restrictions

$$\boldsymbol{\Phi}_1 \operatorname{vec} \mathbf{A}_1 = \boldsymbol{\phi}_1$$

the structure will be identified if

$$\mathbf{A}_1^* = \mathbf{H}_1\bar{\mathbf{A}}$$

where $\mathbf{H}_1$ is some $N \times n$ matrix different from $(\mathbf{I}_N : 0)$. It can then be proved as before that a necessary condition for identification is that

$$\operatorname{rank}\,[\boldsymbol{\Phi}_1(\mathbf{I}_N \otimes \bar{\mathbf{A}}')] = Nn.$$

Applying this to the case where $N = 1$, and $\mathbf{A}_1 = \mathbf{a}'_k$ are the coefficients of equation k and this equation is identified by a total of r_k restrictions, then the order condition for identification becomes

$$r_k \geq n.$$

Notice that in the case of separable constraints, the kth equation can be identified even if the other equations are not.

If the equation constraints are made up of one normalization constraint and $r_k - 1$ zero constraints, and N_k is the total number of variables in the equation then $N_k = 1 + n + m - r_k$ and the condition is equivalent to $m \geq N_k - 1$, i.e. the number of predetermined variables in the system must be greater than or equal to the number of explanatory variables in the kth equation. If $m \geq N_k$, then the kth equation is said to be over-identified (via exclusion restrictions).

3.3 Special Cases: Separable Constraints and Identities

Consider the case of *separable constraints.*

Suppose that there are only single equation restrictions, where $\boldsymbol{\Phi}_k$ gives the restrictions of the kth equation only,

$$\boldsymbol{\Phi}_k\mathbf{a}_k = \boldsymbol{\phi}_k$$

where $\boldsymbol{\Phi}_k$ is the order of $r_k \times (n + m)$. The absence of cross-equation restrictions allows us to write (3.2) as

$$\begin{pmatrix} \boldsymbol{\Phi}_1 & 0 & 0 \\ & \boldsymbol{\Phi}_2 & \\ 0 & & \\ & & 0 \\ 0 & 0 & \boldsymbol{\Phi}_n \end{pmatrix} \operatorname{vec} \mathbf{A} = \begin{pmatrix} \boldsymbol{\phi}_1 \\ \boldsymbol{\phi}_2 \\ \\ \\ \boldsymbol{\phi}_n \end{pmatrix}$$

with $r = \sum_{k=1}^{n} r_k$ as total number of constraints.

As a special case, $\mathbf{\Phi}_k$ may have the form of a selection matrix with some ones and the rest zeroes, each value one picking up the corresponding element of $\mathbf{A}$. This is the case of normalization and zero types of restrictions.

The *rank condition* in this case is,

$$\text{rank}[\mathbf{\Phi}(\mathbf{I} \otimes \bar{\mathbf{A}}')] = \text{rank}\left[\begin{pmatrix} \mathbf{\Phi}_1 & & 0 \\ & \ddots & \\ 0 & & \mathbf{\Phi}_n \end{pmatrix}\begin{pmatrix} \bar{\mathbf{A}}' & & 0 \\ & \ddots & \\ 0 & & \bar{\mathbf{A}}' \end{pmatrix}\right]$$

$$= \text{rank}\begin{pmatrix} \mathbf{\Phi}_1\bar{\mathbf{A}}' & & 0 \\ & \ddots & \\ 0 & & \mathbf{\Phi}_n\bar{\mathbf{A}}' \end{pmatrix} = n^2$$

which implies that

$$\text{rank}\,(\mathbf{\Phi}_k\bar{\mathbf{A}}') = n, \qquad \forall k = 1, \ldots, n$$

and the *order condition,*

$$r_k \geq n, \qquad \forall k = 1, \ldots, n.$$

Consider the case of *identities*:

Let

$$\mathbf{A} = \begin{pmatrix} \mathbf{A}_1 \\ \mathbf{A}_2 \end{pmatrix}$$

where $\mathbf{A}_1 = n_1 \times (n + m)$ and $\mathbf{A}_2 = n_2 \times (n + m)$ and $\mathbf{A}_2$ contains only the coefficients of the identities.

In this case, the transformation $\mathbf{H}$ has the form

$$\mathbf{H} = \begin{pmatrix} \mathbf{H}_1 \\ \hline 0\ \mathbf{I}_{n_2} \end{pmatrix}$$

so that $\mathbf{A}_1^* = \mathbf{H}_1\bar{\mathbf{A}}$, i.e. the transformation, is applied only to the non-identities, since $\mathbf{A}^*$ and $\bar{\mathbf{A}}$ must have the same coefficients for the identities.

Write the constraint satisfied by $\mathbf{A}_1^*$ as

$$\mathbf{\Phi}_1 \text{ vec } \mathbf{A}_1^* = \boldsymbol{\phi}_1$$

where $\mathbf{\Phi}_1$ is of the order $r \times n_1(n + m)$.

Using the same argument as for the general case we obtain the expression

$$\boldsymbol{\Phi}_1(I_{n_1} \otimes \bar{\mathbf{A}}') \text{ vec } [\mathbf{H}_1 - (\mathbf{I}_{n_1}\ 0)] = 0.$$

Thus for $\mathbf{H}_1 = (\mathbf{I}_{n_1}\ 0)$ we need $\boldsymbol{\Phi}_1(\mathbf{I}_{n_1} \otimes \bar{\mathbf{A}}')$ be of full rank, i.e.

$$\text{rank } [\boldsymbol{\Phi}_1(\mathbf{I}_{n_1} \otimes \bar{\mathbf{A}}')] = n_1 n$$

with the corresponding order condition, $r \geq n_1 n$.

3.4 Treatment of General Linear Restrictions

Consider the single equation model

$$\underset{}{\mathbf{y}} = \underset{(T \times n)}{\mathbf{X}} \ \underset{(n \times 1)}{\mathbf{a}} + \mathbf{u} \tag{3.3}$$

subject to a set of r linear restrictions on 'a' of the form

$$\underset{(r \times n)}{\boldsymbol{\Phi}} \ \underset{(n \times 1)}{\mathbf{a}} = \underset{(r \times 1)}{\boldsymbol{\phi}}. \tag{3.4}$$

There are two equivalent ways in which we can get more efficient estimates when estimating under constraints:

(i) Lagrange multiplier technique
(ii) Reparametrization of the constraints

Lagrange multiplier technique: The problem is:

$$\min_{\mathbf{a}} \ \mathbf{u}'\mathbf{u} = (\mathbf{y} - \mathbf{X}\mathbf{a})'(\mathbf{y} - \mathbf{X}\mathbf{a})$$

subject to $\boldsymbol{\Phi}\mathbf{a} = \boldsymbol{\phi}$.

Form the Lagrange minimization function

$$\min_{\mathbf{a}} \ L = \mathbf{u}'\mathbf{u} - \boldsymbol{\lambda}'(\boldsymbol{\Phi}\mathbf{a} - \boldsymbol{\phi})$$

where $\boldsymbol{\lambda}$ is an $(r \times 1)$ vector of Lagrange multipliers.

The first-order conditions (FOCs) are:

$$(\mathbf{X}'\mathbf{X})\,\tilde{\mathbf{a}} - \mathbf{X}'\mathbf{y} - \boldsymbol{\Phi}'\boldsymbol{\lambda} = 0$$

$$\boldsymbol{\Phi}\,\tilde{\mathbf{a}} = \boldsymbol{\phi}$$

where $\tilde{\mathbf{a}}$ is the constrained estimator.

These conditions imply:

$$\tilde{\mathbf{a}} = \hat{\mathbf{a}} + (\mathbf{X}'\mathbf{X})^{-1}\,\mathbf{\Phi}'\boldsymbol{\lambda}$$

$$\mathbf{\Phi}_{\hat{a}} - \phi = -[\mathbf{\Phi}(\mathbf{X}'\mathbf{X})^{-1}\mathbf{\Phi}']\boldsymbol{\lambda} \Rightarrow \boldsymbol{\lambda} = -\,[\mathbf{\Phi}(\mathbf{X}'\mathbf{X})^{-1}\mathbf{\Phi}'](\mathbf{\Phi}\hat{\mathbf{a}} - \phi)$$

where $\hat{\mathbf{a}} = (\mathbf{X}'\mathbf{X})^{-1}\,\mathbf{X}'\mathbf{y}$ is the unconstrained OLS estimator.

Substituting $\boldsymbol{\lambda}$ in $\tilde{\mathbf{a}}$, we obtain the final expression of the constrained estimator for **a**:

$$\tilde{\mathbf{a}} = \hat{\mathbf{a}} - (\mathbf{X}'\mathbf{X})^{-1}\,\mathbf{\Phi}'\,[\mathbf{\Phi}(\mathbf{X}'\mathbf{X})^{-1}\,\mathbf{\Phi}']^{-1}\,(\mathbf{\Phi}\hat{\mathbf{a}} - \phi)$$

with variance matrix:

$$\begin{aligned}\mathrm{Var}(\tilde{\mathbf{a}}) &= \sigma^2(\mathbf{X}'\mathbf{X})^{-1} \\ &\quad - \sigma^2(\mathbf{X}'\mathbf{X})^{-1}\mathbf{\Phi}'\,[\mathbf{\Phi}(\mathbf{X}'\mathbf{X})^{-1}\mathbf{\Phi}']^{-1}\mathbf{\Phi}(\mathbf{X}'\mathbf{X})^{-1}.\end{aligned}$$

Reparameterization of the contraints: Notice that the set of constraints (3.4) determines an $(n-r)$ dimensional subspace of $\mathbf{R}^n$. This fact can be exploited by reparameterizing the constraints.

Consider writing the coefficient vector **a** in the form

$$\underset{(n\times 1)}{\mathbf{a}} = \underset{n\times(n-r)}{\mathbf{S}}\;\underset{(n-r)\times 1}{\gamma} + \underset{(n\times 1)}{\mathbf{s}} \tag{3.5}$$

where $r \leq n$ (otherwise, if $r = n$ we have $\mathbf{a} = \mathbf{s}$), and where S and **s** are known, though not necessarily unique.

For (3.5) to be a valid reparameterization of a, it must satisfy the constraints (3.4) for all values of γ, i.e. $\mathbf{\Phi}(\mathbf{S}\gamma + \mathbf{s}) \equiv \mathbf{\Phi}$.

This implies

$$\mathbf{\Phi}\mathbf{S} = 0 \text{ (see Section 3.6)}$$

$$\mathbf{\Phi}\mathbf{s} = \phi.$$

Substituting (3.5) into (3.3), we obtain the transformed model

$$\mathbf{y} - \mathbf{X}\mathbf{s} = (\mathbf{X}\mathbf{S})\gamma + \mathbf{u}.$$

By the Gauss–Markov Theorem, the Best Linear Unbiased Estimator (BLUE) of γ is,

$$\hat{\gamma} = (\mathbf{S}'\mathbf{X}'\mathbf{X}\mathbf{S})^{-1}\,\mathbf{S}'\mathbf{X}'(\mathbf{y} - \mathbf{X}\mathbf{s}).$$

To obtain now $\tilde{\mathbf{a}}$, from (3.5)

$$\tilde{\mathbf{a}} = \mathbf{S}\hat{\gamma} + \mathbf{s} = \mathbf{S}(\mathbf{S}'\mathbf{X}'\mathbf{X}S)^{-1}S'\mathbf{X}'(\mathbf{y} - \mathbf{X}\mathbf{s}) + \mathbf{s}$$

and

$$(\tilde{\mathbf{a}} - \mathbf{a}) = \mathbf{S}(\hat{\gamma} - \gamma) = \mathbf{S}(\mathbf{S}'\mathbf{X}'\mathbf{X}\mathbf{S})^{-1}\mathbf{S}'\mathbf{X}'\mathbf{u}.$$

If $\mathbf{X}$ is non-stochastic and $E(\mathbf{uu}') = \boldsymbol{\sigma}^2\mathbf{I}$, then the variance of $\tilde{\mathbf{a}}$ is

$$\mathrm{Var}(\tilde{\mathbf{a}}) = \boldsymbol{\sigma}^2\,[\mathbf{S}(\mathbf{S}'\mathbf{X}'\mathbf{X}\mathbf{S})^{-1}\mathbf{S}'].$$

If $\mathbf{X}$ is stochastic, rescaling

$$\sqrt{T}(\tilde{\mathbf{a}} - \mathbf{a}) = \mathbf{S}\left(\frac{\mathbf{S}'\mathbf{X}'\mathbf{X}\mathbf{S}}{T}\right)^{-1}\frac{\mathbf{S}'\mathbf{X}'\mathbf{u}}{\sqrt{T}}$$

and assuming that

$$\operatorname{plim}\frac{\mathbf{S}'\mathbf{X}'\mathbf{X}\mathbf{S}}{T}$$

exists and is a finite positive definite (p.d.) matrix, $\mathbf{M}^*$, we can derive the usual results, i.e.

$$\sqrt{T}(\tilde{\mathbf{a}} - \mathbf{a}) \;\tilde{}\; N(0, \boldsymbol{\sigma}^2\mathbf{S}'\mathbf{M}^{*-1}\mathbf{S}).$$

3.5 Appendix: Computation of S and s

Partition the set of restrictions if necessary by changing the order of the coefficients so that

$$\underset{r \times r}{(\boldsymbol{\Phi}_1} \quad \underset{r \times (n-r)}{\boldsymbol{\Phi}_2)}\begin{pmatrix}\mathbf{a}_1\\ \mathbf{a}_2\end{pmatrix} = \boldsymbol{\Phi}_1\mathbf{a}_1 + \boldsymbol{\Phi}_2\mathbf{a}_2 = \boldsymbol{\phi},$$

such that $\boldsymbol{\Phi}_1$ is a non-singular square matrix. Then

$$\mathbf{a}_1 = -\boldsymbol{\Phi}_1^{-1}\boldsymbol{\Phi}_2\mathbf{a}_2 + \boldsymbol{\Phi}_1^{-1}\boldsymbol{\phi}$$

$$\mathbf{a}_2 = \mathbf{I}_{n-r}\mathbf{a}_2 + 0$$

or compactly

$$\mathbf{a} = \begin{pmatrix}-\boldsymbol{\Phi}_1^{-1}\boldsymbol{\Phi}_2\\ \mathbf{I}_{n-r}\end{pmatrix}\mathbf{a}_2 + \begin{pmatrix}\boldsymbol{\Phi}_1^{-1}\boldsymbol{\phi}\\ 0\end{pmatrix}.$$

This gives *one* reparameterization of $\mathbf{a}$ in terms of $\mathbf{a}_2$, where $\mathbf{a}_2$ belongs to $\mathbf{R}^{n-r}$ and

$$\mathbf{S} = \begin{pmatrix}-\boldsymbol{\Phi}_1^{-1}\boldsymbol{\Phi}_2\\ \mathbf{I}_{n-r}\end{pmatrix} \qquad \mathbf{s} = \begin{pmatrix}\boldsymbol{\Phi}_1^{-1}\boldsymbol{\phi}\\ 0\end{pmatrix}.$$

From this we can also see how $\boldsymbol{\Phi}\mathbf{S} = 0$ and $\boldsymbol{\Phi}\mathbf{s} = \boldsymbol{\phi}$.

4

Estimation of Single Equation Models, 1: The OLS and GLS Estimators

Consider the single equation model

$$y_t = \underset{(1 \times n)}{\mathbf{a}'} \underset{(n \times 1)}{\mathbf{x}_t} + u_t \qquad t = 1, \ldots, T$$

or

$$\underset{(T \times 1)}{\mathbf{y}} = \underset{(T \times n)}{\mathbf{X}} \underset{(n \times 1)}{\mathbf{a}} + \underset{(T \times 1)}{\mathbf{u}} \tag{4.1}$$

4.1 Serially Independent Disturbances

Let $u_t \sim \text{IID}\,(0, \sigma^2)$.

We will consider two cases: the case where the regressors are completely exogenous, and the case where they are stochastic.

4.1.1 Completely Exogenous Regressors

Let $\mathbf{x}_t$ be a vector of strictly exogenous variables. In this case the Gauss–Markov Theorem implies that OLS is the BLUE of $\mathbf{a}$. OLS yields

$$(\mathbf{X}'\mathbf{X})\hat{\mathbf{a}} = \mathbf{X}'\mathbf{y}$$

or

$$(\mathbf{X}'\mathbf{X})\,(\hat{\mathbf{a}} - \mathbf{a}) = \mathbf{X}'\mathbf{u}.$$

Rescaling

$$\frac{\mathbf{X}'\mathbf{X}}{T}\sqrt{T}\,(\hat{\mathbf{a}} - \mathbf{a}) = \frac{\mathbf{X}'\mathbf{u}}{\sqrt{T}} = \mathbf{w}. \tag{4.2}$$

Assume that

$$\lim \frac{\mathbf{X}'\mathbf{X}}{T} = \mathbf{M},$$

where **M** is a p.d. bounded matrix. Then by a central limit theorem discussed in Chapter 1

$$\mathbf{w} \;\widetilde{a}\; \mathrm{N}(0, \sigma^2 M).$$

Therefore from the Slutsky Theorem and the Cramer Linear Transformation Theorem we obtain

$$\sqrt{T}(\hat{\mathbf{a}} - \mathbf{a}) \;\widetilde{a}\; \mathrm{N}(0, \mathbf{M}^{-1}\sigma^2\mathbf{M}\mathbf{M}^{-1}) = \mathrm{N}(0, \sigma^2\mathbf{M}^{-1}).$$

4.1.2 Stochastic Regressors

Let now **X** be stochastic predetermined variables. This happens for example when **X** contains lagged endogenous variables.

The u_ts are independent, so that $\mathrm{E}(\mathbf{x}_t u_t) = 0$, $\forall t$, i.e. uncorrelated contemporaneously. The OLS estimator, once rescaled can be written as (4.2), i.e.

$$\frac{\mathbf{X}'\mathbf{X}}{T}\sqrt{T}\,(\hat{\mathbf{a}} - \mathbf{a}) = \frac{\mathbf{X}'\mathbf{u}}{\sqrt{T}}.$$

Assume that

$$\operatorname{plim} \frac{\mathbf{X}'\mathbf{X}}{T} = \mathbf{M} = \mathrm{E}\left(\frac{\mathbf{X}'\mathbf{X}}{T}\right),$$

which is equivalent to second-order ergodicity on the process generating **X**. The matrix **M** is finite and assumed to be p.d. Then by the previously discussed Central Limit Theorem

$$\mathbf{w} = \frac{\mathbf{X}'\mathbf{u}}{\sqrt{T}} \;\widetilde{a}\; \mathrm{N}(0, \sigma^2\mathbf{M})$$

and therefore can proceed exactly as in the exogenous case to obtain that

$$\sqrt{T}(\hat{\mathbf{a}} - \mathbf{a}) \;\widetilde{a}\; \mathrm{N}(0, \sigma^2\mathbf{M}^{-1}).$$

Notice that the OLS estimator is *not* unbiased in small samples now. However it is clear that the estimator is consistent, and will be shown to be asymptotically efficient in a class of linear estimators later, as a special case of Theorem 1 of Chapter 5.

4.2 Serially Dependent Disturbances

Let $E(\mathbf{uu}') = \sigma^2\mathbf{\Omega}$, where $\mathbf{\Omega}$ is a p.d. serial covariance matrix. Consider again completely exogenous and stochastic regressors.

4.2.1 Completely Exogenous Regressors

Since $\mathbf{\Omega}$ is a p.d. matrix, then there exists a matrix $\mathbf{H}$ such that,

$$\mathbf{HH}' = \mathbf{\Omega}^{-1} \tag{4.3}$$

or

$$\mathbf{H}'\mathbf{\Omega}\mathbf{H} = \mathbf{I}.$$

Applying the transformation $\mathbf{H}'$ to the model (4.1), we obtain

$$\mathbf{H}'\mathbf{y} = \mathbf{H}'\mathbf{Xa} + \mathbf{H}'\mathbf{u} \tag{4.4}$$

or

$$\mathbf{y}^* = \mathbf{X}^*\mathbf{a} + \mathbf{u}^*$$

where

$$\mathbf{y}^* = \mathbf{H}'\mathbf{y} \text{ etc.}$$

Now

$$E(\mathbf{u}^*\mathbf{u}^{*\prime}) = \mathbf{H}'E(\mathbf{uu}')\mathbf{H} = \sigma^2\mathbf{H}'\mathbf{\Omega}\mathbf{H} = \sigma^2\mathbf{I}.$$

Therefore, the Gauss–Markov Theorem ensures that OLS applied to (4.4) gives the BLUE of $\mathbf{a}$. The result is

$$(\mathbf{X}'\mathbf{H}\,\mathbf{H}'\mathbf{X})\,(\hat{\mathbf{a}} - \mathbf{a}) = \mathbf{X}'\mathbf{HH}'\mathbf{u}$$

or

$$(\mathbf{X}'\mathbf{\Omega}^{-1}\mathbf{X})\,(\hat{\mathbf{a}} - \mathbf{a}) = \mathbf{X}\mathbf{\Omega}^{-1}\mathbf{u}.$$

This is the GLS estimator of $\mathbf{a}$ (often referred to as the Aitken GLS estimates). Rescaling

$$\left(\frac{\mathbf{X}'\mathbf{\Omega}^{-1}\mathbf{X}}{T}\right)\sqrt{T}\,(\hat{\mathbf{a}} - \mathbf{a}) = \left(\frac{\mathbf{X}'\mathbf{\Omega}^{-1}\mathbf{u}}{\sqrt{T}}\right): = \mathbf{w} \tag{4.5}$$

and

$$\mathrm{E}(\mathbf{ww}') = \mathrm{E}\left(\frac{\mathbf{X}'\mathbf{\Omega}^{-1}\mathbf{uu}'\mathbf{\Omega}^{-1}\mathbf{X}}{T}\right) = \sigma^2\left(\frac{\mathbf{X}'\mathbf{\Omega}^{-1}\mathbf{X}}{T}\right)$$

since the **X**s are non-stochastic.

If $\mathbf{\Omega}$ is known and **X** is non-stochastic a discussion of asymptotic properties can be conducted as in Section 4.1.

4.2.2 Stochastic Regressors

Suppose that **X** contains lagged endogenous variables. Consider the GLS estimator (4.5).

$$\left(\frac{\mathbf{X}'\mathbf{\Omega}^{-1}\mathbf{X}}{T}\right)\sqrt{T}\,(\hat{\mathbf{a}} - \mathbf{a}) = \frac{\mathbf{X}'\mathbf{\Omega}^{-1}\mathbf{u}}{\sqrt{T}} = \mathbf{w}.$$

In the presence of errors generated by autoregressive processes, the transformation matrix $\mathbf{H}'$ is a lower triangular matrix with ones on the leading diagonal,

$$\mathbf{H}' = \begin{pmatrix} h_{11} & 0 & \ldots & 0 \\ h_{21} & h_{22} & \ldots & 0 \\ h_{31} & h_{32} & \ldots & 0 \\ \cdot & \cdot & \ldots & \cdot \\ h_{T1} & h_{T2} & \ldots & 1 \end{pmatrix}$$

with

$$h_{tt} = 1, \text{ if } t > r_1$$

where the number of rows different from the previous row only by a right-hand shift is r if the AR process is of order r, and $h_{t,t-j} = -p_j$ for $t > r$, where p_j is the coefficient of u_{t-j} in the regression of u_t on $u_1, \ldots, u_{t-1}$.

Thus we are regressing each u_t on all previous u_ts and taking the errors (which will be independent) as new disturbances, i.e.

$$u_t^* = u_t + \sum_{j=1}^{t-1} h_{t,t-j}u_{t-j} = u_t - \sum_{j=1}^{r} p_j u_{t-j}, \qquad \text{if } t > r$$

which ensures that

$$\mathrm{E}(u_t^* u_{t-j}) = 0,\ j \geq 1.$$

Then, for $t > s$

$$\mathrm{E}(u_t^*\, u_s^*) = 0. \tag{4.6}$$

In the case of stochastic regressors

$$E(\mathbf{ww}') = E\left(\frac{\mathbf{X}'\mathbf{\Omega}^{-1}\mathbf{uu}'\mathbf{\Omega}^{-1}\mathbf{X}}{T}\right)$$

as for the non-stochastic model in Section 4.2.1, but now we cannot take the expectations operator over the **X** to apply only to **uu**′ as we did before. However we can derive a similar expression in this case, if the stochastic process of generating the errors is linear with white noise errors given by the u_t^*. Using $\mathbf{HH}' = \mathbf{\Omega}^{-1}$ from (4.3), we can write E(**ww**′) as

$$E\left(\frac{\mathbf{X}'\mathbf{\Omega}^{-1}\mathbf{uu}'\mathbf{\Omega}^{-1}\mathbf{X}}{T}\right) = E\left(\frac{\mathbf{X}^{*\prime}\mathbf{u}^{*}\mathbf{u}^{*\prime}\mathbf{X}^{*}}{T}\right).$$

The *ij*th element of this expression is

$$E\sum_{t=1}^{T}\sum_{s=1}^{T}(x_{it}^{*}\,u_t^{*}\,u_s^{*}\,x_{js}^{*}).$$

For $t > s$, u_t^* is independent of u_s^* from (4.6), and x_{it}^* and x_{js}^* are linear combinations of past xs, therefore all except u_t^* depend only on past values of the u_s^*. Since then u_t^* is independent of all of x_{it}^*, u_s^*, x_{js}^* we can take

$$E(u_t^*)E(x_{it}^*u_s^*x_{js}^*) = 0, \text{ since } E(u_t^*) = 0.$$

So all the elements of E(**ww**′) are going to be zero except for $t = s$, and we have

$$E\left[\sum_t\sum_s(x_{it}^*u_t^*u_t^*u_{js}^*)\right] = \sum_t E[(x_{it}^*x_{jt}^*)u_t^{*2}] = \sigma^2\sum_t E(x_{it}^*x^*{}_{js})$$

and therefore

$$E\left(\frac{\mathbf{X}^{*\prime}\mathbf{u}^{*}\mathbf{u}^{*\prime}\mathbf{X}^{*}}{T}\right) = \sigma^2 E\left(\frac{\mathbf{X}^{*\prime}\mathbf{X}^{*}}{T}\right) = \sigma^2 E\left(\frac{\mathbf{X}'\mathbf{\Omega}^{-1}\mathbf{X}}{T}\right).$$

If $\mathbf{\Omega}$ corresponds to an autoregressive process then the u_t^* are the errors on the autoregressive process for $t > r$, and the same limit is obtained as $T \rightarrow \infty$. Assuming now that

$$\text{plim}\left(\frac{\mathbf{X}'\mathbf{\Omega}^{-1}\mathbf{X}}{T}\right) = \mathbf{M},$$

where **M** is a p.d. matrix, and assuming ergodicity so that plim is equivalent to E, we apply the Hannan Central Limit Theorem, assuming all its conditions are satisfied, to obtain

$$\mathbf{w} = \frac{\mathbf{X}'\boldsymbol{\Omega}^{-1}\mathbf{u}}{\sqrt{T}} = \frac{\mathbf{X}^{*\prime}\mathbf{u}^{*}}{\sqrt{T}} \; \tilde{a} \; \mathrm{N}(0, \sigma^2\mathbf{M})$$

and then by the Cramer Linerar Transformation Theorem

$$\sqrt{T}(\hat{\mathbf{a}} - \mathbf{a}) \; \tilde{a} \; \mathrm{N}(0, \sigma^2\mathbf{M}^{-1}).$$

4.3 Heteroscedastic Disturbances

Let $\mathrm{E}(\mathbf{uu}') = \boldsymbol{\Omega}$ where $\boldsymbol{\Omega}$ is a $(T \times T)$ diagonal matrix with elements σ_t^2, $t = 1, \ldots, T$.

Again by the Aitken Theorem if the X are non-stochastic GLS is the BLUE of $\mathbf{a}$ in (4.1), and we have

$$\left(\frac{\mathbf{X}'\boldsymbol{\Omega}^{-1}\mathbf{X}}{T}\right)\sqrt{T}(\hat{\mathbf{a}} - \mathbf{a}) = \frac{\mathbf{X}'\boldsymbol{\Omega}^{-1}\mathbf{u}}{\sqrt{T}}.$$

The two main characteristics of the model when disturbances are heteroscedastic are the following:

(i) In this case,

$$\operatorname{plim}\left(\frac{\mathbf{X}'\boldsymbol{\Omega}^{-1}\mathbf{X}}{T}\right)$$

may not be O(1), and, if it is rescaled to be O(1), it may not be a p.d. matrix. Even if some elements have non-zero limits as $T \to \infty$, others may have zero limits, and so again the limiting matrix may be singular. The (i, j) element of $(\mathbf{X}'\boldsymbol{\Omega}^{-1}\mathbf{X})$ is

$$\sum_{t=1}^{T}\left(\frac{x_{it}x_{jt}}{\sigma_t^2}\right).$$

If $\sigma_t^2 \to \infty$ then even for $\mathbf{x}$ non-stochastic, the plim might not exist, e.g. let $\mathbf{x}_{it}$ be bounded $\forall i$, $\forall t$ and let $\sigma_t^2 = \boldsymbol{\alpha} + \boldsymbol{\beta}t^2$. In this case the (i, j)th elements would be O(1) rather than O(T) as usual, and therefore by scaling by T, lim $\mathbf{X}'\boldsymbol{\Omega}^{-1}\mathbf{X}/\mathbf{T}$ would not be a p.d. matrix since the elements would tend to zero as $t \to \infty$.

(ii) Since for $\boldsymbol{\Omega}^{-1}$ diagonal

$$\mathbf{w} = \left(\frac{\Sigma_t x_{it}^{*} u_t^{*}}{\sqrt{T}}\right)$$

where $x_{it}^{*} = x_{it}/\sigma_t$, if the x_{it}^{*}s are non-stochastic variables and the

u_t^*s are independent (since off-diagonal elements of $\mathbf{\Omega}$ are zero), we can apply an appropriate central limit theorem to derive the asymptotic distribution. But unless $(\mathbf{X}'\mathbf{\Omega}^{-1}\mathbf{X})$ has latent roots all of which tend to $+\infty$ as $T \rightarrow \infty$, the estimators will not be consistent, and indeed in the special case where

$$\lim_{T\rightarrow\infty}(\mathbf{X}'\mathbf{\Omega}^{-1}\mathbf{X})$$

is finite and non-singular, as could occur for example in the special case considered at the end of Section 4.2.2 $(\hat{\mathbf{a}} - \mathbf{a})$ has an asymptotic distribution, i.e. the errors of $\hat{\mathbf{a}}$ remain finite as $T \rightarrow \infty$, rather than being $O(T^{-1/2})$ as in the homoscedastic case.

5

Estimation of Single Equation Models, 2: The Instrumental Variable and 2SLS Estimators

5.1 The Instrumental Variable (IV) Estimator and the Two-Stage Least Squares (2SLS) Estimator

5.1.1 Number of Instruments Equal to the Number of Regressors

Consider one equation, say the first, out of a set of simultaneous equations and write it

$$\underset{(T \times 1)}{\mathbf{y}_1} = \underset{(T \times n_1)}{\mathbf{X}_1} \underset{(n_1 \times 1)}{\mathbf{a}_1} + \underset{(T \times 1)}{\mathbf{u}_1},$$

$$\mathrm{E}(\mathbf{u}_1) = 0, \ \mathrm{E}(\mathbf{u}_1\mathbf{u}_1') = \sigma_1^2 \mathbf{I}_T$$

and let $\mathbf{Z}$ be a $(T \times m)$ matrix of instrumental variables satisfying in addition to the usual conditions:

Assumption 5.1 (A5.1): rank plim $\dfrac{\mathbf{Z}'\mathbf{Z}}{T} = m.$

Notice that at this stage we are not using $\mathbf{Z}$ in the same sense as it was used in Section 2.1. Each variable in the $\mathbf{Z}$ matrix is predetermined in the sense that it is an exogenous variable, a lagged exogenous variable or a lagged endogenous variable. But $\mathbf{Z}$ does not necessarily include all variables occurring in the $\mathbf{Z}$ matrix of Section 2.1, which can be regarded as containing all the predetermined variables which have a non-zero coefficient in at least one of the structural equations. Also the **Z** matrix of this section may include variables which do not occur in the equations defining the model generating the variables; extra lagged variables may be included in **Z**, both exogenous and endogenous. We wish to discuss a quite general set of variables **Z**, subject only to the general condition discussed below.

A5.1 may not be satisfied in some cases, typically in the case of a large econometric model where the number of predetermined (i.e. exogenous and lagged endogenous) variables may be greater than the number of observations on each variable. See Section 5.1.4.

Consider first the case that $m = n_1$, i.e. the number of instruments is equal to the number of regressors. This for example would be the case if all the predetermined variables were included in the **Z** matrix, and the first equation was exactly identified by means of zero–one restrictions.

The instrumental variable (IV) estimator of $\mathbf{a}_1$ is defined by

$$\mathbf{Z}'\mathbf{X}_1\hat{\mathbf{a}} = \mathbf{Z}'\mathbf{y},$$

leading to

$$\mathbf{Z}'\mathbf{X}_1(\hat{\mathbf{a}}_1 - \mathbf{a}_1) = \mathbf{Z}'\mathbf{u}_1.$$

After rescaling this becomes

$$\frac{\mathbf{Z}'\mathbf{X}_1}{T}\sqrt{T}(\hat{\mathbf{a}}_1 - \mathbf{a}_1) = \frac{\mathbf{Z}'\mathbf{u}_1}{\sqrt{T}}.$$

Assume that:

Assumption 5.2:

$$\operatorname{plim}_{T\to\infty}\frac{\mathbf{X}_1'\mathbf{Z}}{\mathbf{T}} = \mathbf{K}',$$

a non-singular $(n_1 \times n_1)$ matrix, and that A5.1 becomes

Assumption 5.3:

$$\operatorname{plim}_{T\to\infty}\frac{\mathbf{Z}'\mathbf{Z}}{T} = \mathbf{M},$$

a symmetric p.d. $(n_1 \times n_1)$ matrix.

Then, by using an appropriate CLT

$$\mathbf{w} = \frac{\mathbf{Z}'\mathbf{u}_1}{\sqrt{T}} \mathrel{\tilde{a}} \mathrm{N}(0, \sigma_1^2\,\mathbf{M})$$

and so, by the Cramer Linear Transformation Theorem

$$\sqrt{T}(\hat{\mathbf{a}}_1 - \mathbf{a}_1) \stackrel{a}{\sim} \mathrm{N}[0, \sigma_1^2(\mathbf{K}')^{-1}\,\mathbf{M}\mathbf{K}^{-1}]$$

or

$$\sqrt{T}(\hat{\mathbf{a}}_1 - \mathbf{a}_1) \stackrel{a}{\sim} \mathrm{N}[0, \sigma_1^2(\mathbf{K}\mathbf{M}^{-1}\mathbf{K}')^{-1}].$$

Notice that this result is true for any set of instrumental variables. $\mathbf{Z}$ may consist of predetermined (i.e. exogenous and lagged endogenous) variables, the only restriction being that the number of instruments equals the number of regressors in the first equation.

5.1.2 Number of Instruments Greater than the Number of Regressors

Let $m > n_1$, i.e. the number of instruments is greater than the number of regressors. This is true, for example, in the 2SLS case where the first equation is over-identified by means of zero–one restrictions.

Let $\mathbf{H}$ be any $(m \times n_1)$ matrix with rank $(\mathbf{H}) = n_1$. Then $\mathbf{H}$ can be used to transform the original set of instruments so as to reduce their number to n_1. The resulting set of instruments is the $(T \times n_1)$ matrix.

$$\mathbf{Z}^* = \mathbf{Z}\mathbf{H}.$$

Having reduced the number of instruments to n_1 by means of the linear transformation $\mathbf{H}$, we proceed as in Section 5.1.1. The IV estimator of $\mathbf{a}_1$ (depending on the particular choice of $\mathbf{H}$) is defined by

$$\frac{\mathbf{Z}^{*\prime}\mathbf{X}_1}{T}\sqrt{T}\,(\hat{\mathbf{a}}_1 - \mathbf{a}_1) = \frac{\mathbf{Z}^{*\prime}\mathbf{u}_1}{\sqrt{T}}.$$

Then we proceed to minimize the corresponding AVM by choice of $\mathbf{H}$.

We assume that:

Assumption 5.2′: $\mathrm{plim}_{T\to\infty}\,(\mathbf{X}_1'\mathbf{Z}/\mathbf{T}) = \mathbf{K}$, an $(n_1 \times m)$ matrix of full rank n_1.

Assumption 5.3′: $\mathrm{plim}_{T\to\infty}\,(\mathbf{Z}'\mathbf{Z}/\mathbf{T}) = \mathbf{M}$, a symmetric, p.d. $(m \times m)$ matrix.

It then follows that plim $(\mathbf{X}_1'\mathbf{Z}^*/T) = \mathbf{K}\mathbf{H} = \mathbf{K}^*$ and plim $(\mathbf{Z}^{*\prime}\mathbf{Z}^*/T) = \mathbf{H}'\mathbf{M}\mathbf{H} = \mathbf{M}^*$ are both non-singular matrices. Then by the same argument as in Section 5.1.1 we obtain that the IV estimator based on the **H**-transformation is consistent and asymptotically normal

$$\sqrt{T}(\hat{\mathbf{a}}_H - \mathbf{a}_1) \,\tilde{a}\, N[0, \sigma_1^2(\mathbf{K}^*\mathbf{M}^{*-1}\mathbf{K}^{*\prime})^{-1}]$$

where the asymptotic variance matrix of the IV estimator can be written as

$$\begin{aligned}\text{AVM}(\hat{\mathbf{a}}_H) &= \sigma_1^2\,(\mathbf{K}^*\mathbf{M}^{*-1}\mathbf{K}^{*\prime})^{-1} = \sigma_1^2(\mathbf{K}^{*\prime})^{-1}\mathbf{M}^*(\mathbf{K}^*)^{-1}\\ &= \sigma_1^2\,(\mathbf{H}'\mathbf{K}')^{-1}\mathbf{H}'\mathbf{M}\mathbf{H}(\mathbf{K}\mathbf{H})^{-1}.\end{aligned}$$

Clearly the asymptotic efficiency of the IV estimator depends on the choice of **H**. So we consider the problem of choosing the **H**-transformation optimally, in the sense of minimizing the asymptotic variance matrix of the IV estimator.

A 'natural' choice for **H** is the $(m \times n_1)$ asymptotic coefficient matrix of the regression of the $\mathbf{X}_1$ on the **Z**

$$\mathbf{Q}' = \text{plim}\,\frac{(\mathbf{Z}'\mathbf{Z})^{-1}}{T}\,\frac{\mathbf{Z}'\mathbf{X}_1}{T} = \mathbf{M}^{-1}\,\mathbf{K}'.$$

Setting $\mathbf{H} = \mathbf{Q}'$ gives the IV estimator $\hat{\mathbf{a}}_Q$ defined by

$$\mathbf{Q}'\mathbf{Z}\mathbf{X}_1(\hat{\mathbf{a}}_Q - \mathbf{a}_1) = \mathbf{Q}'\mathbf{Z}\mathbf{u}_1 \tag{5.1}$$

with asymptotic variance matrix obtained by substituting in (5.1)

$$\begin{aligned}\text{AVM}(\hat{\mathbf{a}}_Q) &= \sigma_1^2(\mathbf{Q}\mathbf{K}')^{-1}\mathbf{Q}\mathbf{M}\mathbf{Q}'\,(\mathbf{K}\mathbf{Q}')^{-1}\\ &= \sigma_1^2(\mathbf{K}\mathbf{M}^{-1}\mathbf{K}')^{-1}\\ &= \sigma_1^2(\mathbf{Q}\mathbf{M}\mathbf{Q}')^{-1}.\end{aligned}$$

Theorem 1: The IV estimator $\hat{\mathbf{a}}_Q$ is asymptotically efficient in the sense that

$$\text{AVM}(\hat{\mathbf{a}}_H) - \text{AVM}(\hat{\mathbf{a}}_Q)$$

is a positive semi-definite matrix for any choice of **H**.

Proof: We want to show that the asymptotic variance matrix of $\hat{\mathbf{a}}_H$ exceeds that of $\hat{\mathbf{a}}_Q$ by a positive semi-definite (p.s.d.) matrix.

Let

$$\text{AVM}(\hat{\mathbf{a}}_H) = \sigma_1^2(\mathbf{H}'\mathbf{K}')^{-1}\,\mathbf{H}'\mathbf{M}\mathbf{H}(\mathbf{K}\mathbf{H})^{-1} = \sigma_1^2\mathbf{H}^{*\prime}\,\mathbf{M}\mathbf{H}^*$$

$$\text{AVM}(\hat{\mathbf{a}}_Q) = \sigma_1^2(\mathbf{Q}\mathbf{K}')^{-1}\,\mathbf{Q}\mathbf{M}\mathbf{Q}'(\mathbf{K}\mathbf{Q}')^{-1} = \sigma_1^2\mathbf{Q}^*\mathbf{M}\mathbf{Q}^{*\prime}$$

where

$$\mathbf{H}^* = \mathbf{H}(\mathbf{KH})^{-1} \text{ and } \mathbf{Q}^{*\prime} = \mathbf{Q}'(\mathbf{KQ}')^{-1}.$$

Define

$$\boldsymbol{\Delta} = \mathbf{H}^* - \mathbf{Q}^{*\prime}.$$

Then

$$\mathbf{H}^* = \mathbf{Q}^{*\prime} + \boldsymbol{\Delta}$$

and so

$$\begin{aligned}\text{AVM}(\hat{\mathbf{a}}_{\text{H}}) &= \sigma_1^2(\mathbf{Q}^{*\prime} + \boldsymbol{\Delta})' \mathbf{M}(\mathbf{Q}^{*\prime} + \boldsymbol{\Delta}) \\ &= \sigma_1^2(\mathbf{Q}^*\mathbf{MQ}^{*\prime} + \mathbf{Q}^*\mathbf{M}\boldsymbol{\Delta} + \boldsymbol{\Delta}'\mathbf{MQ}^{*\prime} + \boldsymbol{\Delta}'\mathbf{M}\boldsymbol{\Delta}).\end{aligned}$$

We want to show now that

$$\mathbf{Q}^*\mathbf{M}\boldsymbol{\Delta} = 0 = \boldsymbol{\Delta}'\mathbf{MQ}^{*\prime}.$$

First notice that

$$\mathbf{Q}^{*\prime} = \mathbf{Q}'(\mathbf{KQ}')^{-1} = \mathbf{M}^{-1}\,\mathbf{K}'(\mathbf{KM}^{-1}\mathbf{K}')^{-1}$$

from which

$$\mathbf{Q}^*\mathbf{M}\boldsymbol{\Delta} = (\mathbf{KM}^{-1}\mathbf{K}')^{-1}\mathbf{K}\boldsymbol{\Delta}$$

but

$$\mathbf{K}\boldsymbol{\Delta} = \mathbf{KH}^* - \mathbf{KQ}^{*\prime} = \mathbf{KH}(\mathbf{KH})^{-1} - \mathbf{KQ}'(\mathbf{KQ}')^{-1} = 0$$

and so

$$\mathbf{Q}^*\mathbf{M}\boldsymbol{\Delta} = 0 = \boldsymbol{\Delta}'\mathbf{M}^{*\prime}.$$

Therefore

$$\begin{aligned}\text{AVM}(\hat{\mathbf{a}}_{\text{H}}) &= \sigma_1^2\mathbf{Q}^{*\prime}\mathbf{MQ}^* + \sigma_1^2\boldsymbol{\Delta}'\mathbf{M}\boldsymbol{\Delta} \\ &= \text{AVM}(\hat{\mathbf{a}}_{\text{Q}}) + \sigma_1^2\boldsymbol{\Delta}'\mathbf{M}\boldsymbol{\Delta}\end{aligned}$$

where $\sigma_1^2\boldsymbol{\Delta}'\mathbf{M}\boldsymbol{\Delta}$ is a p.s.d. matrix.
(End of proof)

The problem here is that **K** and **M**, and hence **Q**, are in reality unknown and must be approximated in some way. Clearly a simple, consistent estimator of **Q** is

$$\hat{\mathbf{Q}}' = (\mathbf{Z}'\mathbf{Z})^{-1}\,\mathbf{Z}'\mathbf{X}.$$

This suggests choosing as the 'best' set of instruments the optimal linear predictor of the $\mathbf{X}_1$, based on the **Z**, i.e.

$$\mathbf{Z}\hat{\mathbf{Q}}' = \mathbf{Z}(\mathbf{Z}'\mathbf{Z})^{-1}\,\mathbf{Z}'\mathbf{X}_1.$$

Using $\hat{\mathbf{Q}}'$ instead of $\mathbf{Q}'$ to transform the original set $\mathbf{Z}$ of instruments we obtain the estimator of $\mathbf{a}$ defined by

$$(\hat{\mathbf{Q}}\mathbf{Z}'\mathbf{X}_1)(\hat{\mathbf{a}}_1 - \mathbf{a}_1) = \hat{\mathbf{Q}}\mathbf{Z}'\mathbf{u}_1$$

or

$$\mathbf{X}_1'\mathbf{Z}(\mathbf{Z}'\mathbf{Z})^{-1}\,\mathbf{Z}'\mathbf{X}_1\,(\hat{\mathbf{a}}_1 - \mathbf{a}_1) = \mathbf{X}_1'\mathbf{Z}(\mathbf{Z}'\mathbf{Z})^{-1}\mathbf{Z}'\mathbf{u}_1 \tag{5.2}$$

Theorem 2: $\hat{\mathbf{a}}_1$ has the same asymptotic distribution as $\hat{\mathbf{a}}_Q$.

Proof: Rescaling (5.2) by dividing by $\sqrt{T}$ gives

$$\left[\frac{\mathbf{X}_1'\mathbf{Z}}{T}\left(\frac{\mathbf{Z}'\mathbf{Z}}{T}\right)^{-1}\frac{\mathbf{Z}'\mathbf{X}_1}{T}\right]\sqrt{T}(\hat{\mathbf{a}}_1 - \mathbf{a}_1) = \left(\frac{\mathbf{X}_1'\mathbf{Z}}{T}\right)\left(\frac{\mathbf{Z}'\mathbf{Z}^{-1}}{T}\right)\left(\frac{\mathbf{Z}'\mathbf{u}_1}{T}\right).$$

Define the matrix

$$\bar{\mathbf{R}} := \operatorname{plim}\left[\frac{\mathbf{X}_1'\mathbf{Z}}{T}\left(\frac{\mathbf{Z}'\mathbf{Z}}{T}\right)^{-1}\frac{\mathbf{Z}'\mathbf{X}_1}{T}\right] = \mathbf{K}\mathbf{M}^{-1}\mathbf{K}'.$$

Since $\mathbf{K}$ is of full rank (by A5.2′), $\bar{\mathbf{R}}$ is non-singular so that, by the Slutsky Theorem,

$$\operatorname{plim}\left[\frac{\mathbf{X}_1'\mathbf{Z}}{T}\left(\frac{\mathbf{Z}'\mathbf{Z}}{T}\right)^{-1}\left(\frac{\mathbf{Z}'\mathbf{X}_1}{T}\right)\right]^{-1} = \bar{\mathbf{R}}^{-1} = (\mathbf{K}\mathbf{M}^{-1}\mathbf{K}')^{-1}.$$

By the CLT

$$\frac{\mathbf{Z}'\mathbf{u}_1}{\sqrt{T}} \mathrel{\tilde{a}} \mathrm{N}(0, \sigma_1^2\mathbf{M})$$

and so, by the Cramer Linear Transformation Theorem, we obtain the asymptotic distribution of this estimator

$$\sqrt{T}(\hat{\mathbf{a}}_1 - \mathbf{a}_1) \mathrel{\tilde{a}} \mathrm{N}(0, \sigma_1^2\mathbf{V})$$

where

$$\mathbf{V} = \bar{\mathbf{R}}^{-1}\mathbf{K}\mathbf{M}^{-1}\mathbf{M}\mathbf{M}^{-1}\mathbf{K}'\bar{\mathbf{R}}^{-1} = (\mathbf{K}\mathbf{M}^{-1}\mathbf{K}')^{-1} = (\mathbf{Q}\mathbf{M}\mathbf{Q}')^{-1}.$$

Thus the asymptotic distribution of $\hat{\mathbf{a}}_1$ and $\hat{\mathbf{a}}_Q$ are the same.

(End of proof)

An immediate consequence of Theorem 2 is that the estimator $\hat{\mathbf{a}}_1$ is asymptotically efficient in the sense that $\hat{\mathbf{a}}_1$ and $\hat{\mathbf{a}}_Q$ have the same asymptotic variance matrix.

A special case of this IV estimator is the Two-Stage Least Squares

(2SLS) estimator when the set of instrumental variables coincides with the set of predetermined variables which have non-zero coefficients in some equation of the system, i.e. where $\mathbf{Z}$ used in this section is the same as that used in Section 2.1. In the proof of the theorem that follows, we use $\mathbf{Z}$ to mean the set of variables as defined in Section 2.1 and consider adding further instrumental variables to the set. It is clear from Theorem 1 that subtracting variables from this set $\mathbf{Z}$ cannot increase the asymptotic efficiency since it corresponds to constraining the $\mathbf{H}$ matrix introduced in Theorem 1. Is it possible to improve upon the 2SLS estimator by suitably choosing the set of instruments? The answer is negative.

Theorem 3: The 2SLS estimator of $\mathbf{a}_1$ is the most efficient in the class of IV estimators when the data are generated by a simultaneous equation model.

Proof: We want to show that reducing the number of instruments or adding extra instruments to $\mathbf{Z}$ cannot result in a smaller asymptotic variance matrix with relation to the 2SLS estimator. Clearly, reducing the number of instruments cannot reduce the asymptotic variance matrix of the resulting IV estimator compared with the asymptotic variance matrix of the 2SLS estimator.

Consider now adding extra instruments $\mathbf{Z}^+$ to the original set of instruments. The 'enlarged' set of instruments (satisfying the usual conditions) is

$$\underset{T\times(m+m_1)}{\mathbf{Z}^0:} = (\underset{T\times m}{\mathbf{Z}} : \underset{T\times m_1}{\mathbf{Z}^+})$$

The inverse of the asymptotic variance matrix obtained by using $\mathbf{Z}^0$ as the set of instruments is given by

$$\operatorname{plim}\left[\frac{\mathbf{X}_1'\mathbf{Z}^0}{T}\left(\frac{\mathbf{Z}^{0\prime}\mathbf{Z}^0}{T}\right)^{-1}\frac{\mathbf{Z}^{0\prime}\mathbf{X}_1}{T}\right]\Big/\sigma^2. \tag{5.3}$$

Consider the 'augmented' RF equations

$$\underset{n_1\times T}{\mathbf{X}_1'} = \begin{pmatrix}\mathbf{Y}_1'\\ \mathbf{Z}_1\end{pmatrix} = \underset{n_1\times m}{\mathbf{Q}}\ \underset{m\times T}{\mathbf{Z}'} + \underset{n_1\times T}{\mathbf{V}'} \tag{5.4}$$

where

$$\mathbf{Q} = \begin{pmatrix}\mathbf{P}_1 & \\ \mathbf{I}_{m_1} & 0\end{pmatrix}$$

$$\mathbf{V} = \begin{pmatrix}\mathbf{V}_1\\ 0\end{pmatrix}$$

Post-multiplying (5.4) by $\mathbf{Z}^0/T$ and taking the plim using the fact that the variables in $\mathbf{Z}^0$ are independent of the reduced form errors gives

$$\text{plim}\,\frac{\mathbf{X}_1'\mathbf{Z}^0}{T} = \mathbf{Q}\,\text{plim}\,\frac{\mathbf{Z}'\mathbf{Z}^0}{T} + \text{plim}\,\frac{\mathbf{V}'\mathbf{Z}^0}{T} = \mathbf{Q}\,\text{plim}\,\frac{\mathbf{Z}'\mathbf{Z}^0}{T}. \quad (5.5)$$

Using (5.5) the expression (5.3) becomes

$$\mathbf{Q}\left\{\text{plim}\left[\frac{\mathbf{Z}'\mathbf{Z}^0}{T}\left(\frac{\mathbf{Z}^{0\prime}\mathbf{Z}^0}{T}\right)^{-1}\frac{\mathbf{Z}^{0\prime}\mathbf{Z}}{T}\right]\right\}\mathbf{Q}'$$

$$= \mathbf{Q}\left\{\text{plim}\left[(\mathbf{I}_m\!: 0)\,\frac{\mathbf{Z}^{0\prime}\mathbf{Z}}{T}\right]\right\}\mathbf{Q}'$$

$$= \mathbf{QMQ}',$$

which is the same as the inverse of the asymptotic variance matrix of the 2SLS estimator.
(End of proof)

Notice that by partitioning the explanatory variables $\mathbf{X}_1$ as

$$\underset{T\times n_1}{\mathbf{X}_1} = \underset{T\times(n_1-m_1)}{(\mathbf{Y}_1} : \underset{T\times m_1}{\mathbf{Z}_1)}$$

where $\mathbf{Y}_1$ are the endogenous variables in the right hand side of the first equation and $\mathbf{Z}_1$ are the predetermined variables (exogenous and lagged endogenous) and using the fact that

$$(\mathbf{Z}'\mathbf{Z})^{-1}\,\mathbf{Z}'\mathbf{Z}_1 = \begin{pmatrix}\mathbf{I}_{(m_1-n_1)}\\ 0\end{pmatrix}$$

we obtain

$$\mathbf{X}_1'\mathbf{Z}(\mathbf{Z}'\mathbf{Z})^{-1}\mathbf{Z}'\mathbf{X}_1 = \begin{pmatrix}\mathbf{Y}_1'\mathbf{Z}(\mathbf{Z}'\mathbf{Z})^{-1}\mathbf{Z}'\mathbf{Y}_1 & \mathbf{Y}_1'\mathbf{Z}_1\\ \mathbf{Z}_1'\mathbf{Y}_1 & \mathbf{Z}_1'\mathbf{Z}_1\end{pmatrix}$$

$$= \begin{pmatrix}\hat{\mathbf{Y}}_1'\hat{\mathbf{Y}}_1 & \hat{\mathbf{Y}}_1'\mathbf{Z}_1\\ \mathbf{Z}_1'\hat{\mathbf{Y}}_1 & \mathbf{Z}_1'\mathbf{Z}_1\end{pmatrix}$$

and

$$\mathbf{X}_1'\mathbf{Z}(\mathbf{Z}'\mathbf{Z})^{-1}\mathbf{Z}'\mathbf{y}_1 = \begin{pmatrix}\mathbf{Y}_1'\mathbf{Z}(\mathbf{Z}'\mathbf{Z})^{-1}\mathbf{Z}'\mathbf{y}_1\\ \mathbf{Z}'\mathbf{y}_1\end{pmatrix} = \begin{pmatrix}\hat{\mathbf{Y}}_1'\mathbf{y}_1\\ \mathbf{Z}_1'\mathbf{y}_1\end{pmatrix}$$

where

$$\hat{\mathbf{Y}}_1' = (\mathbf{Y}_1'\mathbf{Z})(\mathbf{Z}'\mathbf{Z})^{-1}\mathbf{Z}', \qquad \hat{\mathbf{y}}_1 = \mathbf{Z}(\mathbf{Z}'\mathbf{Z})^{-1}(\mathbf{Z}'\mathbf{y}_1).$$

(Thus the 2SLS procedure can be interpreted as a way of 'purging' the endogenous variables in $\mathbf{Y}_1$ of this stochastic component. This is done by replacing $\mathbf{Y}_1$ by its optimal linear predictor based on the set of instruments $\mathbf{Z}$.)

5.1.3 The Inadequate Sample Size Problem

In the case of a large model, the number of predetermined variables in the model, m, is typically greater than the number of observations, T. In this case A.1 is not satisfied since

$$\text{rank}\ (\mathbf{Z}'\mathbf{Z}) \leq T < m.$$

Since the matrix $\mathbf{Z}'\mathbf{Z}$ is singular the method of 2SLS cannot be applied.

The way of solving this problem consists in 'optimally' choosing some set of IVs in number $m^* < T < m$. This implies choosing an optimal linear transformation $\mathbf{H}$ subject to

$$\underset{T \times m^*}{\mathbf{Z}^*} = \underset{(T \times m)}{\mathbf{Z}} \; \underset{(m \times m^*)}{\mathbf{H}} \cdot$$

If rank $(\mathbf{Z}^*) = m^*$, then

$$\text{rank}\ (\mathbf{Z}^{*\prime}\mathbf{Z}^*) = m^*$$

and the method of instrumental variables can be applied by using the reduced set of instruments $\mathbf{Z}^*$.

There are two possible ways of doing so:

(i) If we could allow $T \rightarrow \infty$ as m remains constant we know that $\mathbf{H} = \mathbf{Q}'$ would be an optimal choice. Unfortunately we can no longer estimate $\mathbf{Q}$ by using an OLS estimator. There are various methods of using iterative techniques to derive estimates of Q (see, for example, Brundy and Jorgenson, 1971).

(ii) The principal component method involves transforming the original set of instruments $\mathbf{Z}$ by a matrix $\mathbf{H}$ formed by the latent vectors of $\mathbf{Z}'\mathbf{Z}$ corresponding to the largest latent roots, $m^* \ll T$.

Both methods have the disadvantage that for realistic models where the $\mathbf{Z}$ matrix includes lagged endogenous variables, only asymptotic theory is available to discuss the sampling properties of the estimators; this depends on considering the limit as $T \rightarrow \infty$ while m and n remain finite. Such theory is not likely to yield a satisfactory approximation to a case where $T < m$.

5.2 The IV Estimator of the Model with Linear Restrictions

Consider a single equation, out of a system of simultaneous equations, say

$$\mathbf{y} = \mathbf{Xa} + \mathbf{u} \qquad \mathrm{E}(\mathbf{u}) = 0,\ \mathrm{E}(\mathbf{uu}') = \sigma^2\mathbf{I}_T \tag{5.6}$$

where the parameter vector $\mathbf{a}'$ is subject to a set of $r \leq n$ linear restrictions of the form

$$\underset{(r \times n)}{\boldsymbol{\Phi}} \ \underset{(n \times 1)}{\mathbf{a}} = \underset{(r \times 1)}{\boldsymbol{\phi}}. \tag{5.7}$$

Notice that this implies that the restrictions on the first equation are separable.

The set of constraints (5.7) can be parameterized as

$$\mathbf{a} = \underset{(n \times p)}{\mathbf{S}} \ \underset{(p \times 1)}{\boldsymbol{\alpha}} + \underset{(n \times 1)}{\mathbf{s}} \tag{5.8}$$

where $p = n - r$ and rank $(\mathbf{S}) = p \leq n$. We recall here that for (5.8) to be a valid parameterization of (5.7) we must have $\boldsymbol{\Phi}\mathbf{S} = 0$ and $\boldsymbol{\Phi}\mathbf{s} = \boldsymbol{\phi}$.

Substituting (5.8) into (5.6) and rearranging gives the transformed model

$$\mathbf{y}^* = \mathbf{X}^*\boldsymbol{\alpha} + \mathbf{u} \tag{5.9}$$

where

$$\mathbf{y}^*: = \mathbf{y} - \mathbf{Xs} \text{ and } \mathbf{X}^*: = \mathbf{XS}.$$

The p-dimensional parameter vector $\boldsymbol{\alpha}$ can then be estimated by applying IV to the transformed model (5.9).

Let $\mathbf{Z}$ be a $(T \times m)$ matrix of valid instruments, with $m \geq p$ satisfying the assumption at the beginning of this chapter. The IV estimator of $\boldsymbol{\alpha}$ is therefore given by

$$(\mathbf{X}^{*\prime}\mathbf{Z})(\mathbf{Z}'\mathbf{Z})^{-1}\mathbf{Z}'\mathbf{X}^*\hat{\boldsymbol{\alpha}} = (\mathbf{X}^{*\prime}\mathbf{Z})(\mathbf{Z}'\mathbf{Z})^{-1}\mathbf{Z}'\mathbf{y}^*$$

i.e.

$$\mathbf{S}'\mathbf{X}'\mathbf{Z}(\mathbf{Z}'\mathbf{Z})^{-1}\mathbf{Z}'\mathbf{XS}\hat{\boldsymbol{\alpha}} = \mathbf{S}'\mathbf{X}'\mathbf{Z}(\mathbf{Z}'\mathbf{Z})^{-1}\mathbf{Z}(\mathbf{y} - \mathbf{Xs}). \tag{5.10}$$

If $m = p$, then the IV estimator of $\boldsymbol{\alpha}$ is simply given by

$$\mathbf{Z}'\mathbf{X}^*\hat{\boldsymbol{\alpha}} = \mathbf{Z}'\mathbf{y}$$

i.e.

$$\mathbf{Z}'\mathbf{X}\mathbf{S}\hat{\boldsymbol{\alpha}} = \mathbf{Z}'(\mathbf{y} - \mathbf{X}\mathbf{s}).$$

Notice that the estimator $\hat{\boldsymbol{\alpha}}$ can be regarded as the solution to the problem

$$\text{Min}_{\boldsymbol{\alpha}}\mathbf{u}'\mathbf{Z}(\mathbf{Z}'\mathbf{Z})^{-1}\mathbf{Z}'\mathbf{u} = (\mathbf{y}^* - \mathbf{X}^*\boldsymbol{\alpha})'\mathbf{Z}(\mathbf{Z}'\mathbf{Z})^{-1}\mathbf{Z}'(\mathbf{y}^* - \mathbf{X}^*\boldsymbol{\alpha}).$$

Alternatively we can directly obtain the restricted IV estimator of **a** by solving the problem

$$\text{Min}_{\mathbf{a}}(\mathbf{y} - \mathbf{X}\mathbf{a})'\mathbf{Z}(\mathbf{Z}'\mathbf{Z})^{-1}\mathbf{Z}'(\mathbf{y} - \mathbf{X}\mathbf{a}) \tag{5.11}$$

subject to

$$\boldsymbol{\Phi}\mathbf{a} = \boldsymbol{\phi}.$$

If the latter problem is solved by the use of Lagrange multipliers the solution must be the same as in the parameterized version of the problem, and this is a matter of algebraic manipulation.

The notation used here might have been modified to distinguish between the true parameter vector (and the true error term) as distinct from a general value for the parameter vector used in setting up various criterion by optimization, or from the corresponding estimators. In general $\boldsymbol{\theta}$ or **a** without any affix is used for the general value of the parameter; $\bar{\boldsymbol{\theta}}$ or $\bar{\mathbf{a}}$ is used for the true value of the parameter vector, and various affixes such as $\hat{\boldsymbol{\theta}}$, $\tilde{\boldsymbol{\theta}}$, $\boldsymbol{\theta}^*$, $\hat{\mathbf{a}}$, $\tilde{\mathbf{a}}$, $\mathbf{a}^+$ are used for various estimators. For example in the case of Section 5.2, the true model, i.e. equation (5.1), might have ben denoted by

$$\mathbf{y} = \mathbf{X}\bar{\mathbf{a}} + \mathbf{u}, \qquad \text{E}(\mathbf{u}) = 0, \text{E}(\mathbf{u}\mathbf{u}') = \sigma^2\mathbf{I}_T.$$

The set of restrictions on **a** would then be denoted by

$$\boldsymbol{\Phi}\mathbf{a} = \boldsymbol{\phi}$$

and the corresponding parameterization by

$$\mathbf{a} = \mathbf{S}\boldsymbol{\alpha} + \mathbf{s}.$$

A generic value of **a** or $\boldsymbol{\alpha}$ would be denoted by **a** (or $\boldsymbol{\alpha}$), and the associated residual by **e** particularly when we are thinking of **e** as the function of **a**, $\mathbf{e} = \mathbf{e}(\mathbf{a})$. The constrained 2SLS estimator of $\bar{\mathbf{a}}$, denoted $\hat{\mathbf{a}}$, would then be obtained by solving the problem

$$\text{Min}_{\mathbf{a}}\mathbf{e}'\mathbf{Z}(\mathbf{Z}'\mathbf{Z})^{-1}\mathbf{Z}'\mathbf{e}$$

subject to

$$\boldsymbol{\Phi}\mathbf{a} = \boldsymbol{\phi}.$$

The 2SLS estimator of $\bar{\boldsymbol{\alpha}}$, denoted by $\hat{\boldsymbol{\alpha}}$, would be obtained by solving

$$\text{Min}_{\alpha}\mathbf{e}'\mathbf{Z}(\mathbf{Z}'\mathbf{Z})^{-1}\mathbf{Z}'\mathbf{e}$$

where

$$\mathbf{e} = \mathbf{y}^* - \mathbf{X}^* \boldsymbol{\alpha}$$

and would be defined by

$$\mathbf{X}^{*\prime}\mathbf{Z}(\mathbf{Z}'\mathbf{Z})^{-1}\mathbf{Z}'\mathbf{X}^*\hat{\boldsymbol{\alpha}} = \mathbf{X}^{*\prime}\mathbf{Z}(\mathbf{Z}'\mathbf{Z})^{-1}\mathbf{Z}'\mathbf{y}^*.$$

The residual associated with the 2SLS estimator of $\bar{\boldsymbol{\alpha}}$ would then be denoted by $\hat{\mathbf{e}} = \mathbf{y}^* - \mathbf{X}^*\hat{\boldsymbol{\alpha}}$.

In practice we use $\mathbf{u}$ indiscriminately to mean $\mathbf{u} = \mathbf{y} - \mathbf{X}\bar{\mathbf{a}}$, where it is obvious from the context that this is so, and also for $\mathbf{u} = \mathbf{y} - \mathbf{X}\mathbf{a}$ for general values of $\mathbf{a}$, with an accompanying footnote to make the discrimination where it is not obvious from the context. On the other hand where the $\mathbf{u}$ are residuals corresponding to some particular estimator they will be labelled with the same affix as the estimator, such as

$$\hat{\mathbf{u}} = \mathbf{y} - \mathbf{X}\hat{\mathbf{a}},\ \tilde{\mathbf{u}} = \mathbf{y} - \mathbf{X}\tilde{\mathbf{a}},\ \mathbf{u}^+ = \mathbf{y} - \mathbf{X}\mathbf{a}^+.$$

We assume that:

Assumption 5.4: plim $(\mathbf{X}^{*\prime}\mathbf{Z}/\mathbf{T}) = \mathbf{K}^*$, a $(p \times m)$ matrix of full rank p.

Assumption 5.5: plim $(\mathbf{Z}'\mathbf{Z}/\mathbf{T}) = \mathbf{M}$, a finite p.d. $(m \times m)$ matrix.

Notice that if rank $(\mathbf{S}) = p$, then A5.4 requires that the rank of $\mathbf{X}'\mathbf{Z}$ is not smaller than p, which implies that we must have at least as many instruments as there are unknown parameters $\boldsymbol{\alpha}$.

We now prove the following:

Theorem 4: Under A5.4 and A5.5 the estimator $\hat{\boldsymbol{\alpha}}$ is consistent for $\bar{\boldsymbol{\alpha}}$.

Proof: Let $\bar{\boldsymbol{\alpha}}$ be the true value of $\boldsymbol{\alpha}$. Consistency requires that the plim of the (rescaled) criterion function (5.11) exists and achieves a unique global minimum at $\boldsymbol{\alpha} = \bar{\boldsymbol{\alpha}}$.

After dividing by T the criterion function becomes

$$\frac{\mathbf{y}^{*\prime}\mathbf{Z}}{T}\frac{(\mathbf{Z}'\mathbf{Z})^{-1}}{T}\frac{\mathbf{Z}'\mathbf{y}^*}{T} - 2\frac{\mathbf{y}^{*\prime}\mathbf{Z}}{T}\frac{(\mathbf{Z}'\mathbf{Z})^{-1}}{T}\frac{\mathbf{Z}'\mathbf{X}^*}{T}\boldsymbol{\alpha} + \boldsymbol{\alpha}'\frac{\mathbf{X}^*\mathbf{Z}}{T}\frac{(\mathbf{Z}'\mathbf{Z})^{-1}}{T}\frac{\mathbf{Z}'\mathbf{X}^*}{T}\boldsymbol{\alpha}. \quad (5.12)$$

Notice that since plim $(\mathbf{u}'\mathbf{Z}/T) = 0$ and since the equation (5.9) is only satisfied at the true value $\bar{\boldsymbol{\alpha}}$ we have

$$\text{plim}\ \frac{\mathbf{y}^{*\prime}\mathbf{Z}}{T} = \text{plim}\ \frac{(\mathbf{X}^*\bar{\boldsymbol{\alpha}} + \mathbf{u})'\mathbf{Z}}{T} = \bar{\boldsymbol{\alpha}}'\ \text{plim}\ \frac{\mathbf{X}^{*\prime}\mathbf{Z}}{T} = \bar{\boldsymbol{\alpha}}'\mathbf{K}^*.$$

Then the plim of the criterion function (5.12) exists and is given by

$$\bar{\boldsymbol{\alpha}}'\mathbf{K}^*\mathbf{M}^{-1}\,\mathbf{K}^{*\prime}\bar{\boldsymbol{\alpha}} - 2\boldsymbol{\alpha}'\mathbf{K}^*\mathbf{M}^{-1}\,\mathbf{K}^{*\prime}\boldsymbol{\alpha} + \boldsymbol{\alpha}'\mathbf{K}^*\mathbf{M}^{-1}\,\mathbf{K}^{*\prime}\boldsymbol{\alpha}$$
$$= (\bar{\boldsymbol{\alpha}} - \boldsymbol{\alpha})'\,\mathbf{K}^*\mathbf{M}^{-1}\,\mathbf{K}^{*\prime}\,(\bar{\boldsymbol{\alpha}} - \boldsymbol{\alpha}). \quad (5.13)$$

Since $\mathbf{M}$ is p.d. and $\mathbf{K}^*$ is of full rank, the quadratic form (5.13) achieves a unique global minimum of zero at $\boldsymbol{\alpha} = \bar{\boldsymbol{\alpha}}$.
(End of proof)

This discussion is intended as a case study of the use of our global identification theorem, since it is only necessary to take plims of equation (5.10) to obtain the same result. If the conditions of Theorem 1 are satisfied then, by proceeding as in Section 5.1, it is straightforward to show that

$$\sqrt{T}(\hat{\boldsymbol{\alpha}} - \boldsymbol{\alpha}) \mathrel{\tilde{a}} \mathrm{N}(0, \sigma^2\mathbf{V}_\alpha)$$

where

$$\mathbf{V}_\alpha = \text{plim}\left[\frac{\mathbf{X}^{*\prime}\mathbf{Z}}{T}\left(\frac{\mathbf{Z}'\mathbf{Z}}{T}\right)^{-1}\frac{\mathbf{Z}'\mathbf{X}^*}{T}\right]^{-1} = \left[\mathbf{S}'\mathbf{K}\mathbf{M}^{-1}\,\mathbf{K}'\mathbf{S}\right]^{-1}.$$

The properties of the constrained IV estimator of $\mathbf{a}$ follow immediately from those of $\hat{\boldsymbol{\alpha}}$, for

$$\hat{\mathbf{a}} - \mathbf{a} = \mathbf{S}(\hat{\boldsymbol{\alpha}} - \boldsymbol{\alpha}).$$

Thus, under A.1 and A.2 $\hat{\mathbf{a}}$ is consistent and asymptotically normal

$$\sqrt{T}\,(\hat{\mathbf{a}} - \mathbf{a}) \mathrel{\tilde{a}} \mathrm{N}(0, \sigma^2\mathbf{V}_{\mathrm{a}})$$

where

$$\mathbf{V}_{\mathrm{a}} = \mathbf{S}\mathbf{V}_\alpha\mathbf{S}' = \mathbf{S}(\mathbf{S}'\mathbf{K}\mathbf{M}^{-1}\mathbf{K}'\mathbf{S})^{-1}\mathbf{S}'.$$

5.3 The IV Estimator of the Non-Linear in Parameter Model

Consider the single equation out of a set of simultaneous equations

$$\underset{}{\mathbf{y}} = \underset{(T \times n)}{\mathbf{X}}\ \underset{(n \times 1)}{\mathbf{a}(\boldsymbol{\theta})} + \mathbf{u}, \qquad \mathrm{E}(\mathbf{u}) = 0,\ \mathrm{E}(\mathbf{u}\mathbf{u}') = \sigma^2\mathbf{I}_T \quad (5.14)$$

where the coefficient vector $\mathbf{a}$ is a non-linear function of a $(p \times 1)$ vector of unknown parameters $\boldsymbol{\theta}$, with $p \leq n$.

Since $\mathbf{a}(\boldsymbol{\theta})$ can be interpreted as a set of general non-linear restrictions on the coefficient vector $\mathbf{a}$, parameterized in terms of $\boldsymbol{\theta}$, model (5.14) is a generalization of the model with linear restrictions in Section 5.2.

We assume that

Assumption 5.6: $\mathbf{a}(\boldsymbol{\theta})$ is a function with first-order derivatives continuous at $\boldsymbol{\theta} = \bar{\boldsymbol{\theta}}$, the true value of $\boldsymbol{\theta}$.

Let $\mathbf{Z}$ be a $(T \times m)$ matrix of valid instruments, satisfying rank $(\mathbf{Z}'\mathbf{Z}) = m$.

5.3.1 Number of Instruments Equal to the Number of Parameters

Let $m = p$, i.e. the number of instruments is equal to the number of unknown parameters in $\boldsymbol{\theta}$. Then $\mathbf{Z}$ is a $(T \times p)$ matrix.

The IV estimator of $\boldsymbol{\theta}$, denoted by $\hat{\boldsymbol{\theta}}$, is the solution to the problem

$$\mathrm{Min}_{\boldsymbol{\theta}} \mathbf{u}'\mathbf{Z}(\mathbf{Z}'\mathbf{Z})^{-1}\mathbf{Z}'\mathbf{u} = [\mathbf{y} - \mathbf{X}\mathbf{a}(\boldsymbol{\theta})]'\mathbf{Z}(\mathbf{Z}'\mathbf{Z})^{-1}\mathbf{Z}'[\mathbf{y} - \mathbf{X}\mathbf{a}(\boldsymbol{\theta})] \tag{5.15}$$

which leads to the system of non-linear equations

$$\mathbf{Z}'\mathbf{X}\mathbf{a}(\hat{\boldsymbol{\theta}}) = \mathbf{Z}'\mathbf{y}. \tag{5.16}$$

We assume that

Assumption 5.7: plim $(\mathbf{X}'\mathbf{Z}/T)$: $= \mathbf{K}$, an $(n \times p)$ matrix of full column rank p.

Assumption 5.8: plim $(\mathbf{Z}'\mathbf{Z}/T)$: $= \mathbf{M}$, a finite, p.d. $(p \times p)$ matrix.

We then have the following result:

Theorem 5: Under A5.6, A5.7 and A5.8 the IV estimator $\hat{\boldsymbol{\theta}}$ is a consistent estimator if $\mathbf{K}'\mathbf{a}(\boldsymbol{\theta}) = \mathbf{K}'\mathbf{a}(\bar{\boldsymbol{\theta}})$ implies $\boldsymbol{\theta} = \bar{\boldsymbol{\theta}}$.

Proof: Dividing by T, the criterion function (5.15) becomes

$$\frac{\mathbf{y}'\mathbf{Z}}{T}\left(\frac{\mathbf{Z}'\mathbf{Z}}{T}\right)^{-1}\frac{\mathbf{Z}'\mathbf{y}}{T} - 2\frac{\mathbf{y}'\mathbf{Z}}{T}\left(\frac{\mathbf{Z}'\mathbf{Z}}{T}\right)^{-1}\frac{\mathbf{Z}'\mathbf{X}}{T}\mathbf{a}(\boldsymbol{\theta})$$
$$+ \mathbf{a}'(\boldsymbol{\theta})\frac{\mathbf{X}'\mathbf{Z}}{T}\left(\frac{\mathbf{Z}'\mathbf{Z}}{T}\right)^{-1}\frac{\mathbf{Z}'\mathbf{X}}{T}\mathbf{a}(\boldsymbol{\theta}). \tag{5.17}$$

Notice that since plim $(\mathbf{u}'\mathbf{Z}/T) = 0$ we have

$$\text{plim}\,\frac{\mathbf{y}'\mathbf{Z}}{T} = \mathbf{a}'(\bar{\boldsymbol{\theta}})\,\text{plim}\,\frac{\mathbf{X}'\mathbf{Z}}{T} = \mathbf{a}'(\boldsymbol{\theta})\mathbf{K}.$$

Then the plim of (5.17) exists and is given by

$$\mathbf{a}'(\bar{\boldsymbol{\theta}})\mathbf{K}\mathbf{M}^{-1}\,\mathbf{K}'\mathbf{a}(\boldsymbol{\theta}) - 2\mathbf{a}'(\bar{\boldsymbol{\theta}})\mathbf{K}\mathbf{M}^{-1}\,\mathbf{K}'\mathbf{a}(\boldsymbol{\theta}) + \mathbf{a}'(\boldsymbol{\theta})\mathbf{K}\mathbf{M}^{-1}\,\mathbf{K}'\mathbf{a}(\boldsymbol{\theta})$$

$$= [\mathbf{a}'(\bar{\boldsymbol{\theta}}) - \mathbf{a}'(\boldsymbol{\theta})]'\,\mathbf{K}\mathbf{M}^{-1}\,\mathbf{K}'[\mathbf{a}'(\bar{\boldsymbol{\theta}}) - \mathbf{a}(\boldsymbol{\theta})]. \tag{5.18}$$

Since $\mathbf{M}^{-1}$ is p.d., the criterion function (5.18) achieves a unique global minimum at $\boldsymbol{\theta} = \bar{\boldsymbol{\theta}}$, if and only if, $\mathbf{a}'(\bar{\boldsymbol{\theta}})\,\mathbf{K} = \mathbf{a}'(\boldsymbol{\theta})\,\mathbf{K}$ implies that $\bar{\boldsymbol{\theta}} = \boldsymbol{\theta}$.
(End of proof)

Notice that in regular cases the asymptotic variance matrix is proportional to the inverse of the Hessian matrix of the plim of the rescaled criterion function (5.18). If the plim of the Hessian matrix is positive definite the condition for consistency will be satisfied. Also if

$$\frac{\partial \mathbf{a}'}{\partial \boldsymbol{\theta}}\mathbf{K}$$

is of full rank at $\bar{\boldsymbol{\theta}}$ then the asymptotic distribution of the non-linear estimator of $\bar{\boldsymbol{\theta}}$ will be a joint normal distribution.

Theorem 6: If the conditions of Theorem 5 are satisfied and

$$\mathbf{K}'\frac{\partial \mathbf{a}}{\partial \boldsymbol{\theta}'}$$

is of rank p at $\bar{\boldsymbol{\theta}}$, then

$$\sqrt{T}(\hat{\boldsymbol{\theta}} - \boldsymbol{\theta}) \mathrel{\tilde{a}} \text{N}(0, \sigma^2\mathbf{V}_\theta)$$

where

$$\mathbf{V}_\theta = \left[\left(\frac{\partial \mathbf{a}}{\partial \boldsymbol{\theta}'}\right)_{\bar{\boldsymbol{\theta}}}'\mathbf{K}\mathbf{M}^{-1}\mathbf{K}'\left(\frac{\partial \mathbf{a}}{\partial \boldsymbol{\theta}'}\right)_{\bar{\boldsymbol{\theta}}}\right]^{-1}$$

Proof: Rescaling (5.16) by dividing by $\sqrt{T}$ and rearranging gives

$$\frac{\mathbf{Z}'\mathbf{X}}{T}\sqrt{T}[\mathbf{a}(\hat{\boldsymbol{\theta}}) - \mathbf{a}(\bar{\boldsymbol{\theta}})] = \frac{\mathbf{Z}'\mathbf{u}}{\sqrt{T}}. \tag{5.19}$$

Since, by A5.6 the function $\mathbf{a}(\cdot)$ is continuous with continuous first derivatives in a neighbourhood of $\bar{\boldsymbol{\theta}}$ we can expand around $\boldsymbol{\theta} = \bar{\boldsymbol{\theta}}$ by using the Taylor Series expansion

$$\mathbf{a}(\hat{\boldsymbol{\theta}}) - \mathbf{a}(\bar{\boldsymbol{\theta}}) = \left(\frac{\partial \mathbf{a}}{\partial \boldsymbol{\theta}}\right)_{\boldsymbol{\theta}^*}(\hat{\boldsymbol{\theta}} - \bar{\boldsymbol{\theta}})$$

where

$$\boldsymbol{\theta}^* = c\hat{\boldsymbol{\theta}} + (1 - c)\bar{\boldsymbol{\theta}}, \qquad 0 \leq c \leq 1.$$

Substituting into (5.19) gives

$$\left[\frac{\mathbf{Z}'\mathbf{X}}{T}\left(\frac{\partial \mathbf{a}}{\partial \boldsymbol{\theta}}\right)_{\boldsymbol{\theta}^*}\right]\sqrt{T}\,(\hat{\boldsymbol{\theta}} - \bar{\boldsymbol{\theta}}) = \frac{\mathbf{Z}'\mathbf{u}}{\sqrt{T}}$$

where by standard CLT

$$\frac{\mathbf{Z}'\mathbf{u}}{\sqrt{T}} \mathrel{\tilde{a}} \mathrm{N}(0, \sigma^2\mathbf{M}).$$

By assumption $(p \times p)$ matrix $\mathbf{K}'(\partial \mathbf{a}/\partial \boldsymbol{\theta})_{\bar{\boldsymbol{\theta}}}$ is non-singular. Therefore by the Slutsky Theorem

$$\operatorname{plim}\left[\frac{\mathbf{Z}'\mathbf{X}}{T}\left(\frac{\partial \mathbf{a}}{\partial \boldsymbol{\theta}}\right)_{\boldsymbol{\theta}^*}\right]^{-1} = \left[\mathbf{K}'\left(\frac{\partial \mathbf{a}}{\partial \boldsymbol{\theta}}\right)_{\bar{\boldsymbol{\theta}}}\right]^{-1}$$

and so by the Cramer Linear Transformation Theorem

$$\sqrt{T}\,(\hat{\boldsymbol{\theta}} - \boldsymbol{\theta}) \mathrel{\tilde{a}} \mathrm{N}(0, \sigma^2\mathbf{V}_\theta)$$

where

$$\mathbf{V}_\theta = \left\{\left[\mathbf{K}'\left(\frac{\partial \mathbf{a}}{\partial \boldsymbol{\theta}}\right)_{\bar{\boldsymbol{\theta}}}\right]^{-1}\mathbf{M}\left[\left(\frac{\partial \mathbf{a}}{\partial \boldsymbol{\theta}}\right)'_{\bar{\boldsymbol{\theta}}}\mathbf{K}\right]^{-1}\right\}$$

$$= \left[\left(\frac{\partial \mathbf{a}}{\partial \boldsymbol{\theta}}\right)'_{\bar{\boldsymbol{\theta}}}\mathbf{K}\mathbf{M}^{-1}\mathbf{K}'\left(\frac{\partial \mathbf{a}}{\partial \boldsymbol{\theta}}\right)_{\bar{\boldsymbol{\theta}}}\right]^{-1}$$

(End of proof)

5.3.2 Number of Instruments Greater than the Number of Parameters in $\boldsymbol{\theta}$

Now consider the case where $m > p$. We want to choose an 'optimal' linear transformation of the instruments, defined by an $(m \times p)$ matrix $\mathbf{H}$ of full rank p, so as to reduce the number of instruments to p.

Consider the minimization problem

$$\mathrm{Min}_{\boldsymbol{\theta}}\mathbf{u}'\mathbf{Z}(\mathbf{Z}'\mathbf{Z})^{-1}\mathbf{Z}'\mathbf{u} = [\mathbf{y} - \mathbf{X}\mathbf{a}(\boldsymbol{\theta})]'\mathbf{Z}(\mathbf{Z}'\mathbf{Z})^{-1}\mathbf{Z}'[\mathbf{y} - \mathbf{X}\mathbf{a}(\boldsymbol{\theta})].$$

The FOCs for this problem give the non-linear IV estimator of

$$\left(\frac{\partial \mathbf{a}}{\partial \boldsymbol{\theta}'}\right)'_{\hat{\boldsymbol{\theta}}}\mathbf{X}'\mathbf{Z}(\mathbf{Z}'\mathbf{Z})^{-1}\mathbf{Z}'\mathbf{X}\mathbf{a}(\hat{\boldsymbol{\theta}}) = \left(\frac{\partial \mathbf{a}}{\partial \boldsymbol{\theta}'}\right)'_{\hat{\boldsymbol{\theta}}}\mathbf{X}'\mathbf{Z}(\mathbf{Z}'\mathbf{Z})^{-1}\mathbf{Z}'\mathbf{y}. \tag{5.20}$$

Compare the expressions (5.16) and (5.20) when $m = p$. Equation (5.16) is premultiplied by the matrix $(\partial \mathbf{a}/\partial \boldsymbol{\theta})'\mathbf{X}'\mathbf{Z}(\mathbf{Z}'\mathbf{Z})^{-1}$. This can be shown to be a consistent estimator of the optimal matrix $\mathbf{H}$ to transform the original set of instruments using a proof similar to that of Theorem 5. Notice that

$$\mathbf{Z}^* = \mathbf{Z}\mathbf{H} = \mathbf{Z}(\mathbf{Z}'\mathbf{Z})^{-1}\mathbf{Z}'\mathbf{X}\left(\frac{\partial \mathbf{a}}{\partial \boldsymbol{\theta}'}\right)_{\hat{\boldsymbol{\theta}}}$$

can be interpreted as the matrix of optimal linear predictors of

$$\mathbf{X}\frac{\partial \mathbf{a}}{\partial \boldsymbol{\theta}'}$$

based on the set of instruments $\mathbf{Z}$.

It is straightforward to show, by simply repeating the argument in Section 5.3.1 that if the conditions of Theorem 5 are satisfied then this non-linear IV estimator of $\boldsymbol{\theta}$ is consistent and asymptotically normal

$$\sqrt{T}\,(\hat{\boldsymbol{\theta}} - \boldsymbol{\theta}) \;\tilde{a}\; N(0, \sigma^2\mathbf{V}_\theta)$$

where

$$\mathbf{V}_\theta = \left[\left(\frac{\partial \mathbf{a}}{\partial \boldsymbol{\theta}'}\right)'\mathbf{K}\mathbf{M}^{-1}\mathbf{K}'\left(\frac{\partial \mathbf{a}}{\partial \boldsymbol{\theta}'}\right)_{\bar{\boldsymbol{\theta}}}\right]^{-1} \tag{5.21}$$

and this is the most efficient choice of $\mathbf{H}$.

Notice that the asymptotic variance matrix of $\hat{\boldsymbol{\theta}}$ may be estimated consistently by

$$s^2\left[\left(\frac{\partial \mathbf{a}}{\partial \boldsymbol{\theta}'}\right)'_{\hat{\boldsymbol{\theta}}}(\mathbf{X}'\mathbf{Z})(\mathbf{Z}'\mathbf{Z})^{-1}(\mathbf{Z}'\mathbf{X})\left(\frac{\partial \mathbf{a}}{\partial \boldsymbol{\theta}'}\right)_{\hat{\boldsymbol{\theta}}}/T\right]^{-1}$$

where

$$s^2 := \frac{\hat{\mathbf{u}}'\hat{\mathbf{u}}}{T - p} \text{ and } \hat{\mathbf{u}} = \mathbf{y} - \mathbf{X}\mathbf{a}(\hat{\boldsymbol{\theta}}).$$

Also, by exactly the same argument as in Section 5.1.3, one can show that the non-linear 2SLS estimator is the most efficient in the class of IV estimators where data are generated by a non-linear in parameter simultaneous equation model, in the sense that by adding extra instruments one cannot obtain a smaller asymptotic variance matrix. 2SLS is used to mean the IV estimator using the set of variables summarized in Section 5.1.2.

5.3.3 An Illustration: The Model with Autoregressive Disturbances

Consider a single equation, out of a set of simultaneous equations

$$\mathbf{y}_t = \mathbf{x}_t^{*}\boldsymbol{\alpha} + \eta_t, \qquad t = 1, \ldots, T \tag{5.22}$$

where the η_ts are generated by an AR(r) process

$$\eta_t = \sum_{s=1}^{r}\phi_s\eta_{t-s} + u_t, \qquad u_t \sim \text{IID}(0, \sigma^2). \tag{5.23}$$

Substituting (5.23) into (5.22) and rearranging gives

$$y_t = \mathbf{x}_t^{*}\boldsymbol{\alpha} + -\sum_{s=1}^{r}\phi_s y_{t-s} - \sum_{s=1}^{r}\phi_s\mathbf{x}_{t-s}^{*}\boldsymbol{\alpha} + u_t \tag{5.24}$$

or

$$y_t = \mathbf{x}^{**}_t\mathbf{a}(\boldsymbol{\theta}) + u_t$$

where

$$\mathbf{x}_t^{**} = (\mathbf{x}_t^{*}, \mathbf{x}_{t-1}^{*}, \ldots, \mathbf{x}_{t-r}^{*}, \mathbf{y}_{t-1}, \ldots, \mathbf{y}_{t-s})'$$

$$\mathbf{a}(\boldsymbol{\theta}) = (\boldsymbol{\alpha}', -\ \phi_1\boldsymbol{\alpha}', \ldots, -\ \phi_s\boldsymbol{\alpha}', \phi_1, \ldots, \phi_s)'$$

and

$$\underset{(n+r)\times 1}{\boldsymbol{\theta}} = (\boldsymbol{\alpha}', \boldsymbol{\phi}')', \qquad \boldsymbol{\phi} = (\phi_1, \ldots, \phi_s)'.$$

Equation (5.24) is in the form of a non-linear in parameter equation. The non-linear 2SLS estimator of θ is therefore obtained by solving the problem

$$\text{Min}_{\boldsymbol{\theta}}\mathbf{u}'\mathbf{Z}(\mathbf{Z}'\mathbf{Z})^{-1}\mathbf{Z}'\mathbf{u}$$

where $\mathbf{u} = \mathbf{y} - \mathbf{X}^{*}\mathbf{a}(\boldsymbol{\theta})$, and is defined by the FOCs

$$\left(\frac{\partial\mathbf{a}}{\partial\boldsymbol{\theta}}\right)'\mathbf{X}^{*\prime}\mathbf{Z}(\mathbf{Z}'\mathbf{Z})^{-1}\mathbf{Z}'\mathbf{u} = 0.$$

This system of non-linear equations must be solved by numerical methods.

One possible procedure is the following. First notice that equation (5.24) can be rearranged as

$$y_t - \sum_{s=1}^{r}\phi_s y_{t-s} = (\mathbf{x}_t - \sum_{s=1}^{r}\phi_s\mathbf{x}_{t-s})'\boldsymbol{\alpha} + u_t$$

or

$$y_t^+ = \mathbf{x}_t{}' \boldsymbol{\alpha} + u_t$$

where $y_t^+ = y_t - \Sigma_{s=1}^r \phi_s y_{t-s}$ and $\mathbf{x}_t^+ = \mathbf{x}_t - \Sigma_{s=1}^r \phi_s \mathbf{x}_{t-s}$ are often called the autoregressive transformations of y_t and $\mathbf{x}_t$.

The non-linear 2SLS estimator of $\boldsymbol{\theta} = (\boldsymbol{\alpha}', \boldsymbol{\phi}')$ is therefore the

$$\text{Min}_{\boldsymbol{\alpha},\boldsymbol{\phi}} \mathbf{u}'\mathbf{Z}(\mathbf{Z}'\mathbf{Z})^{-1}\mathbf{Z}'\mathbf{u} \tag{5.25}$$

where now $\mathbf{u} = \mathbf{y}^+ - \mathbf{X}^+\boldsymbol{\alpha}$. Problem (5.25) can be solved by a 'zig-zag' procedure. Start off from initial consistent estimates $\boldsymbol{\phi}^{(0)}$ of $\boldsymbol{\phi}$ and minimize with relation to $\boldsymbol{\alpha}$ holding $\boldsymbol{\phi}^{(0)}$ constant. This gives the FOCs

$$\mathbf{X}^{+\prime}\mathbf{Z}(\mathbf{Z}'\mathbf{Z})^{-1}\mathbf{Z}'\mathbf{u} = 0$$

giving the immediate solution

$$\boldsymbol{\alpha}^{(1)} = [(\mathbf{X}^{+}\mathbf{Z})(\mathbf{Z}'\mathbf{Z})^{-1}\ (\mathbf{Z}'\mathbf{X}^{+})]^{-1}\ (\mathbf{X}^{+\prime}\mathbf{Z})(\mathbf{Z}'\mathbf{Z})^{-1}\ \mathbf{Z}'\mathbf{y}^{+}.$$

Then, holding $\boldsymbol{\alpha}^{(1)}$ fixed, minimize with relation to $\boldsymbol{\phi}$. This gives the FOCs

$$\left(\frac{\partial \mathbf{u}}{\partial \phi_s}\right)' \mathbf{Z}(\mathbf{Z}'\mathbf{Z})^{-1}\ \mathbf{Z}'\mathbf{u} = -\eta^*_{-s}\ \mathbf{Z}(\mathbf{Z}'\mathbf{Z})^{-1}\ \mathbf{Z}'\mathbf{u} = 0$$

where $\eta_{-s}\colon = (\eta_{1-s}, \ldots, \eta_{T-s})'$, from which an estimate $\boldsymbol{\phi}^{(1)}$ can be derived. The entire procedure may be repeated until convergence. This method of alternating minimization, often called the Cochrane–Orcutt iterative procedure, holds under suitable regularity conditions for any criterion function depending on two separate sets of parameters $(\boldsymbol{\theta}_1, \boldsymbol{\theta}_2)$ where it is possible to solve explicitly for the values of $\boldsymbol{\theta}_i$, which minimize the criterion function with relation to $\boldsymbol{\theta}_i$, $i = 1, 2$.

5.4 The IV Estimator of the Model with Serially Dependent Disturbances

Consider a single equation out of a set of simultaneous equations

$$\mathbf{y} = \mathbf{Xa} + \mathbf{u}, \qquad \mathrm{E}(\mathbf{u}) = 0, \qquad \mathrm{E}(\mathbf{uu}') = \sigma^2\boldsymbol{\Omega},\ \boldsymbol{\Omega} \neq \mathbf{I}_T$$

i.e. the errors in the equation are serially correlated.

If $\boldsymbol{\Omega}$ is a p.d. matrix, then there exists a p.d. $(T \times T)$ matrix $\mathbf{H}$ subject to $\mathbf{H}'\mathbf{H} = \boldsymbol{\Omega}^{-1}$ or $\mathbf{H}\boldsymbol{\Omega}\mathbf{H}' = \mathbf{I}_T$.

The matrix $\mathbf{H}$ can be used to transform the observation. This gives the transformed model

$$\mathbf{y}^* = \mathbf{X}^*\mathbf{a} + \mathbf{u}^*$$

where

$$\mathbf{y}^* = \mathbf{H}\mathbf{y},\ \mathbf{X}^* = \mathbf{H}\mathbf{X} \text{ and } \mathbf{u}^* = \mathbf{H}\mathbf{u}$$

with

$$\mathrm{E}(\mathbf{u}^*) = 0 \text{ and } \mathrm{E}(\mathbf{u}^*\mathbf{u}^{*\prime}) = \sigma^2\mathbf{H}\boldsymbol{\Omega}\mathbf{H} = \mathbf{I}_T$$

i.e. the transformed errors are serially uncorrelated. Similarly, let $\mathbf{Z}^* = \mathbf{HZ}$ be the transformed set of instruments.

We want to compare the properties of two alternative IV estimators; the 'crude' IV estimator which takes no account of serial correlation in the errors, and the estimator obtained by applying IV to the transformed model.

5.4.1 The 'Crude' IV Estimator

The 'crude' IV estimator of $\mathbf{a}$ is defined by

$$\mathbf{X}'\mathbf{Z}(\mathbf{Z}'\mathbf{Z})^{-1}\mathbf{Z}'\mathbf{X}\hat{\mathbf{a}} = \mathbf{X}'\mathbf{Z}(\mathbf{Z}'\mathbf{Z})^{-1}\,\mathbf{Z}'\mathbf{y}. \tag{5.26}$$

In what follows we will assume that

Assumption 5.9: plim $(\mathbf{X}'\mathbf{Z}/\mathbf{T}) = \mathbf{K}$, and $(n \times m)$ matrix of full rank $n < m$.

Assumption 5.10: plim $(\mathbf{Z}'\mathbf{Z}/\mathbf{T}) = \mathbf{M}$, a finite, p.d. $(m \times m)$ matrix.

Recall that the set of instruments $\mathbf{Z}$ may contain lagged endogenous as well as exogenous variables.

Theorem 7: If $\mathbf{Z}$ contains lagged endogenous variables and the errors are serially correlated, then the IV estimator $\hat{\mathbf{a}}$, as defined by (5.3), is an inconsistent estimator of $\mathbf{a}$.

Proof: Let $\mathbf{R} = \mathbf{X}'\mathbf{Z}(\mathbf{Z}'\mathbf{Z})^{-1}\mathbf{Z}'\mathbf{X}$, then (5.3) can be rearranged to obtain

$$\frac{\mathbf{R}}{T}(\hat{\mathbf{a}} - \mathbf{a}) = \frac{\mathbf{X}'\mathbf{Z}}{T}\,\frac{\mathbf{Z}'\mathbf{Z}^{-1}}{T}\,\frac{\mathbf{Z}'\mathbf{u}}{T}$$

where under the stated assumptions

$$\text{plim }(\mathbf{Z}'\mathbf{u}/T) \neq 0.$$

Thus $\hat{\mathbf{a}}$ will not in general be consistent.

Notice, however, that if $\mathbf{u}_t$ is generated by a finite order MA process, say MA(s), then the 'crude' IV estimator is consistent if $\mathbf{Z}$ excludes endogenous variables lagged by less than $(s + 1)$ time periods. This is because for an MA(s) process, $\mathbf{u}_t$ apart more than s time periods are independent.
(End of proof)

Theorem 8: If $\mathbf{Z}$ contains only exogenous variables and the errors are serially correlated then

$$\sqrt{T}(\hat{\mathbf{a}} - \mathbf{a}) \mathrel{\tilde{a}} \mathrm{N}[0, (\bar{\mathbf{R}}^{-1}\mathbf{K}\mathbf{M}^{-1}\mathbf{M}^{+}\mathbf{N}^{-1}\mathbf{K}'\bar{\mathbf{R}}^{-1})]$$

where

$$\bar{\mathbf{R}} = \mathbf{K}\mathbf{M}^{-1}\mathbf{K}' \text{ and } \mathbf{M}^{+} = \lim_{T\to\infty}(\mathbf{Z}'\boldsymbol{\Omega}\mathbf{Z}/T).$$

Proof: Since $\mathbf{Z}$ is completely non-stochastic, then by standard CLT

$$\mathbf{w} \mathrel{\tilde{a}} \mathrm{N}(0, \sigma^2\mathbf{V}_{\mathrm{w}})$$

where

$$\sigma^2\mathbf{V}_{\mathrm{w}} = \lim_{T\to\infty}\mathrm{E}\left(\frac{\mathbf{Z}'\mathbf{u}\mathbf{u}'\mathbf{Z}}{T}\right) = \lim_{T\to\infty}\frac{\mathbf{Z}'\mathrm{E}(\mathbf{u}\mathbf{u}')\mathbf{Z}}{T} = \sigma^2\mathbf{M}^{+}.$$

By A5.9 and A5.10

$$\bar{\mathbf{R}} = \operatorname{plim}\frac{\mathbf{R}}{T} = \mathbf{K}\mathbf{M}^{-1}\mathbf{K}'$$

is a non-singular matrix and so by the Slutsky Theorem

$$\operatorname{plim}\left(\frac{\mathbf{R}}{T}\right)^{-1} = \bar{\mathbf{R}}^{-1}.$$

Then, by the Cramer Linear Transformation Theorem

$$\sqrt{T}(\hat{\mathbf{a}} - \mathbf{a}) \mathrel{\tilde{a}} \mathrm{N}[0, \sigma^2(\bar{\mathbf{R}}^{-1}\mathbf{K}\mathbf{M}^{-1}\mathbf{M}^{+}\mathbf{M}^{-1}\mathbf{K}'\bar{\mathbf{R}}^{-1})]. \tag{5.27}$$

(End of proof)

Notice that if $\boldsymbol{\Omega} = \mathbf{I}_T$, i.e. the errors are serially uncorrelated, then $\mathbf{M}^{+} = \mathbf{M}$ and (5.27) becomes

$$\sqrt{T}(\hat{\mathbf{a}} - \mathbf{a}) \mathrel{\tilde{a}} \mathrm{N}[0, \sigma^2(\mathbf{K}\mathbf{M}^{-1}\mathbf{K}')^{-1}]$$

which is precisely the result obtained in Section 5.1.3.

Thus, the extra terms in the expression for the asymptotic variance matrix in (5.27) are the effect of serial correlation in the errors.

5.4.2 The IV Estimator of the Transformed Model

The estimator obtained by applying IV to the transformed model is

$$\mathbf{X}^{*\prime}\mathbf{Z}^{*}(\mathbf{Z}^{*\prime}\mathbf{Z}^{*})^{-1}\mathbf{Z}^{*\prime}\mathbf{X}^{*}\,\tilde{\mathbf{a}} = \mathbf{X}^{*\prime}\mathbf{Z}^{*}(\mathbf{Z}^{*\prime}\mathbf{Z}^{*})^{-1}\mathbf{Z}^{*}\mathbf{y}^{*}$$

where

$$\mathbf{Z}^{*} = \mathbf{HZ}$$

or

$$\mathbf{X}'\boldsymbol{\Omega}^{-1}\mathbf{X}(\mathbf{Z}'\boldsymbol{\Omega}^{-1}\mathbf{Z})^{-1}\mathbf{Z}'\boldsymbol{\Omega}^{-1}\mathbf{X}\,\tilde{\mathbf{a}} = \mathbf{X}'\boldsymbol{\Omega}^{-1}\mathbf{Z}(\mathbf{Z}'\boldsymbol{\Omega}^{-1}\mathbf{Z})^{-1}\mathbf{Z}'\boldsymbol{\Omega}\mathbf{y}. \tag{5.28}$$

This estimator is consistent even if $\mathbf{Z}$ includes lagged endogenous variables as can be seen by using the methods of Section 1.3.2.

Theorem 9: If $\mathbf{Z}$ contains lagged endogenous variables and the errors are serially correlated, then the IV estimator $\tilde{\mathbf{a}}$ defined by (5.28) is a consistent and asymptotic normal estimator of $\mathbf{a}$.

Proof: Define the matrix

$$\mathbf{R}^{*} = \mathbf{X}^{*\prime}\mathbf{Z}^{*}(\mathbf{Z}^{*\prime}\mathbf{Z}^{*})^{-1}\mathbf{Z}^{*\prime}\mathbf{X}^{*} = \mathbf{X}'\boldsymbol{\Omega}^{-1}\mathbf{Z}(\mathbf{Z}'\boldsymbol{\Omega}^{-1}\dot{\mathbf{Z}})^{-1}\mathbf{Z}'\boldsymbol{\Omega}^{-1}\mathbf{X}. \tag{5.29}$$

Then by rearranging (5.28) we obtain

$$\frac{\mathbf{R}^{*}}{T}\sqrt{T}\,(\tilde{\mathbf{a}} - \mathbf{a}) = \frac{\mathbf{X}'\boldsymbol{\Omega}^{-1}\mathbf{Z}}{T}\left(\frac{\mathbf{Z}'\boldsymbol{\Omega}^{-1}\mathbf{Z}}{T}\right)^{-1}\mathbf{w}^{*}$$

where

$$\mathbf{w}^{*} = \mathbf{Z}'\boldsymbol{\Omega}^{-1}\,\mathbf{u}/\sqrt{T} \text{ and } \mathrm{E}(\mathbf{Z}'\boldsymbol{\Omega}^{-1}\mathbf{u}) = \mathrm{E}(\mathbf{Z}^{*\prime}\mathbf{u}^{*}) = 0$$

since the transformed errors and the transformed instruments are uncorrelated.

Consistency follows from the conditions

$$\text{plim}\,\frac{\mathbf{Z}'\boldsymbol{\Omega}^{-1}\mathbf{u}}{T} = 0$$

even if $\mathbf{Z}$ contains lagged endogenous variables. Under suitable conditions on $\mathbf{HZ}$, we have from Hannan's CLT that

$$\mathbf{w}^{*}\ \tilde{a}\ \mathrm{N}(0,\,\sigma^{2}\mathbf{V}^{*}_{\mathrm{w}})$$

where

$$\sigma^2 \mathbf{V}^*_{\mathrm{w}} = \lim_{T\to\infty} \mathrm{E}(\mathbf{w}^*\mathbf{w}^{*\prime}) = \lim_{T\to\infty} \mathrm{E}\left(\frac{\mathbf{Z}'\boldsymbol{\Omega}^{-1}\mathbf{u}\mathbf{u}'\boldsymbol{\Omega}^{-1}\mathbf{Z}}{T}\right).$$

The use of the Cramer Linear Transformation Theorem then gives

$$\sqrt{T}(\widetilde{\mathbf{a}} - \mathbf{a}) \;\widetilde{a}\; \mathrm{N}[0, \sigma^2(\mathbf{K}^*\mathbf{M}^{*-1}\mathbf{K}^{*\prime})^{-1}]$$

where

$$\mathbf{K}^* = \operatorname{plim}\left(\frac{\mathbf{X}'\boldsymbol{\Omega}^{-1}\mathbf{Z}}{T}\right)$$

$$\mathbf{M}^* = \operatorname{plim}\left(\frac{\mathbf{Z}'\boldsymbol{\Omega}^{-1}\mathbf{Z}}{T}\right).$$

(End of proof)

Theorem 10: If **Z** contains only exogenous variables and the errors are serially correlated, then

$$\sqrt{T}\,(\widetilde{\mathbf{a}} - \mathbf{a}) \;\widetilde{a}\; \mathrm{N}[0, \sigma^2(\mathbf{Q}\mathbf{M}^*\mathbf{Q}')]^{-1}$$

where

$$\mathbf{M}^* = \lim_{T\to\infty}(\mathbf{Z}'\boldsymbol{\Omega}^{-1}\mathbf{Z}/T), \text{ and } \mathbf{Q} = \mathbf{K}\mathbf{M}^{-1}.$$

Proof: From the proof of Theorem 3

$$\mathbf{w}^* \;\widetilde{a}\; \mathrm{N}(0, \sigma^2\mathbf{V}^*_{\mathrm{w}})$$

where if **Z** is completely non-stochastic

$$\sigma^2\mathbf{V}^*_{\mathrm{w}} = \lim_{T\to\infty}\frac{\mathbf{Z}'\boldsymbol{\Omega}^{-1}\mathrm{E}(\mathbf{u}\mathbf{u}')\boldsymbol{\Omega}^{-1}\mathbf{Z}}{T} = \sigma^2 \lim_{T\to\infty}\frac{\mathbf{Z}'\boldsymbol{\Omega}^{-1}\mathbf{Z}}{T} = \sigma^2\mathbf{M}^*.$$

To evaluate plim $\mathbf{R}^*/T$ consider the transformed Reduced Form (RF) equations

$$\mathbf{X}^{*\prime} = \mathbf{Q}\mathbf{Z}^{*\prime} + \mathbf{V}^{*\prime} = \begin{pmatrix}\mathbf{P}\\ \mathbf{I}\end{pmatrix}\mathbf{Z}^{*\prime} + \mathbf{V}^{*\prime}.$$

Post-multiplying by $\mathbf{Z}^*$ dividing by T and then taking the plim of the resulting expression gives

$$\operatorname{plim}\frac{\mathbf{X}^{*\prime}\mathbf{Z}^*}{T} = \mathbf{Q}\operatorname{plim}\frac{\mathbf{Z}^{*\prime}\mathbf{Z}^*}{T} + \operatorname{plim}\frac{\mathbf{V}^{*\prime}\mathbf{Z}^*}{T} = \mathbf{Q}\mathbf{M}^*$$

since plim $(\mathbf{V}^{*\prime}\mathbf{Z}^*/T)$ = plim $(\mathbf{Z}'\boldsymbol{\Omega}^{-1}\mathbf{V}/T) = 0$. It is worth noticing that this would not be true if **Z** contained lagged endogenous variables since then the transformed IV would in general include lagged values of the reduced form errors that would be correlated with the lagged endogenous variables in **Z**. Thus

$$\text{plim}\,\frac{\mathbf{R}^*}{T} = \mathbf{QM}^*\mathbf{M}^{*-1}\mathbf{M}^*\mathbf{Q}' = \mathbf{QM}^*\mathbf{Q}'$$
$$= \mathbf{KM}^{-1}\mathbf{M}^*\mathbf{M}^{-1}\mathbf{K}'$$

a non-singular matrix. Then by the Slutsky Theorem and the Cramer Linear Transformation Theorem

$$\sqrt{T}\,(\tilde{\mathbf{a}} - \mathbf{a}) \,\tilde{a}\, N[0, \sigma^2(\mathbf{KM}^{-1}\mathbf{M}^*\mathbf{M}^{-1}\mathbf{K}')^{-1}]. \quad (5.30)$$

(End of proof)

Notice that if $\mathbf{\Omega} = \mathbf{I}$, i.e. the errors are serially uncorrelated, then $\mathbf{M}^* = \mathbf{M}$ so that (5.30) becomes

$$\sqrt{T}\,(\tilde{\mathbf{a}} - \mathbf{a}) \,\tilde{a}\, N[0, \sigma^2(\mathbf{KM}^{-1}\mathbf{K}')^{-1}].$$

Also note that as a special case $\mathbf{V}^*$ might be serially independent. This exceptional case was first discussed by Theil. The method of estimation is then consistent and efficient even if **Z** contains lagged endogenous variables.

5.4.3 Relative Efficiency of the Two Estimators

In the case where **Z** contains purely exogenous variables the 'crude' IV estimator $\hat{\mathbf{a}}$ defined by (5.26) is consistent. It is therefore interesting to compare its asymptotic variance matrix with the asymptotic variance matrix of the estimator $\tilde{\mathbf{a}}$.

Theorem 11: If **Z** does not contain lagged endogenous variables and the errors are serially correlated then the estimator $\tilde{\mathbf{a}}$ is more efficient than the estimator $\hat{\mathbf{a}}$.

Proof: We want to show that the asymptotic variance matrix of $\hat{\mathbf{a}}$ exceeds the asymptotic variance matrix of $\tilde{\mathbf{a}}$ by a p.s.d. matrix. The asymptotic variance matrices of $\hat{\mathbf{a}}$ and $\tilde{\mathbf{a}}$ are respectively

$$\text{AVM}(\hat{\mathbf{a}}) = \sigma^2\bar{\mathbf{R}}^{-1}\mathbf{KM}^{-1}\mathbf{M}^+\mathbf{K}'\bar{\mathbf{R}}^{-1}$$
$$= \sigma^2(\mathbf{QMQ}')^{-1}\mathbf{QM}^+\mathbf{Q}'(\mathbf{QMQ}')^{-1}$$

and

$$\text{AVM}(\tilde{\mathbf{a}}) = \sigma^2\,(\mathbf{KM}^{-1}\mathbf{M}^*\mathbf{MK}')^{-1}$$
$$= \sigma^2(\mathbf{QM}^*\mathbf{Q}')^{-1}$$

where

$$\bar{\mathbf{R}} = \mathbf{KM}^{-1}\mathbf{K}' = \mathbf{KM}^{-1}\mathbf{MM}^{-1}\mathbf{K}' = \mathbf{QMQ}'.$$

First notice that

$$\text{AVM}(\hat{\mathbf{a}}) - \text{AVM}(\tilde{\mathbf{a}}) = \text{p.s.d. matrix}$$

is equivalent to

$$\mathbf{QM}^*\mathbf{Q}' - \mathbf{QMQ}'(\mathbf{QM}^+\mathbf{Q}')^{-1}\mathbf{QMQ} = \text{p.s.d. matrix.} \qquad (5.31)$$

It is therefore sufficient to show that for all p.d. matrices one has that

$$\frac{\mathbf{QZ}'\mathbf{\Omega}^{-1}\mathbf{ZQ}'}{T} - \frac{\mathbf{QZ}'\mathbf{ZQ}}{T}\left(\frac{\mathbf{QZ}'\mathbf{\Omega}\mathbf{ZQ}'}{T}\right)^{-1}\frac{\mathbf{QZ}'\mathbf{ZQ}'}{T}$$
$$= \text{p.s.d. matrix.} \qquad (5.32)$$

Then by taking the plim of (5.32) the inequality (5.30) will be obtained.

Let $\mathbf{QZ}'/\sqrt{T} = \mathbf{C}$, then (5.32) can be written as

$$\mathbf{C\Omega}^{-1}\mathbf{C}' - \mathbf{CC}'(\mathbf{C\Omega C}')^{-1}\mathbf{CC}'.$$

Since $\mathbf{\Omega}$ is p.d. we can find a p.d. matrix $\mathbf{H}$ subject to $\mathbf{H}'\mathbf{H} = \mathbf{\Omega}^{-1}$. By setting $\boldsymbol{\psi} = \mathbf{CH}$ the above equation becomes

$$\boldsymbol{\psi\psi}' - \boldsymbol{\psi}(\mathbf{CH}^{-1})(\mathbf{CH}^{-1}\mathbf{H}'^{-1}\mathbf{C}')^{-1}(\mathbf{CH}^{-1})\boldsymbol{\psi}'$$

i.e.

$$\boldsymbol{\psi}[\mathbf{I} - (\mathbf{CH}^{-1})'(\mathbf{CH}^{-1}\mathbf{H}'^{-1}\mathbf{C}')^{-1}(\mathbf{CH}^{-1})]\boldsymbol{\psi}'$$

which is a p.s.d. matrix since the matrix into square brackets is idempotent.
(End of proof)

Note that this latter algebraic result is used in Section 6.3 to show that 3SLS applied to a set of simultaneous equations is at least as efficient as 2SLS applied to each equation is isolation.

5.5 The 2SLS Estimator of the General Non-Linear Model

Consider one equation out of a set of simultaneous equations

$$u_t = f(\mathbf{x}_t, \boldsymbol{\theta}), \qquad u_t \sim \text{IID}(0, \sigma^2), \qquad t = 1, \ldots, T \qquad (5.33)$$

where $\mathbf{x}_t$ is an $(n + m) \times 1$ vector of endogenous and predetermined (exogenous and lagged endogenous) variables and $\boldsymbol{\theta}$ is a $(p \times 1)$ vector of unknown parameters.

Model(5.33) is very general and encompasses all the models discussed so far.

Let Z be a $(T \times m)$ matrix of instruments with $m \geq p$. Then the non-linear 2SLS estimator of $\boldsymbol{\theta}$ is the solution to the problem

$$\text{Min}_{\boldsymbol{\theta}} \mathbf{u}'\mathbf{Z}(\mathbf{Z}'\mathbf{Z})^{-1}\mathbf{Z}'\mathbf{u}$$

which leads to the system of non-linear equations

$$\left[\left(\frac{\partial \mathbf{u}}{\partial \boldsymbol{\theta}'}\right)'_{\hat{\boldsymbol{\theta}}} \mathbf{Z}(\mathbf{Z}'\mathbf{Z})^{-1}\right]\mathbf{Z}'\mathbf{u} = 0 \tag{5.34}$$

where $\hat{\boldsymbol{\theta}}$ denotes the non-linear 2SLS estimator of $\boldsymbol{\theta}$. Notice that the $(p \times m)$ matrix in square brackets in (5.34) is the matrix of regression coefficients of $\partial\mathbf{u}/\partial\boldsymbol{\theta}'$ on the instruments $\mathbf{Z}$.

It is not difficult to show by an argument similar to the one in Section 5.3 that if appropriate plims exist, and $\mathbf{w} = (\mathbf{Z}'\mathbf{u}/\sqrt{T})$ has the usual asymptotic normal distribution the IV estimator is consistent and asymptotic normal

$$\sqrt{T}\,(\hat{\boldsymbol{\theta}} - \boldsymbol{\theta}) \;\tilde{a}\; \mathrm{N}(0, \mathbf{V}_{\theta})$$

with

$$\mathbf{V}_{\theta} = \text{plim}\left[\frac{1}{T}\left(\frac{\partial \mathbf{u}}{\partial \boldsymbol{\theta}}\right)'_{\bar{\boldsymbol{\theta}}} \mathbf{Z}(\mathbf{Z}'\mathbf{Z})^{-1}\mathbf{Z}'\left(\frac{\partial \mathbf{u}}{\partial \boldsymbol{\theta}}\right)_{\bar{\boldsymbol{\theta}}}\right]^{-1}$$

where $\bar{\boldsymbol{\theta}}$ denotes the true value of $\boldsymbol{\theta}$.

6

IV Estimation of a Set of Simultaneous Equations

6.1 Notation

Consider a set of N simultaneous equations (where N is not necessarily assumed to be equal to the number of endogenous variables in the system, i.e. we can have an incomplete system $N < n$):

$$\underset{(T \times 1)}{\mathbf{y}_i} = \underset{(T \times n_i)}{\mathbf{X}_i} \underset{(n_i \times 1)}{\mathbf{a}_i} + \underset{(T \times 1)}{\mathbf{u}_i}, \quad i = 1, \ldots, N. \tag{6.1}$$

These single N equations can be now blocked into a single one, by letting

$$\underset{(TN \times 1)}{\mathbf{y}^*} = \begin{pmatrix} \mathbf{y}_1 \\ \vdots \\ \mathbf{y}_N \end{pmatrix}, \quad \underset{(TN \times M)}{\mathbf{X}^*} = \begin{pmatrix} \mathbf{X}_1 & \ldots & 0 \\ . & \ldots & . \\ 0 & \ldots & \mathbf{X}_N \end{pmatrix},$$

$$\underset{(M \times 1)}{\mathbf{a}^*} = \begin{pmatrix} \mathbf{a}_1 \\ \vdots \\ \mathbf{a}_N \end{pmatrix}, \quad \underset{(TN \times 1)}{\mathbf{u}^*} = \begin{pmatrix} \mathbf{u}_1 \\ \\ \mathbf{u}_N \end{pmatrix}$$

as

$$\mathbf{y}^* = \mathbf{X}^*\mathbf{a}^* + \mathbf{u}^*. \tag{6.2}$$

We assume we have a set of IV, $\mathbf{Z}$, of order $(T \times m)$, which is the same for all the equations, and therefore we can write

$$\underset{(TN \times NM)}{\mathbf{Z}^*} = \begin{pmatrix} \mathbf{Z} & \dots & 0 \\ . & \dots & . \\ 0 & \dots & \mathbf{Z} \end{pmatrix} = (\mathbf{I}_N \otimes \mathbf{Z})$$

where $\otimes$ denotes the Kronecker product.

The disturbances are assumed to be contemporaneously correlated across equations, but serially independent, i.e.

$$\begin{aligned} \mathrm{E}(u_{it}u_{js}) &= 0, \qquad t \neq s, \\ &= \omega_{ij}, \qquad t = s. \end{aligned}$$

Therefore

$$\mathrm{E}(\mathbf{u}^*\mathbf{u}^{*\prime}) = \underset{(TN \times TN)}{\boldsymbol{\Omega}^*} = \begin{pmatrix} \omega_{11}\mathbf{I}_T & \dots\dots & \omega_{1N}\mathbf{I}_T \\ \omega_{N1}\mathbf{I}_T & \dots\dots & \omega_{NN}\mathbf{I}_T \end{pmatrix} = \underset{(N \times N)}{\boldsymbol{\Omega}_{\mathrm{u}}} \times \mathbf{I}_T.$$

6.2 Three-Stage Least Squares (3SLS) as an IV Estimator

Given that $\boldsymbol{\Omega}^*$ is not the identity matrix, we cannot apply directly a simple IV estimator to $\mathbf{y}^* = \mathbf{X}^*\mathbf{a}^* + \mathbf{u}^*$. The obvious way out is to treat it like a case of serial correlation in the disturbances seen in previous chapters; that is, we consider a square $(N \times N)$ matrix $\mathbf{H}$ such that

$$\mathbf{H}\mathbf{H}' = \boldsymbol{\Omega}_{\mathrm{u}}^{-1} \text{ or } \mathbf{H}'\boldsymbol{\Omega}_{\mathrm{u}}\mathbf{H} = \mathbf{I}_N.$$

From this, define

$$\mathbf{H}^* = (\mathbf{H} \otimes \mathbf{I}_T).$$

Hence

$$\begin{aligned} \mathbf{H}^{*\prime}\boldsymbol{\Omega}^*\mathbf{H}^* &= (\mathbf{H} \otimes \mathbf{I}_T)' \, (\boldsymbol{\Omega}_{\mathrm{u}} \otimes \mathbf{I}_T) \, (\mathbf{H} \otimes \mathbf{I}_T) = (\mathbf{I}_N \otimes \mathbf{I}_T) \\ &= \mathbf{I}_{NT}. \end{aligned}$$

Proceeding as we did for a single equation, we now transform the model and $\mathbf{Z}^*$ to obtain the best linear combination of IV, which yields

$$\begin{aligned} &(\mathbf{X}^{*\prime}\boldsymbol{\Omega}^{*-1}\mathbf{Z}^*) \, (\mathbf{Z}^{*\prime}\boldsymbol{\Omega}^{*-1}\mathbf{Z}^*)^{-1} \, (\mathbf{Z}^{*\prime}\boldsymbol{\Omega}^{*-1}\mathbf{X}^*) \, \widetilde{\mathrm{a}}^* \\ &\qquad = (\mathbf{X}^{*\prime}\boldsymbol{\Omega}^{-1}\mathbf{Z}^*)(\mathbf{Z}^{*\prime}\boldsymbol{\Omega}^{*-1}\mathbf{Z})^{-1}(\mathbf{Z}^{*\prime}\boldsymbol{\Omega}^{*-1}\mathbf{y}^*). \qquad (6.3) \end{aligned}$$

Using Kronecker products algebra we can now simplify the expression. Consider the left-hand side element as an example:

$$\begin{aligned}
&[\mathbf{X}^{*\prime}\mathbf{H}^{*}\mathbf{H}^{*\prime}(\mathbf{I}\otimes\mathbf{Z})][(\mathbf{I}\otimes\mathbf{Z})'\,\mathbf{H}^{*}\mathbf{H}^{*\prime}(\mathbf{I}\otimes\mathbf{Z})]^{-1}[(\mathbf{I}\otimes\mathbf{Z})'\mathbf{H}^{*}\mathbf{H}^{*\prime}\mathbf{X}^{*}]\\
&\quad = [\mathbf{X}^{*\prime}(\mathbf{H}\otimes\mathbf{I})(\mathbf{H}'\otimes\mathbf{I})(\mathbf{I}\otimes\mathbf{Z})]\times\\
&\qquad [(\mathbf{I}\otimes\mathbf{Z}')(\mathbf{H}\otimes\mathbf{I})(\mathbf{H}'\otimes\mathbf{I})(\mathbf{I}\otimes\mathbf{Z})]^{-1}\times\\
&\qquad [(\mathbf{I}\otimes\mathbf{Z}')\,(\mathbf{H}\otimes\mathbf{I})\,(\mathbf{H}'\otimes\mathbf{I})\mathbf{X}^{*}]\\
&\quad = \mathbf{X}^{*\prime}(\mathbf{HH}'\otimes\mathbf{Z})\,[(\mathbf{HH}'\otimes\mathbf{Z}'\mathbf{Z})^{-1}]\,(\mathbf{HH}'\otimes\mathbf{Z}')\mathbf{X}^{*}\\
&\quad = \mathbf{X}^{*\prime}(\boldsymbol{\Omega}_{\mathrm{u}}^{-1}\otimes\mathbf{Z})\,[\boldsymbol{\Omega}_{\mathrm{u}}\otimes(\mathbf{Z}'\mathbf{Z})^{-1}]\,(\boldsymbol{\Omega}_{\mathrm{u}}^{-1}\otimes\mathbf{Z}')\mathbf{X}^{*}\\
&\quad = \mathbf{X}^{*\prime}[\boldsymbol{\Omega}_{\mathrm{u}}^{-1}\otimes\mathbf{Z}(\mathbf{Z}'\mathbf{Z})^{-1}\mathbf{Z}']\mathbf{X}^{*}.
\end{aligned}$$

Therefore equation (6.3) becomes

$$\mathbf{X}^{*\prime}[\boldsymbol{\Omega}_{\mathrm{u}}^{-1}\otimes\mathbf{Z}(\mathbf{Z}'\mathbf{Z})^{-1}\mathbf{Z}']\mathbf{X}^{*}\,\widetilde{\mathbf{a}}^{*} = \mathbf{X}^{*\prime}[\boldsymbol{\Omega}_{\mathrm{u}}^{-1}\otimes\mathbf{Z}(\mathbf{Z}'\mathbf{Z})^{-1}\mathbf{Z}']\mathbf{y}^{*}.$$

We will call this the Three-Stage Instrumental Variables (3SIV) estimator. It will be the same as the 3SLS estimator if the $\mathbf{Z}$ is not restricted to the same variable as we assumed for 2SLS. In practice we replace $\boldsymbol{\Omega}_{\mathrm{u}}^{-1}$ by $\hat{\boldsymbol{\Omega}}_{\mathrm{u}}^{-1}$, where $\hat{\boldsymbol{\Omega}}$ is obtained from the residuals of each single equation estimated by IV, i.e.

$$\hat{\boldsymbol{\Omega}}_{\mathrm{u}} = (\hat{\omega}_{ij}),\qquad \hat{\omega}_{ij} = \frac{1}{T}\,(\mathbf{y}_i - \mathbf{X}_i\,\widetilde{\mathbf{a}}_i)'\,(\mathbf{y}_j - \mathbf{X}_j\,\widetilde{\mathbf{a}}_j),\qquad i, j = 1, \ldots, N$$

where $\widetilde{\mathbf{a}}$ is the single equation IV estimator.

An alternative expression of the 3SIV estimator is obtained by considering explicitly the zero–one restrictions imposed on the simultaneous model to obtain the single equations (6.1), i.e. consider the structural form

$$\underset{N\times(n+m)}{\mathbf{A}}\quad\underset{(n+m)\times T}{\mathbf{X}'}\quad=\quad\underset{NXT}{\mathbf{U}'}$$

where

$$\mathbf{X} = \underset{T\times n\;\; T\times m}{(\mathbf{Y}\,\vdots\,\mathbf{Z})},\qquad \text{and } \mathrm{E}[\mathrm{vec}\,\mathbf{U}'\,(\mathrm{vec}\,\mathbf{U}')'] = (\boldsymbol{\Omega}_{\mathrm{u}}\otimes\mathbf{I}_T)$$

and impose the zero–one restrictions on $\mathbf{A}$ which can be reparameterized as

$$\underset{[N(n+m)\times 1]}{\mathrm{vec}\;\mathbf{A}} \;=\; \underset{[N(n+m)\times M]}{\mathbf{S}}\;\underset{(M\times 1)}{\boldsymbol{\alpha}} \;+\; \underset{[N(n+m)\times 1]}{\mathbf{s}}$$

as in Chapter 5.

In the next section it will be shown that

$$\boldsymbol{\alpha} = -\,\mathbf{a}^{*}.$$

The **S** matrix and the vector **s** are defined as

$$\mathbf{S} = \begin{pmatrix} \mathbf{S}_1 & \cdots & 0 \\ & \ddots & \\ 0 & \cdots & \mathbf{S}_N \end{pmatrix}, \ \mathbf{s} = \begin{pmatrix} \mathbf{s}_1 \\ \vdots \\ \mathbf{s}_n \end{pmatrix}$$

The submatrices $\mathbf{S}_i$ are therefore selection matrices that pick up from **X** all the explanatory variables corresponding to non-zero elements of **A** in the *i*th equation, i.e.

$$\underset{[T \times (n + M)]}{\mathbf{X}} \ \underset{[(n + m) \times n_i]}{\mathbf{S}_i} = \underset{[T \times n_i]}{\mathbf{X}_i}.$$

Equivalently the subvectors $\mathbf{s}_i$ are selection vectors that pick up the endogenous variable on the left-hand side of the *i*th equation, i.e.

$$\mathbf{X}\mathbf{s}_i = \mathbf{y}_i.$$

Therefore we can write

$$\mathbf{X}^* = (\mathbf{I}_N \otimes \mathbf{X})\,\mathbf{S}$$

$$\mathbf{y}^* = (\mathbf{I}_N \otimes \mathbf{X})\,\mathbf{s}.$$

From the definition of $\mathbf{X}^*$, $\mathbf{Z}^*$ and $\mathbf{\Omega}^*$ we then obtain

$$\begin{aligned} \mathbf{X}^{*\prime}\mathbf{\Omega}^{*-1}\mathbf{Z}^* &= \mathbf{S}'(\mathbf{I}_N \otimes \mathbf{X}')\,(\mathbf{\Omega}_{\mathrm{u}}^{-1} \otimes \mathbf{I}_T)\,(\mathbf{I}_N \otimes \mathbf{Z}) \\ &= \mathbf{S}'(\mathbf{\Omega}_{\mathrm{u}}^{-1} \otimes \mathbf{X}'\mathbf{Z}) \end{aligned}$$

$$\mathbf{Z}^{*\prime}\mathbf{\Omega}^{*-1}_{\mathrm{u}}\mathbf{Z}^* = (\mathbf{I}_N \otimes \mathbf{Z}')\,(\mathbf{\Omega}_{\mathrm{u}}^{-1} \otimes \mathbf{I}_T)\,(\mathbf{I}_N \otimes \mathbf{Z}) = (\mathbf{\Omega}_{\mathrm{u}}^{-1} \otimes \mathbf{Z}'\mathbf{Z})$$

and equation (6.3) can be written as

$$\mathbf{S}'[\mathbf{\Omega}_{\mathrm{u}}^{-1} \otimes \mathbf{X}'\mathbf{Z}(\mathbf{Z}'\mathbf{Z})^{-1}\mathbf{Z}'\mathbf{X}]\mathbf{S}\hat{\mathbf{a}}^* = \mathbf{S}[\mathbf{\Omega}_{\mathrm{u}}^{-1} \otimes \mathbf{X}'\mathbf{Z}(\mathbf{Z}'\mathbf{Z})^{-1}\mathbf{Z}'\mathbf{X}]\mathbf{s} \tag{6.4}$$

which is the 3SIV when $\mathbf{\Omega}_{\mathrm{u}}^{-1}$ is replaced by $\hat{\mathbf{\Omega}}_{\mathrm{u}}^{-1}$ as before.

Let $\mathbf{R} = \mathbf{X}'\mathbf{Z}(\mathbf{Z}'\mathbf{Z})^{-1}\mathbf{Z}'\mathbf{X}$, with $\mathbf{R}_{ij} = \mathbf{X}_i'\mathbf{Z}(\mathbf{Z}'\mathbf{Z})^{-1}\mathbf{Z}'\mathbf{X}_j$ and let $\mathbf{\Omega}_{\mathrm{u}}^{-1} = (\omega^{ij})$, then we can write (6.4) as

$$\begin{pmatrix} \omega^{11}\mathbf{R}_{11} & \omega^{12}\mathbf{R}_{12} & \cdots & \omega^{1N}\mathbf{R}_{1N} \\ \\ \omega^{N1}\mathbf{R}_{N1} & \omega^{N2}\mathbf{R}_{N2} & \cdots & \omega^{NN}\mathbf{R}_{NN} \end{pmatrix} \hat{\alpha}^* = \begin{pmatrix} \mathbf{r}_1 \\ \vdots \\ \mathbf{r}_N \end{pmatrix}$$

where $\mathbf{r}_j = \Sigma_{k=1}^{N}\,\omega^{jk}\mathbf{X}_j\mathbf{Z}(\mathbf{Z}'\mathbf{Z})^{-1}\mathbf{Z}'\mathbf{y}_k$.

6.3 Asymptotic Distribution of the 3SLS Estimator

Take the block equation $\mathbf{y}^* = \mathbf{X}^*\mathbf{a}^* + \mathbf{u}^*$, and write it using the selection matrices and vectors:

$$\mathbf{y}^* - \mathbf{X}\mathbf{a}^* = (\mathbf{I} \otimes \mathbf{X})\mathbf{s} - (\mathbf{I} \otimes \mathbf{X})\mathbf{S}\mathbf{a}^* = \mathbf{u}^*. \tag{6.5}$$

Also from the structural form $\mathbf{AX}' = \mathbf{U}'$, using the general result that $\text{vec}\,(\mathbf{ABC}) = (\mathbf{A} \otimes \mathbf{C}')\,\text{vec}\,\mathbf{B}$, we obtain

$$(\mathbf{I} \otimes \mathbf{X})\,\text{vec}\,\mathbf{A} = \text{vec}\,\mathbf{U}' = \mathbf{u}^*.$$

Comparing this with (6.5) we have the expression for the reparameterization

$$\text{vec}\,\mathbf{A} = \mathbf{s} - \mathbf{S}\mathbf{a}^* = \mathbf{s} + \mathbf{S}\boldsymbol{\alpha}$$

showing that $\mathbf{a}^* = -\boldsymbol{\alpha}$.

Now consider equation (6.4) with $\hat{\boldsymbol{\Omega}}_u^{-1}$:

$$\mathbf{S}'(\hat{\boldsymbol{\Omega}}_u^{-1} \otimes \mathbf{R})\mathbf{S}\hat{\mathbf{a}}^* = \mathbf{S}'(\hat{\boldsymbol{\Omega}}_u^{-1} \otimes \mathbf{R})\mathbf{s}$$

and subtract $\mathbf{S}'(\hat{\boldsymbol{\Omega}}_u^{-1} \otimes \mathbf{R})\mathbf{S}\mathbf{a}^*$ from both sides

$$\mathbf{S}'(\hat{\boldsymbol{\Omega}}_u^{-1} \otimes \mathbf{R})\,[\mathbf{S}(\hat{\mathbf{a}}^* - \mathbf{a}^*)] = \mathbf{S}'(\hat{\boldsymbol{\Omega}}_u^{-1} \otimes \mathbf{R})\,(\mathbf{s} - \mathbf{S}\mathbf{a}^*). \tag{6.6}$$

Consider the right-hand side term,

$$\begin{aligned}
\mathbf{S}'(\hat{\boldsymbol{\Omega}}^{-1} \otimes \mathbf{R})(\mathbf{s} - \mathbf{S}\mathbf{a}^*) &= \mathbf{S}'[\hat{\boldsymbol{\Omega}}_u^{-1} \otimes \mathbf{X}'\mathbf{Z}(\mathbf{Z}'\mathbf{Z})^{-1}\mathbf{Z}'\mathbf{X}]\,\text{vec}\,\mathbf{A} \\
&= \mathbf{S}'[\hat{\boldsymbol{\Omega}}_u^{-1} \otimes \mathbf{X}'\mathbf{Z}(\mathbf{Z}'\mathbf{Z})^{-1}\mathbf{Z}']\,(\mathbf{I} \otimes \mathbf{X})\,\text{vec}\,\mathbf{A} \\
&= \mathbf{S}'[\hat{\boldsymbol{\Omega}}_u^{-1} \otimes \mathbf{X}'\mathbf{Z}(\mathbf{Z}'\mathbf{Z})^{-1}\mathbf{Z}']\,\text{vec}\,\mathbf{U}' \\
&= \mathbf{S}'[\hat{\boldsymbol{\Omega}}_u^{-1} \otimes \mathbf{X}'\mathbf{Z}(\mathbf{Z}'\mathbf{Z})^{-1}]\,(\mathbf{I} \otimes \mathbf{Z}')\,\text{vec}\,\mathbf{U}' \\
&= \mathbf{S}'[\hat{\boldsymbol{\Omega}}_u^{-1} \otimes \mathbf{X}'\mathbf{Z}(\mathbf{Z}'\mathbf{Z})^{-1}]\,\text{vec}\,\mathbf{U}'\mathbf{Z}
\end{aligned}$$

and so, rescaling, (6.6) can be written as

$$\begin{aligned}
&\mathbf{S}'\left(\hat{\boldsymbol{\Omega}}_u^{-1} \otimes \frac{\mathbf{R}}{T}\right)\mathbf{S}\,\sqrt{T}\,(\hat{\mathbf{a}}^* - \mathbf{a}^*) \\
&\qquad = \mathbf{S}'\left[\hat{\boldsymbol{\Omega}}_u^{-1} \otimes \frac{\mathbf{X}'\mathbf{Z}}{T}\left(\frac{\mathbf{Z}'\mathbf{Z}}{T}\right)^{-1}\right]\text{vec}\,\frac{\mathbf{U}'\mathbf{Z}}{\sqrt{T}}.
\end{aligned} \tag{6.7}$$

Since the $\mathbf{Z}$ has only predetermined variables, and the disturbances are serially uncorrelated, then we can apply the Hannan CLT, or even the Lindeberg–Feller CLT (see Cramer, 1946) if $\mathbf{Z}$ has only non-stochastic variables to obtain

$$\text{vec}\,\frac{\mathbf{U}'\mathbf{Z}}{\sqrt{T}} = \frac{(\mathbf{I} \otimes \mathbf{Z}')\mathbf{u}^*}{\sqrt{T}} = \frac{\begin{pmatrix} \mathbf{Z}' & \ldots & 0 \\ 0 & \ldots & \mathbf{Z}' \end{pmatrix}\begin{pmatrix} \mathbf{u}_1 \\ \mathbf{u}_N \end{pmatrix}}{\sqrt{T}} = \begin{pmatrix} \dfrac{\mathbf{Z}'\mathbf{u}_1}{\sqrt{T}} \\ \vdots \\ \dfrac{\mathbf{Z}'\mathbf{u}_N}{\sqrt{T}} \end{pmatrix}$$

$$= \begin{pmatrix} \mathbf{w}_1^* \\ \vdots \\ \mathbf{w}_N^* \end{pmatrix} = \mathbf{w}^*$$

$$\mathbf{w}^* \overset{a}{\sim} \mathrm{N}(0, \boldsymbol{\Omega}_u \otimes \mathbf{M})$$

where

$$\mathbf{M} = \operatorname{plim} \frac{\mathbf{Z}'\mathbf{Z}}{T} = \lim \mathrm{E}\left(\frac{\mathbf{Z}'\mathbf{Z}}{T}\right)$$

by ergodicity which is a finite p.d. $(m \times m)$ matrix (or $M = \lim \frac{\mathbf{Z}'\mathbf{Z}}{T}$ for $\mathbf{Z}$ non-stochastic).

Now denote

$$\mathbf{E} = \mathbf{S}'\left(\hat{\boldsymbol{\Omega}}_u^{-1} \otimes \frac{\mathbf{R}}{\mathbf{T}}\right)\mathbf{S}.$$

Then

$$\bar{\mathbf{E}} = \operatorname{plim} \mathbf{E} = \mathbf{S}'(\boldsymbol{\Omega}_u^{-1} \otimes \mathbf{K}\mathbf{M}^{-1}\mathbf{K}')\mathbf{S}$$

where $\mathbf{K} = \operatorname{plim} \frac{\mathbf{X}'\mathbf{Z}}{T}$

and so the asymptotic variance matrix (AVM) of the errors $\sqrt{T}(\hat{\mathbf{a}}^* - \mathbf{a}^*)$ is, from (6.7), using the Slutsky Theorem and the Cramer Linear Transformation Theorem,

$$\begin{aligned}
&\mathrm{AVM}[\sqrt{T}(\hat{\mathbf{a}}^* - \mathbf{a}^*)] \\
&\quad = \bar{\mathbf{E}}^{-1}[\mathbf{S}(\boldsymbol{\Omega}_u^{-1} \otimes \mathbf{K}\mathbf{M}^{-1}]\,[\boldsymbol{\Omega}_u \otimes \mathbf{M})\,(\boldsymbol{\Omega}_u^{-1} \otimes \mathbf{M}^{-1}\mathbf{K}')\mathbf{S}']\bar{\mathbf{E}}^{-1} \\
&\quad = \bar{\mathbf{E}}^{-1}\bar{\mathbf{E}}\bar{\mathbf{E}}^{-1} \\
&\quad = \bar{\mathbf{E}}^{-1}
\end{aligned}$$

i.e.

$$\sqrt{T}(\hat{\mathbf{a}}^* - \mathbf{a}^*) \overset{a}{\sim} \mathrm{N}(0, \bar{\mathbf{E}}^{-1})$$

where

$$\bar{\mathbf{E}} = \mathbf{S}'(\boldsymbol{\Omega}_u^{-1} \otimes \mathbf{K}\mathbf{M}^{-1}\mathbf{K}')\mathbf{S}.$$

We can obtain a consistent estimate of this asymptotic variance by

$$\hat{\mathbf{E}}^{-1} = \left\{\mathbf{S}'\left[\hat{\boldsymbol{\Omega}}_u^{-1} \otimes \frac{\mathbf{X}'\mathbf{Z}(\mathbf{Z}'\mathbf{Z})^{-1}\mathbf{Z}'\mathbf{X}}{T}\right]\mathbf{S}\right\}^{-1},$$

and can derive from this likelihood ratio (LR) tests and t-ratio tests which are asymptotically valid.

Also, notice that since $\text{vec}\,\mathbf{A} = \mathbf{s} - \mathbf{Sa}^*$, then $\text{vec}(\hat{\mathbf{A}} - \mathbf{A}) = -\mathbf{S}(\hat{\mathbf{a}}^* - \mathbf{a}^*)$ and therefore

$$\sqrt{T}\ \text{vec}(\hat{\mathbf{A}} - \mathbf{A}) \ \tilde{a}\ \text{N}(0, \mathbf{S}\bar{\mathbf{E}}^{-1}\mathbf{S}').$$

6.4 3SLS Derived from a Criterion Function Minimization

As in the case of simple equation IV, we can show that 3SIV can be obtained by minimizing a criterion function.

Consider the structural form of the model, $\mathbf{AX}' = \mathbf{U}'$, and the criterion function minimization

$$\min_{\text{vec}\,\mathbf{A}} \text{tr}[\hat{\mathbf{\Omega}}_u^{-1}\mathbf{U}'\mathbf{Z}(\mathbf{Z}'\mathbf{Z})^{-1}\mathbf{Z}'\mathbf{U}]. \tag{6.8}$$

Using the fact that $\text{tr}(\mathbf{AB}) = \text{tr}(\mathbf{BA})$ gives

$$\min_{\text{vec}\,\mathbf{A}} \text{tr}[\mathbf{Z}'\mathbf{U}\hat{\mathbf{\Omega}}_u^{-1}\mathbf{U}'\mathbf{Z}(\mathbf{Z}'\mathbf{Z})^{-1}].$$

Then since $\text{tr}\,\mathbf{A}'\mathbf{B} = (\text{vec}\,\mathbf{A})'\ \text{vec}\,\mathbf{B}$, this becomes

$$\min_{\text{vec}\,\mathbf{A}} (\text{vec}\,\mathbf{U}'\mathbf{Z})'\ \text{vec}[\hat{\mathbf{\Omega}}_u^{-1}\mathbf{U}'\mathbf{Z}(\mathbf{Z}'\mathbf{Z})^{-1}]$$

$$= \min_{\text{vec}\,\mathbf{A}} (\text{vec}\,\mathbf{U}'\mathbf{Z})'[\hat{\mathbf{\Omega}}_u^{-1} \otimes (\mathbf{Z}'\mathbf{Z})^{-1}]\ \text{vec}\,\mathbf{U}'\mathbf{Z}.$$

Now, $\text{vec}\,\mathbf{U}'\mathbf{Z} = (\mathbf{I} \otimes \mathbf{Z})\ \text{vec}\,\mathbf{U}'$, and so we obtain

$$\min\ (\text{vec}\,\mathbf{U}')'\ (\mathbf{I} \otimes \mathbf{Z})\ [\hat{\mathbf{\Omega}}_u^{-1} \otimes (\mathbf{Z}'\mathbf{Z})^{-1}]\ (\mathbf{I} \otimes \mathbf{Z})\ \text{vec}\,\mathbf{U}'$$

$$= \min\ (\text{vec}\,\mathbf{U}')'\ [\hat{\mathbf{\Omega}}_u^{-1} \otimes \mathbf{Z}(\mathbf{Z}'\mathbf{Z})^{-1}\mathbf{Z}']\ \text{vec}\,\mathbf{U}'.$$

Now, from $\mathbf{AX}' = \mathbf{U}'$, $(\mathbf{I} \otimes \mathbf{X})\ \text{vec}\,\mathbf{A} = \text{vec}\,\mathbf{U}'$, Therefore, substituting, we have

$$\min\ (\text{vec}\,\mathbf{A})'\ [\hat{\mathbf{\Omega}}_u^{-1} \otimes \mathbf{X}'\mathbf{Z}(\mathbf{Z}'\mathbf{Z})^{-1}\mathbf{Z}'\mathbf{X}]\ \text{vec}\,\mathbf{A}.$$

Recalling that the zero–one restrictions can be reparameterized as

$$\text{vec}\,\mathbf{A} = \mathbf{s} - \mathbf{Sa}^*,$$

substituting we have

$$\min_{\mathbf{a}}\ (\mathbf{s} - \mathbf{Sa}^*)'\ [\hat{\mathbf{\Omega}}_u^{-1} \otimes \mathbf{X}'\mathbf{Z}(\mathbf{Z}'\mathbf{Z})^{-1}\mathbf{Z}'\mathbf{X}]\ (\mathbf{s} - \mathbf{Sa}^*). \tag{6.9}$$

The 3SLS is given by the FOC of this criterion function i.e.

$$\text{FOC: } -\mathbf{S}'\,[\hat{\boldsymbol{\Omega}}_u^{-1} \otimes \mathbf{X}'\mathbf{Z}(\mathbf{Z}'\mathbf{Z})^{-1}\mathbf{Z}'\mathbf{X}]\,(\mathbf{s} - \mathbf{S}\hat{\mathbf{a}}^*) = 0$$

$$\text{or } \mathbf{S}'(\hat{\boldsymbol{\Omega}}_u^{-1} \otimes \mathbf{X}'\mathbf{Z})\,(\mathbf{Z}'\mathbf{Z})^{-1}\mathbf{Z}'\mathbf{X}\mathbf{s} = \mathbf{S}'[\hat{\boldsymbol{\Omega}}_u^{-1} \otimes \mathbf{Z}'\mathbf{X}(\mathbf{Z}'\mathbf{Z})^{-1}\mathbf{Z}'\mathbf{X}]\mathbf{S}\hat{\mathbf{a}}^*$$

which is precisely the 3SLS estimation expression (6.4).

Linear and non-linear constraints can easily be introduced here. For the non-linear case, we consider $\mathbf{A}(\boldsymbol{\theta})$ rather than $\mathbf{A}$, and minimize with respect to $\boldsymbol{\theta}$, the FOC now being

$$\left(\frac{\delta \operatorname{vec} \mathbf{A}(\hat{\boldsymbol{\theta}})}{\delta \boldsymbol{\theta}'}\right)'[\hat{\boldsymbol{\Omega}}_u^{-1} \otimes \mathbf{X}'\mathbf{Z}(\mathbf{Z}'\mathbf{Z})^{-1}\mathbf{Z}'\mathbf{X}] \operatorname{vec} \mathbf{A}(\hat{\boldsymbol{\theta}}) = 0.$$

For the general linear constraints case, we have $\mathbf{r}$ constraints of the form

$$\underset{r \times N(n+m)}{\boldsymbol{\Phi}} \quad \underset{N(n+m) \times 1}{\operatorname{vec} \mathbf{A}} = \underset{(r \times 1)}{\phi}$$

We parameterize these constraints as

$$\operatorname{vec} \mathbf{A} = \underset{N(n+m) \times p}{\mathbf{S}} \quad \underset{p \times 1}{\mathbf{a}^*} + \underset{N(n+m) \times 1}{\mathbf{s}}$$

where $\boldsymbol{\Phi} S = 0$ and $\boldsymbol{\Phi} s = -\phi$, and the expression that we get is just identical to (6.4), though now $\mathbf{S}$ and $\mathbf{s}$ are generalizations of those in (6.4) where only zero–one restrictions are considered.

6.5 3SIV Consistency and Asymptotic Distribution and their Relation to Identification Conditions

We are going to consider consistency and asymptotic distribution of 3SIV for both the general linear constraints case, and the non-linear in parameters case. Let us take them in turn.

6.5.1 General Linear Restrictions Case: $\boldsymbol{\Phi} \operatorname{vec} A = \phi$

As we saw above, after reparameterizing the constraints we obtain a criterion function expression identical to (6.9).

Since this criterion function is quadratic, the 3SLS estimator (6.4) defines a unique global minimum of (6.9) provided that the matrix plim $\mathbf{S}'(\hat{\boldsymbol{\Omega}}_u^{-1} \otimes \mathbf{R})\mathbf{S}/\mathbf{T}$, i.e.

$$\operatorname{plim} \mathbf{S}'[\hat{\mathbf{\Omega}}_{\mathrm{u}}^{-1} \otimes \mathbf{X}'\mathbf{Z}(\mathbf{Z}'\mathbf{Z})^{-1}\mathbf{Z}'\mathbf{X}]\mathbf{S}/\mathbf{T}$$

is non-singular. We can write this as

$$\operatorname{plim} \mathbf{S}'(\mathbf{I}_N \otimes \mathbf{X}'\mathbf{Z})\, [\hat{\mathbf{\Omega}}_{\mathrm{u}}^{-1} \otimes (\mathbf{Z}'\mathbf{Z})^{-1}]\, (\mathbf{I}_N \otimes \mathbf{Z}'\mathbf{X})\mathbf{S}.$$

Since $\mathbf{\Omega}_{\mathrm{u}}$ and

$$\operatorname{plim} \frac{\mathbf{Z}'\mathbf{Z}}{T}$$

are assumed to be non-singular, the condition is satisfied if

$$\operatorname{plim}\left(\mathbf{I}_N \otimes \frac{\mathbf{Z}'\mathbf{X}}{T}\right)\mathbf{S}$$

has full rank p, i.e. if

$$\operatorname{rank}\left[\operatorname{plim}\left(\mathbf{I} \otimes \frac{\mathbf{Z}'\mathbf{X}}{T}\right)\mathbf{S}\right] = \operatorname{rank}(\mathbf{I}_N \otimes \mathbf{K}')\mathbf{S} = p$$

then the plim of the criterion function has a unique global minimum at the true value of $\mathbf{a}^*$, and therefore the 3SLS estimator (6.4) is *consistent*. With respect to the asymptotic distribution, consider the following proposition, for the standard 3SLS case where $N = n$ and $\mathbf{Z}$ coincides with the set of predetermined variables with non-zero coefficients in at least one equation of the structural model.

Theorem 1: A necessary and sufficient condition for the AVM $\bar{\mathbf{E}}^{-1}$ to be well defined and so the 3SLS estimator to have the asymptotic distribution of Section 6.3 is that the model satisfies the usual condition for identification.

Proof: We shall consider only the case of general linear restrictions, For this case we have

$$\bar{\mathbf{E}} = \mathbf{S}'(\mathbf{\Omega}_{\mathrm{u}}^{-1} \otimes \bar{\mathbf{R}})\, \mathbf{S}$$

where $\bar{\mathbf{R}} = \mathbf{K}\mathbf{M}^{-1}\mathbf{K}'$.

The proof has two parts, in the first we show that the rank condition for identification of Section 3.2 is a necessary and sufficient condition for $\bar{\mathbf{E}}$ to be non-singular, and therefore for the asymptotic distribution to exist. Then we show how this rank condition is just the usual rank condition for identification.

Consider the reduced form equations

$$\mathbf{X}' = \mathbf{Q}\mathbf{Z}' + \mathbf{V}'$$

where $\mathbf{Z}$ contains only predetermined variables. Therefore

$$\text{plim}\,\frac{\mathbf{X}'\mathbf{Z}}{T} = \mathbf{K} = \text{plim}\,\frac{\mathbf{Q}\mathbf{Z}'\mathbf{Z}}{T} = \mathbf{QM}$$

since $\text{plim}\,\dfrac{\mathbf{V}'\mathbf{Z}}{T} = 0$ we can write

$$\bar{\mathbf{E}} = \mathbf{S}'(\mathbf{I} \otimes \mathbf{K})\,(\boldsymbol{\Omega}_{\mathrm{u}}^{-1} \otimes \mathbf{M}^{-1})\,(\mathbf{I} \otimes \mathbf{K}')\mathbf{S}$$

as

$$\begin{aligned} &\mathbf{S}'(\mathbf{I} \otimes \mathbf{QM})\,(\boldsymbol{\Omega}_{\mathrm{u}}^{-1} \otimes \mathbf{M}^{-1})\,(\mathbf{I} \otimes \mathbf{MQ}')\mathbf{S} \\ &= \mathbf{S}'(\mathbf{I} \otimes \mathbf{Q})\,(\boldsymbol{\Omega}_{\mathrm{u}}^{-1} \otimes \mathbf{M})\,(\mathbf{I} \otimes \mathbf{Q}')\mathbf{S}. \end{aligned} \tag{6.10}$$

Therefore the condition that $\bar{\mathbf{E}}$ is of full rank p, is equivalent to the condition that rank $(\mathbf{I} \otimes \mathbf{Q}')\mathbf{S} = p$. Clearly when this rank condition is satisfied the 3SLS is consistent as we just saw before and the model is identified since the estimator is consistent. Conversely if the model is identified we now show that $\bar{\mathbf{E}}$ is non-singular.

The proof is by contradiction, i.e. if $\bar{\mathbf{E}}$ is singular the model is unidentified. If $\bar{\mathbf{E}}$ is singular, then for a non-zero vector $\boldsymbol{\delta}$, we have

$$\boldsymbol{\delta}'\bar{\mathbf{E}}\boldsymbol{\delta} = \boldsymbol{\delta}'\mathbf{S}'(\mathbf{I} \otimes \mathbf{Q})\,(\boldsymbol{\Omega}_{\mathrm{u}}^{-1} \otimes \mathbf{M})\,(\mathbf{I} \otimes \mathbf{Q}')\mathbf{S}\boldsymbol{\delta} = 0.$$

Since $(\boldsymbol{\Omega}_{\mathrm{u}}^{-1} \otimes \mathbf{M})$ is a p.d. matrix, this will happen only if

$$(\mathbf{I} \otimes \mathbf{Q}')\mathbf{S}\boldsymbol{\delta} = 0.$$

Since

$$\mathbf{X}' = \begin{pmatrix} \mathbf{Y}' \\ \mathbf{Z}' \end{pmatrix} = \begin{pmatrix} \mathbf{P}\ \ \mathbf{Z}' + \mathbf{V}_1 \\ \mathbf{Z} \end{pmatrix}$$

this implies

$$\mathbf{X}' = \begin{pmatrix} \mathbf{P} \\ \mathbf{I}_{\mathrm{m}} \end{pmatrix} \mathbf{Z}' + \begin{pmatrix} \mathbf{V}_1 \\ 0 \end{pmatrix}$$

i.e.

$$\mathbf{Q} = \begin{pmatrix} \mathbf{P} \\ \mathbf{I}_{\mathrm{m}} \end{pmatrix}.$$

Now, since $\mathbf{A} = (\mathbf{BC})$, then

$$\mathbf{AQ} = 0$$

since

$$\mathbf{AQ} = (\mathbf{BC})\begin{pmatrix}\mathbf{P}\\ \mathbf{I}_m\end{pmatrix} = \mathbf{BP} + \mathbf{C} = \mathbf{B}(-\mathbf{B}^{-1}\mathbf{C}) + \mathbf{C} = 0.$$

Both **A** and **Q** are of full rank: **A** because it includes the matrix of endogenous variables **B** and **Q** because it contains the identity matrix $\mathbf{I}_m$. Thus, $\mathbf{AQ} = 0$ indicate that each of these is an annihilator of the other, i.e. **A** is a row kernel of **Q** and **Q** is a column kernel of **A**. Then each vector that annihilates **Q** is a linear combination of columns of **A**.

$\mathbf{AQ} = 0$ also implies that equivalently $(\mathbf{I}_N \otimes \mathbf{Q}')\ (\mathbf{I}_N \otimes \mathbf{A}') = 0$. Then each vector $\boldsymbol{\mu}$ such that

$$(\mathbf{I}_N \otimes \mathbf{Q}')\boldsymbol{\mu} = 0$$

is a linear combination of $(\mathbf{I}_N \otimes \mathbf{A}')$, i.e.

$$\boldsymbol{\mu} = (\mathbf{I}_N \otimes \mathbf{A}')\boldsymbol{\lambda}. \qquad (\boldsymbol{\lambda} \neq 0).$$

Hence in our case

$$\mathbf{S}\boldsymbol{\delta} = (\mathbf{I}_N \otimes \mathbf{A}')\boldsymbol{\lambda}.$$

Recall that **S** is a non-singular matrix such that $\boldsymbol{\Phi}\mathbf{S} = 0$, thus

$$\boldsymbol{\Phi}\mathbf{S}\boldsymbol{\delta} = 0 = \boldsymbol{\Phi}(\mathbf{I}_N \otimes \mathbf{A}')\boldsymbol{\lambda}$$

which implies,

$$\text{rank } \boldsymbol{\Phi}(\mathbf{I}_N \otimes \mathbf{A}') < N^2$$

which is precisely the sufficient rank condition for unidentification. So the usual local identifiability condition, rank $\boldsymbol{\Phi}(\mathbf{I}_N \otimes \mathbf{A}') = N^2$, ensure that the AVM of error of the 3SLS estimator is non-singular, and therefore the 3SLS has a non-degenerate asymptotic distribution.

(End of proof)

6.5.2 Non-Linear in Parameters Case: $\mathbf{A}(\bar{\boldsymbol{\theta}})\mathbf{X}' = \mathbf{U}'$

Consider the non-linear in parameters model

$$\mathbf{A}(\bar{\boldsymbol{\theta}})\mathbf{x}_t = \mathbf{u}_t \qquad t = 1, \ldots, T$$

where $\boldsymbol{\theta}$ is a $(p \times 1)$ vector of unknown parameters. As we showed in Section 6.4 the estimators can be derived from the criterion function

$$\min_{\boldsymbol{\theta}} \text{tr}[\hat{\boldsymbol{\Omega}}_u^{-1}\mathbf{U}'\mathbf{Z}(\mathbf{Z}'\mathbf{Z})^{-1}\mathbf{Z}'\mathbf{U}]$$

$$= \min_{\boldsymbol{\theta}} \operatorname{tr}[\hat{\boldsymbol{\Omega}}_u^{-1}\mathbf{A}(\boldsymbol{\theta})\mathbf{X}'\mathbf{Z}(\mathbf{Z}'\mathbf{Z})^{-1}\mathbf{Z}'\mathbf{X}\mathbf{A}(\boldsymbol{\theta})']$$

and we saw that it has as FOC the expression of the non-linear 3SLS:

$$\left(\frac{\partial \operatorname{vec} \mathbf{A}(\hat{\boldsymbol{\theta}})}{\partial \boldsymbol{\theta}'}\right)(\hat{\boldsymbol{\Omega}}_u^{-1} \otimes \mathbf{R}) \operatorname{vec} \mathbf{A}(\hat{\boldsymbol{\theta}}) = 0. \tag{6.11}$$

In order to obtain the asymptotic distribution of $\hat{\boldsymbol{\theta}}$ we need $\hat{\boldsymbol{\theta}}$ to be a *consistent* estimator of $\boldsymbol{\theta}$, since only at true $\bar{\boldsymbol{\theta}}$ do we obtain

$$\operatorname{vec} \frac{\mathbf{U}'\mathbf{Z}}{\sqrt{T}} \; \tilde{a} \; \mathrm{N}(0, \boldsymbol{\Omega}_u \otimes \mathbf{M})$$

(see Section 6.3) and $\mathbf{A}(\bar{\boldsymbol{\theta}})\mathbf{X}' = \mathbf{U}$.

Therefore we need a condition to ensure that the solution to the minimization problem has a unique minimum equal to the true value $\bar{\boldsymbol{\theta}}$. Replacing $\hat{\boldsymbol{\Omega}}_u^{-1}$ and $\mathbf{R}$ by their plim values, $\boldsymbol{\Omega}_u^{-1}$ and $\bar{\mathbf{R}}$ we require that the only solution to

$$\min_{\boldsymbol{\theta}}[\operatorname{vec} \mathrm{A}(\boldsymbol{\theta})]' (\boldsymbol{\Omega}_u^{-1} \otimes \bar{\mathbf{R}}) \operatorname{vec} \mathbf{A}(\boldsymbol{\theta})$$

where

$$\bar{\mathbf{R}} = \mathbf{K}\mathbf{M}^{-1}\mathbf{K}'$$

be

$$\boldsymbol{\theta} = \bar{\boldsymbol{\theta}}.$$

This criterion function can be written as

$$[\operatorname{vec} \mathbf{A}(\boldsymbol{\theta})]' (\mathbf{I} \otimes \mathbf{K}) (\boldsymbol{\Omega}_u^{-1} \otimes \mathbf{M}^{-1}) (\mathbf{I} \otimes \mathbf{K}') \operatorname{vec} \mathbf{A}(\boldsymbol{\theta}),$$

where $(\boldsymbol{\Omega}_u^{-1} \otimes \mathbf{M}^{-1}) = (\boldsymbol{\Omega}_u \otimes \mathbf{M})^{-1}$ is a p.d. matrix, and thus, the quadratic criterion function will achieve its minimum, i.e. zero where

$$(\mathbf{I} \otimes \mathbf{K}') \operatorname{vec} \mathbf{A}(\boldsymbol{\theta}) = 0, \tag{6.12}$$

i.e. if $\operatorname{vec}[\mathbf{A}(\boldsymbol{\theta})\mathbf{K}] = 0$, which is equivalent to

$$\operatorname{vec}[\operatorname{plim} \mathbf{T}^{-1}\mathbf{A}(\boldsymbol{\theta})\mathbf{X}'\mathbf{Z}] = 0.$$

But $\mathbf{A}(\bar{\boldsymbol{\theta}})\mathbf{X}' = \mathbf{U}$, and therefore at $\boldsymbol{\theta} = \bar{\boldsymbol{\theta}}$ this is just

$$\operatorname{vec}(\operatorname{plim} \mathbf{T}^{-1}\mathbf{U}'\mathbf{Z}) = 0.$$

Therefore $\operatorname{vec}[\mathbf{A}(\boldsymbol{\theta})\mathbf{K}] = 0$ when $\boldsymbol{\theta} = \bar{\boldsymbol{\theta}}$. For identification a sufficient condition is then that the equation (6.12) have the unique solution

$\boldsymbol{\theta} = \bar{\boldsymbol{\theta}}$. A less general (sufficient) condition, which ensures that there is no other minimum within some neighbourhood of $\bar{\boldsymbol{\theta}}$, a condition usually described as a condition for local identification, is given in the following definition due to Fisher:

Definition 1: We say that $\bar{\boldsymbol{\theta}}$ is locally identifiable if there does not exist a sequence $\boldsymbol{\theta}_i$ such that

$$(\mathbf{I} \otimes \mathbf{K}')\,\mathrm{vec}\,\mathbf{A}(\boldsymbol{\theta}_i) = 0$$

for the sequence $\boldsymbol{\theta}_i \to \bar{\boldsymbol{\theta}}$ as $i \to \infty$.

Local identification can be shown to be a necessary condition for the usual asymptotic distribution of $\hat{\boldsymbol{\theta}}$ to exist. Let us see this in the two following propositions:

Theorem 2: A sufficient condition for the true value of $\boldsymbol{\theta}$, $\bar{\boldsymbol{\theta}}$, to be locally identifiable is that the $(Nm \times p)$ matrix

$$(\mathbf{I}_N \otimes \mathbf{K}')\left(\frac{\partial\,\mathrm{vec}\,\mathbf{A}(\boldsymbol{\theta})}{\partial \boldsymbol{\theta}}\right) \tag{6.13}$$

is of full rank p at $\boldsymbol{\theta} = \bar{\boldsymbol{\theta}}$.

Proof: Suppose that the true parameter is locally unidentified. Then by Fisher's definition of local identification, there exists in a neighbourhood of $\bar{\boldsymbol{\theta}}$ an infinite set of solutions to the criterion function minimization problem, i.e.

$$(\mathbf{I}_N \otimes \mathbf{K}')\,\mathrm{vec}\,\mathbf{A}(\boldsymbol{\theta}_i) = 0$$

where $\boldsymbol{\theta}_i \to \bar{\boldsymbol{\theta}}$ as $i \to \infty$.

If the first derivatives of $\mathbf{A}(\boldsymbol{\theta})$ with respect to $\boldsymbol{\theta}$ are continuous at $\bar{\boldsymbol{\theta}}$ we can apply the Mean Value Theorem to obtain

$$(\mathbf{I}_N \otimes \mathbf{K}')\left(\frac{\partial\,\mathrm{vec}\,\mathbf{A}(\boldsymbol{\theta})}{\partial \boldsymbol{\theta}'}\right)_{\boldsymbol{\theta}_i^*}(\boldsymbol{\theta}_i - \bar{\boldsymbol{\theta}}) = 0 \tag{6.14}$$

where the derivatives are evaluated at some point $\boldsymbol{\theta}_i^*$ such that $\boldsymbol{\theta}_i \leqslant \boldsymbol{\theta}_i^* \leqslant \bar{\boldsymbol{\theta}}$.

Now rescale $(\boldsymbol{\theta}_i - \bar{\boldsymbol{\theta}})$ by its norm and denote it by

$$\boldsymbol{\delta}_i = \left| \frac{\boldsymbol{\theta}_i - \bar{\boldsymbol{\theta}}}{|\boldsymbol{\theta}_i - \bar{\boldsymbol{\theta}}|} \right|,$$

which implies $||\boldsymbol{\delta}_i|| = 1$, i.e. bounded. Therefore by construction, $\boldsymbol{\delta}_i$ is a sequence in a compact set, and therefore $\{\boldsymbol{\delta}_i\}$ has a limit point, $\boldsymbol{\delta}^*$ say, within the compact set.

One can also extract a subsequence from the sequence $\{\boldsymbol{\delta}_i\}$ such that it converges to $\boldsymbol{\delta}^*$, and therefore we can state that

$$(\mathbf{I}_N \otimes \mathbf{K}')\left(\frac{\partial \operatorname{vec} \mathbf{A}(\boldsymbol{\theta})}{\partial \boldsymbol{\theta}'}\right)\boldsymbol{\theta}_i^* \boldsymbol{\delta}_i = 0 \underset{i\to\infty}{\rightarrow}$$

$$(\mathbf{I}_N \otimes \mathbf{K}')\left(\frac{\partial \operatorname{vec} \mathbf{A}(\boldsymbol{\theta})}{\partial \boldsymbol{\theta}'}\right)\bar{\boldsymbol{\theta}}\, \boldsymbol{\delta}^* = 0.$$

Since $\boldsymbol{\delta}^* \neq 0$ by construction, it follows that

$$(\mathbf{I}_N \otimes \mathbf{K}')\left(\frac{\partial \operatorname{vec} \mathbf{A}(\boldsymbol{\theta})}{\partial \boldsymbol{\theta}'}\right)_{\bar{\boldsymbol{\theta}}}$$

is not of full rank p.

This proposition implies that a *sufficient condition* for local identification is that

$$\operatorname{rank}\,(\mathbf{I}_N \otimes \mathbf{K}')\left(\frac{\partial \operatorname{vec} \mathbf{A}(\boldsymbol{\theta})}{\partial \boldsymbol{\theta}'}\right)_{\bar{\boldsymbol{\theta}}} = p.$$

If this condition is satisfied then, in a sufficiently small neighbourhood of $\bar{\boldsymbol{\theta}}$, there will be no other solution, and therefore $\hat{\boldsymbol{\theta}}$ will be consistent, if the solution is known to lie in some sufficiently small neighbourhood of $\bar{\boldsymbol{\theta}}$.
(End of proof)

However, this condition is not a necessary condition for local identification. Let us see now the corresponding extension of the asymptotic distribution after the derivation of (local) consistency of $\hat{\boldsymbol{\theta}}$.

Theorem 3: Assume that the rank solution for local identification is satisfied. Then, under the assumptions stated in this chapter for the linear 3SLS plus continuity of the first derivatives of $\mathbf{A}(\boldsymbol{\theta})$ at $\bar{\boldsymbol{\theta}}$

$$\sqrt{T}(\hat{\boldsymbol{\theta}} - \bar{\boldsymbol{\theta}}) \;\tilde{a}\; \mathrm{N}(0, \mathbf{V}_e)$$

where $\hat{\boldsymbol{\theta}}$ is the non-linear 3SLS estimator defined by (6.11), and

$$\mathbf{V}_\theta = \left[\left(\frac{\partial \operatorname{vec} \mathbf{A}(\boldsymbol{\theta})}{\partial \boldsymbol{\theta}'}\right)'_{\bar{\boldsymbol{\theta}}} (\boldsymbol{\Omega}_u^{-1} \otimes \mathbf{K}\mathbf{M}^{-1}\mathbf{K}')\left(\frac{\partial \operatorname{vec} \mathbf{A}(\boldsymbol{\theta})}{\partial \boldsymbol{\theta}'}\right)_{\bar{\boldsymbol{\theta}}}\right]^{-1}.$$

Proof: By the Mean Value Theorem

$$\operatorname{vec} \mathbf{A}(\hat{\theta}) = \operatorname{vec} \mathbf{A}(\bar{\boldsymbol{\theta}}) + \left(\frac{\partial \operatorname{vec} \mathbf{A}(\boldsymbol{\theta})}{\partial \boldsymbol{\theta}}\right)_{\boldsymbol{\theta}^*}(\hat{\boldsymbol{\theta}} - \bar{\boldsymbol{\theta}})$$

for some $\boldsymbol{\theta}^*$ in the line joining $\hat{\boldsymbol{\theta}}$ and $\bar{\boldsymbol{\theta}}$.

Substituting in the FOC (6.11) we obtain

$$\left[\left(\frac{\partial \operatorname{vec} \mathbf{A}(\boldsymbol{\theta})}{\partial \boldsymbol{\theta}'}\right)'_{\hat{\boldsymbol{\theta}}}\left(\hat{\boldsymbol{\Omega}}_{\mathrm{u}}^{-1} \otimes \frac{\mathbf{R}}{T}\right)\left(\frac{\partial \operatorname{vec} \mathbf{A}(\boldsymbol{\theta})}{\partial \boldsymbol{\theta}'}\right)_{\boldsymbol{\theta}^*}\right] \sqrt{T}\,(\hat{\boldsymbol{\theta}} - \bar{\boldsymbol{\theta}})$$
$$= -\left(\frac{\partial \operatorname{vec} \mathbf{A}(\boldsymbol{\theta})}{\partial \boldsymbol{\theta}'}\right)'_{\hat{\boldsymbol{\theta}}}\left(\hat{\boldsymbol{\Omega}}_{\mathrm{u}}^{-1} \otimes \frac{\mathbf{R}}{\sqrt{T}}\right) \operatorname{vec} \mathbf{A}(\bar{\boldsymbol{\theta}}).$$

Consider the right-hand side element:

$$-\left(\frac{\partial \operatorname{vec} \mathbf{A}(\boldsymbol{\theta})}{\partial \boldsymbol{\theta}'}\right)'_{\hat{\boldsymbol{\theta}}} [\hat{\boldsymbol{\Omega}}_{\mathrm{u}}^{-1} \otimes \mathbf{X}'\mathbf{Z}(\mathbf{Z}'\mathbf{Z})^{-1}]\, \frac{\mathbf{Z}'\mathbf{X}}{\sqrt{T}} \operatorname{vec} \mathbf{A}(\bar{\boldsymbol{\theta}})$$
$$= -\left(\frac{\partial \operatorname{vec} \mathbf{A}(\boldsymbol{\theta})}{\partial \boldsymbol{\theta}'}\right)'_{\hat{\boldsymbol{\theta}}} [\hat{\boldsymbol{\Omega}}_{\mathrm{u}}^{-1} \otimes \mathbf{X}'\mathbf{Z}(\mathbf{Z}'\mathbf{Z})^{-1}] \left(\mathbf{I} \otimes \frac{\mathbf{Z}'\mathbf{X}}{\sqrt{T}}\right) \operatorname{vec} \mathbf{A}(\bar{\boldsymbol{\theta}}).$$

Now

$$\left(\mathbf{I} \otimes \frac{\mathbf{Z}'\mathbf{X}}{\sqrt{T}}\right) \operatorname{vec} \mathbf{A}(\bar{\boldsymbol{\theta}}) = \operatorname{vec} \mathbf{A}(\bar{\boldsymbol{\theta}})\, \frac{\mathbf{X}'\mathbf{Z}}{\sqrt{T}} = \operatorname{vec} \frac{\mathbf{U}'\mathbf{Z}}{\sqrt{T}}$$

which as we saw in Section 6.3, applying the Central Limit Theorem has

$$\operatorname{vec} \frac{\mathbf{U}'\mathbf{Z}}{\sqrt{T}} \;\tilde{a}\; \mathrm{N}(0, \boldsymbol{\Omega}_{\mathrm{u}} \otimes M).$$

On the left-hand side, assume that the matrix in square brackets has plim, and has the form

$$\underset{(p \times p)}{\bar{\mathbf{E}}} = \operatorname{plim} \mathbf{E}$$
$$= \left(\frac{\partial \operatorname{vec} \mathbf{A}(\boldsymbol{\theta})}{\partial \boldsymbol{\theta}'}\right)'_{\bar{\boldsymbol{\theta}}} (\boldsymbol{\Omega}_{\mathrm{u}}^{-1} \otimes \bar{\mathbf{R}}) \left(\frac{\partial \operatorname{vec} \mathbf{A}(\boldsymbol{\theta})}{\partial \boldsymbol{\theta}'}\right)_{\bar{\boldsymbol{\theta}}}.$$
$$[p \times N(n+m)]$$

Fisher's condition for local identification, ensures that this is a p.d. matrix (see Theorem 2).

Then by the Slutsky Theorem and the Cramer Linear Transformation Theorem

$$\sqrt{T}(\hat{\boldsymbol{\theta}} - \bar{\boldsymbol{\theta}}) \;\tilde{a}\; \mathrm{N}(0, \mathbf{V}_{\theta})$$

where

$$\mathbf{V}_{\theta} =$$
$$\bar{\mathbf{E}}^{-1}\left|\left(\frac{\partial \operatorname{vec} \mathbf{A}(\boldsymbol{\theta})}{\partial \boldsymbol{\theta}'}\right)_{\bar{\boldsymbol{\theta}}}(\boldsymbol{\Omega}_{\mathrm{u}}^{-1} \otimes \mathbf{K}\mathbf{M}^{-1})(\boldsymbol{\Omega}_{\mathrm{u}} \otimes \mathbf{M})(\boldsymbol{\Omega}_{\mathrm{u}}^{-1} \otimes \mathbf{M}^{-1}\mathbf{K}')\left(\frac{\partial \operatorname{vec} \mathbf{A}(\boldsymbol{\theta})}{\partial \boldsymbol{\theta}'}\right)_{\bar{\boldsymbol{\theta}}}\right| \bar{\mathbf{E}}^{-1}$$
$$\equiv \bar{\mathbf{E}}^{-1}\bar{\mathbf{E}}\bar{\mathbf{E}}^{-1} = \bar{\mathbf{E}}^{-1}.$$

(End of proof)

Notice that in the case of linear constraints, instead of $\text{vec}\,\mathbf{A} = \text{vec}\,\mathbf{A}(\boldsymbol{\theta})$, we have $\text{vec}\,\mathbf{A} = \mathbf{s} - \mathbf{S}\mathbf{a}^*$, and therefore

$$\frac{\partial\,\text{vec}\,\mathbf{A}(\boldsymbol{\theta})}{\partial\boldsymbol{\theta}'}$$

becomes

$$\frac{\partial\,\text{vec}\,\mathbf{A}}{\partial\mathbf{a}^*} = -\,\mathbf{S},$$

therefore substituting in $\mathbf{V}_\theta$ we obtain precisely the AVM of $\sqrt{T}(\hat{\mathbf{a}}^* - \mathbf{a}^*)$ of Section 6.3.

6.6 Relative Efficiency of 3SIV and Single Equation IV

In general 3SIV is more efficient than single equation IV. A proof can be found, for example, in Schmidt (1976, p. 209), which uses the same algebraic result as the one used to prove the relative efficiency of the IV estimator that accounts for autocorrelation as compared with the 'crude' IV estimator, or can directly be derived from Theorem 1 of Chapter 5, when it is considered that 3SIV has been proved to be the most efficient IV estimator for equation (5.2), whereas separate IV estimators correspond to the 'crude' IV estimator of Section 5.4.

The heuristic is that 3SIV accounts for correlation between the single equations and this information used by the 3SIV estimator makes it more efficient than single equation IV estimators. There are however several special cases where the 3SIV estimator is *not* more efficient than the single equation estimator asymptotically.

Consider again the set of N equations

$$\mathbf{A}\mathbf{X}' = \mathbf{U}', \qquad \mathrm{E}[\text{vec}\,\mathbf{U}'(\text{vec}\,\mathbf{U}')'] = (\boldsymbol{\Omega}_{\mathrm{u}} \otimes \mathbf{I}_T)$$

subject to a set of r restrictions of the form

$$\boldsymbol{\Phi}\,\text{vec}\,\mathbf{A} = \boldsymbol{\phi}$$

or alternatively

$$\text{vec}\,\mathbf{A} = \mathbf{s} - \mathbf{S}\mathbf{a}^*, \qquad \boldsymbol{\Phi}\mathbf{s} = \boldsymbol{\phi},\ \boldsymbol{\Phi} = 0.$$

Partition the model in two blocks

$$\mathbf{A}_1\mathbf{X}' = \mathbf{U}_1' \qquad (N_1 \text{ equations})$$

$$\mathbf{A}_2\mathbf{X}' = \mathbf{U}_2' \qquad (N_2 = N - N_1 \text{ equations})$$

and correspondingly partition the covariance matrix $\mathbf{\Omega}_u$ and its inverse $\mathbf{\Omega}_u^{-1}$ as

$$\mathbf{\Omega}_u = \begin{pmatrix} \mathbf{\Omega}_{11} & \mathbf{\Omega}_{12} \\ \mathbf{\Omega}_{21} & \mathbf{\Omega}_{22} \end{pmatrix} \mathbf{\Omega}_u^{-1} = \begin{pmatrix} \mathbf{\Omega}^{11} & \mathbf{\Omega}^{12} \\ \mathbf{\Omega}^{21} & \mathbf{\Omega}^{22} \end{pmatrix}.$$

For our equivalence results we need the constraints to be separable. The constraints $\mathbf{\Phi}\,\text{vec}\,\mathbf{a} = \boldsymbol{\phi}$ are separable if we can write them in two blocks, each affecting one block of the system, i.e.

$$\begin{matrix} \mathbf{\Phi}_1 \,\text{vec}\,\mathbf{A}_1 = \boldsymbol{\phi}_1 \\ \mathbf{\Phi}_2 \,\text{vec}\,\mathbf{A}_2 = \boldsymbol{\phi}_2 \end{matrix} \quad \textit{or} \quad \begin{pmatrix} \text{vec}\,\mathbf{A}_1 \\ \text{vec}\,\mathbf{A}_2 \end{pmatrix} = \begin{pmatrix} \mathbf{s}_1 \\ \mathbf{s}_2 \end{pmatrix} - \begin{pmatrix} \mathbf{S}_1 & 0 \\ 0 & \mathbf{S}_2 \end{pmatrix} \begin{pmatrix} \mathbf{a}_1^* \\ \mathbf{a}_2^* \end{pmatrix}$$

Under these assumptions, the 3SLS estimator becomes, using (6.4),

$$\mathbf{S}_1'(\hat{\mathbf{\Omega}}^{11} \otimes \mathbf{R})\mathbf{S}_1\hat{\mathbf{a}}_1^* + \mathbf{S}_1'(\hat{\mathbf{\Omega}}^{12} \otimes \mathbf{R})\mathbf{S}_2\hat{\mathbf{a}}_2^* = \mathbf{S}_1'(\hat{\mathbf{\Omega}}^{11} \otimes \mathbf{R})\mathbf{s}_1 + \mathbf{S}_1'(\hat{\mathbf{\Omega}}^{12} \otimes \mathbf{R})\mathbf{s}_2 \quad (6.15a)$$

$$\mathbf{S}_2'(\hat{\mathbf{\Omega}}^{21} \otimes \mathbf{R})\mathbf{S}_1\hat{\mathbf{a}}_1^* + \mathbf{S}_2'(\hat{\mathbf{\Omega}}^{22} \otimes \mathbf{R})\mathbf{S}_2\hat{\mathbf{a}}_2^* = \mathbf{S}_2'(\hat{\mathbf{\Omega}}^{21} \otimes \mathbf{R})\mathbf{s}_1 + \mathbf{S}_2'(\hat{\mathbf{\Omega}}^{22} \otimes \mathbf{R})\mathbf{s}_2, \quad (6.15b)$$

where $\hat{\mathbf{\Omega}}^{11}$, $\hat{\mathbf{\Omega}}^{12}$, etc. are the estimates of $\mathbf{\Omega}^{11}$, $\mathbf{\Omega}^{12}$, etc.

The cases we are going to examine for which 3SIV and 2SIV estimators are asymptotically equivalent are the following:

(i) Disturbances are not correlated across equations, i.e. $\mathbf{\Omega}_u$ is a diagonal matrix, and all the restrictions apply to separate equations (i.e. $\mathbf{\Phi}$ is completely separable).

(ii) No correlation between the two blocks of equations, i.e. $\mathbf{\Omega}_{12} = \mathbf{\Omega}_{21} = 0$.

(iii) The first block of equations is over-identified and the second block is exactly identified.

Theorem 4: If the constraints are separable and the disturbances are not correlated across equations, then the 3SLS estimator is exactly the same as the 2SLS estimator of each equation in isolation, provided $\hat{\mathbf{\Omega}}_u$ is also constrained to be diagonal.

Proof: In the case of separable constraints and uncorrelated disturbances across equations, i.e. $\hat{\mathbf{\Omega}}_u = \hat{\mathbf{D}}$, where $\hat{\mathbf{D}}$ is a diagonal matrix the 3SLS (6.4) can be written as,

$$\mathbf{S}'(\hat{\mathbf{D}} \otimes \mathbf{R})\mathbf{S}\hat{\mathbf{a}}^* = \mathbf{S}'(\hat{\mathbf{D}} \otimes \mathbf{R})\mathbf{s}.$$

But then $\mathbf{S}'(\hat{\mathbf{D}} \otimes \mathbf{R})\mathbf{S}$ is a block diagonal matrix, and if the jth block of equations is considered, it will be found that $\hat{\mathbf{d}}_j$ can be cancelled to yield the equation,

$$\mathbf{S}_j'(\mathbf{R})\mathbf{S}_j\mathbf{a}_j^* = \mathbf{S}_j'(\mathbf{R})\mathbf{s}_j, \qquad i = 1, \ldots, N.$$

Also if the restrictions are zero–one restrictions, then we obtain the usual 2SLS estimators of the ith equation

$$\mathbf{X}_i'\mathbf{Z}(\mathbf{Z}'\mathbf{Z})^{-1}\mathbf{Z}'\mathbf{X}_i\hat{\mathbf{a}}_i^* = \mathbf{X}_i'\mathbf{Z}(\mathbf{Z}'\mathbf{Z})^{-1}\mathbf{Z}'\mathbf{y}_i, \qquad i = 1, \ldots, N$$

(End of proof)

Theorem 5: If the model is divided into two submodels and the constraints are separable, and there is no correlation across the two blocks of equations, then the IV estimator of each block of equations in isolation has the same AVM as the IV estimator of the entire system simultaneously.

Proof: As we saw in Section 6.3, the AVM of the 3SLS estimator has the form

$$\text{AVM } \sqrt{T}(\hat{\mathbf{a}}^* - \mathbf{a}^*) = [\mathbf{S}'(\boldsymbol{\Omega}_u^{-1} \otimes \bar{\mathbf{R}})\mathbf{S}]^{-1}$$

where $\bar{\mathbf{R}} = \operatorname{plim} \mathbf{R}/T = \mathbf{KM}^{-1}\mathbf{K}'$.

From the assumption of separable constraints and $\boldsymbol{\Omega}_{12} = \boldsymbol{\Omega}_{21} = 0$, this can be written, using

$$\boldsymbol{\Omega}_u^{-1} = \begin{pmatrix} \boldsymbol{\Omega}_{11}^{-1} & 0 \\ 0 & \boldsymbol{\Omega}_{22}^{-1} \end{pmatrix}$$

$$\begin{pmatrix} \mathbf{S}_1'(\boldsymbol{\Omega}_{11}^{-1} \otimes \bar{\mathbf{R}})\mathbf{S}_1 & 0 \\ 0 & \mathbf{S}_2'(\boldsymbol{\Omega}_{22}^{-1} \otimes \bar{\mathbf{R}})\mathbf{S}_2 \end{pmatrix}^{-1} =$$

$$\begin{pmatrix} [\mathbf{S}_1'(\boldsymbol{\Omega}_{11}^{-1} \otimes \bar{\mathbf{R}})\mathbf{S}_1]^{-1} & 0 \\ 0 & [\mathbf{S}_2'(\boldsymbol{\Omega}_{22}^{\vee} \otimes \bar{\mathbf{R}})\mathbf{S}_2]^{-1} \end{pmatrix},$$

i.e. the AVM of the 3SLS estimator errors is the same as that of the IV estimator errors of each block in isolation.
(End of proof)

As a particular case, when one of the blocks is composed of just one equation, then 2SIV and 3SIV estimators have the same AVM for that equation. Of course if $\boldsymbol{\Omega}_u$ is not block diagonal, the 3SIV estimates for the whole model will be more efficient than the separate estimator but a notable exception is provided by the next theorem.

Despite the asymptotic equivalence of 2SIV and 3SIV, estimators under these assumptions, the estimators can be different, since though $\mathbf{\Omega}_u$ is block diagonal, $\hat{\mathbf{\Omega}}_u$ will not usually be due to sampling errors. Of course if the block diagonality of $\mathbf{\Omega}_u$ was known *a priori*, we would set $\hat{\mathbf{\Omega}}_{21} = 0$ and the two estimates would be identical.

Theorem 6: If constraints are separable, and if one of the two blocks is over-identified whereas the other is just identified, then the 3SIV estimator of the over-identified block of equations in isolation is *identical* to the 3SIV estimator for the whole model.

Proof: Consider that the over-identified block is the first one, and the second block is just identified. Recall that under separable constraints, the 3SIV estimator expression is given by (6.15a) and (6.15b).

Consider the second block of just identified equations:

$$\mathbf{S}_2'(\hat{\mathbf{\Omega}}^{21} \otimes \mathbf{R})\mathbf{S}_1\hat{\mathbf{a}}_1^* + \mathbf{S}_2'(\hat{\mathbf{\Omega}}^{22} \otimes \mathbf{R})\mathbf{S}_2\hat{\mathbf{a}}_2^* = \mathbf{S}_2'(\hat{\mathbf{\Omega}}^{21} \otimes \mathbf{R})\mathbf{s}_1 + \mathbf{S}_2'(\hat{\mathbf{\Omega}}^{22} \otimes \mathbf{R})\mathbf{s}_2.$$

If the second block of equations is just identified, then

$$(\mathbf{I}_{N_2} \otimes \mathbf{Z}'\mathbf{X})\mathbf{S}_2$$

is a square matrix, and

$$\text{plim}\,\frac{\mathbf{Z}'\mathbf{X}\mathbf{S}_2}{T}$$

is a non-singular ensured by identification (see Section 6.5.1), hence $(\mathbf{I}_{N_2} \otimes \mathbf{Z}'\mathbf{X})\mathbf{S}_2$ has an inverse with probability one.

Recall that

$$\mathbf{R} = \mathbf{X}'\mathbf{Z}(\mathbf{Z}'\mathbf{Z})^{-1}\mathbf{Z}'\mathbf{X} = \mathbf{X}'\mathbf{Z}\hat{\mathbf{Q}}'.$$

Taking $\mathbf{S}_2'(\mathbf{I}_{N_2} \otimes \mathbf{X}'\mathbf{Z})$ as a common factor from the second block of equations

$$\mathbf{S}_2'(\mathbf{I}_{N_2} \otimes \mathbf{X}'\mathbf{Z})\{(\hat{\mathbf{\Omega}}^{21} \otimes \hat{\mathbf{Q}}')\mathbf{S}_1\hat{\mathbf{a}}_1^* + [\hat{\mathbf{\Omega}}^{22} \otimes (\mathbf{Z}'\mathbf{Z})^{-1}](\mathbf{I} \otimes \mathbf{Z}'\mathbf{X})\mathbf{S}_2\hat{\mathbf{a}}_2^* - (\hat{\mathbf{\Omega}}^{21} \otimes \hat{\mathbf{Q}}')\mathbf{s}_1 + (\hat{\mathbf{\Omega}}^{22} \otimes \hat{\mathbf{Q}}')\mathbf{s}_2\} = 0.$$

Pre-multiplying by $[\mathbf{S}_2'(\mathbf{I}_{N_2} \otimes \mathbf{X}'\mathbf{Z})]^{-1}$, the term $\mathbf{S}_2'(\mathbf{I}_{N_2} \otimes \mathbf{X}'\mathbf{Z})$ disappears; and now pre-multiplying by

$$[\hat{\mathbf{\Omega}}^{22} \otimes (\mathbf{Z}'\mathbf{Z})^{-1}] = [(\hat{\mathbf{\Omega}}^{22})^{-1} \otimes (\mathbf{Z}'\mathbf{Z})]$$

yields

$$[(\hat{\mathbf{\Omega}}^{22})^{-1}\hat{\mathbf{\Omega}}^{21} \otimes \mathbf{Z}'\mathbf{X})\mathbf{S}_1\hat{\mathbf{a}}_1^* + (\mathbf{I} \otimes \mathbf{Z}'\mathbf{X})\mathbf{S}_2\hat{\mathbf{a}}_2^* = [(\hat{\mathbf{\Omega}}^{22})^{-1}\hat{\mathbf{\Omega}}^{21} \otimes \mathbf{Z}'\mathbf{X}]\mathbf{s}_1 + (\mathbf{I} \otimes \mathbf{Z}'\mathbf{X})\mathbf{s}_2.$$

Pre-multiplying by $\mathbf{S}_1'(\hat{\mathbf{\Omega}}^{12} \otimes \hat{\mathbf{Q}})$ gives

$$\mathbf{S}_1'[\hat{\mathbf{\Omega}}^{12}(\hat{\mathbf{\Omega}}^{22})^{-1}\hat{\mathbf{\Omega}}^{21} \otimes \mathbf{R}]\mathbf{S}_1\hat{\mathbf{a}}_1^* + \mathbf{S}_1'(\hat{\mathbf{\Omega}}^{12} \otimes \mathbf{R})\mathbf{S}_2\hat{\mathbf{a}}_2^* = \mathbf{S}_1'[\hat{\mathbf{\Omega}}^{12}(\hat{\mathbf{\Omega}}^{22})^{-1}\hat{\mathbf{\Omega}}^{21} \otimes \mathbf{R}]\mathbf{s}_1 + \mathbf{S}_1'(\hat{\mathbf{\Omega}}^{12} \otimes \mathbf{R})\mathbf{s}_2.$$

Subtracting this from (6.15a) yields

$$\mathbf{S}_1'(\hat{\mathbf{\Omega}}^{11} \otimes \mathbf{R})\mathbf{S}_1\hat{\mathbf{a}}_1^* - \mathbf{S}_1'[\hat{\mathbf{\Omega}}^{12}(\hat{\mathbf{\Omega}}^{22})^{-1}\hat{\mathbf{\Omega}}^{21} \otimes \mathbf{R}]\mathbf{S}_1\hat{\mathbf{a}}_1^* = \mathbf{S}_1'(\hat{\mathbf{\Omega}}^{11} \otimes \mathbf{R})\mathbf{s}_1 - \mathbf{S}_1'[\hat{\mathbf{\Omega}}^{12}(\hat{\mathbf{\Omega}}^{22})^{-1}\hat{\mathbf{\Omega}}^{21} \otimes \mathbf{R}]\mathbf{s}_1.$$

By the formula of the inverse of a partitioned matrix we have

$$\hat{\mathbf{\Omega}}_{11} = [\hat{\mathbf{\Omega}}^{11} - \hat{\mathbf{\Omega}}^{12}(\hat{\mathbf{\Omega}}^{22})^{-1}\hat{\mathbf{\Omega}}^{21}]^{-1}$$

thus

$$\hat{\mathbf{\Omega}}_{11}^{-1} = \hat{\mathbf{\Omega}}^{11} - \hat{\mathbf{\Omega}}^{12}(\hat{\mathbf{\Omega}}^{22})^{-1}\hat{\mathbf{\Omega}}^{21}$$

and substituting the above equation becomes

$$\mathbf{S}_1'(\hat{\mathbf{\Omega}}_{11}^{-1} \otimes \mathbf{R})\mathbf{S}_1\hat{\mathbf{a}}_1^* = \mathbf{S}_1'(\hat{\mathbf{\Omega}}_{11}^{-1} \otimes \mathbf{R})\mathbf{s}_1$$

which is just the 3SIV estimator of the first block of over-identified equations in isolation.
(End of proof)

This proposition therefore shows how we cannot improve the estimation of over-identified equations by considering the just identified equations. This however does not mean that we have to ignore the just identified block since of the predetermined variables in **Z** can belong to that block only, i.e. the just identified block only affects the estimation of the over-identified block by providing instruments.

The equivalence between 3SIV and 2SIV happens in the case when the over-identified block consists of a single equation. With respect to the second block, the estimates are not the same as those of 2SIV.

Grouping common terms in (6.16), we have

$$(\mathbf{I} \otimes \mathbf{Z}'\mathbf{X})\mathbf{S}_2\hat{\mathbf{a}}_2^* = [(\hat{\mathbf{\Omega}}^{22})^{-1}\,\mathbf{\Omega}^{21} \otimes \mathbf{Z}'\mathbf{X}]\,(\mathbf{s}_1 - \mathbf{S}_1\hat{\mathbf{a}}_1^*) + (\mathbf{I} \otimes \mathbf{Z}'\mathbf{X})\mathbf{s}_2\hat{\mathbf{a}}_2^*,$$

and so

$$\hat{\mathbf{a}}_2^* = [(\mathbf{I} \otimes \mathbf{Z}'\mathbf{X})\mathbf{S}_2]^{-1} [(\hat{\mathbf{\Omega}}^{22})^{-1}\hat{\mathbf{\Omega}}^{21} \otimes \mathbf{Z}'\mathbf{X}] (\mathbf{s}_1 - \mathbf{S}_1\hat{\mathbf{a}}_1^*)$$
$$+ [\mathbf{I} \otimes \mathbf{Z}'\mathbf{X})\mathbf{S}_2]^{-1} (\mathbf{I} \otimes \mathbf{Z}'\mathbf{X})\mathbf{s}_2$$

where the last term is the usual 2SIV estimator for just identified equations. Therefore 3SIV estimators of the just identified equations are equal to the 2SIV estimators plus a term which is a linear combination of the estimators of the over-identified equations.

6.7 3SIV Estimation with Identities

Consider a model with identities, and partition it in the form

$$\mathbf{A}_1\mathbf{x}_t = \mathbf{u}_t$$

$$\mathbf{A}_2\mathbf{x}_t = 0$$

i.e. the second block includes all, and only, the identities, and $\mathbf{A}_2$ is a known matrix of coefficients.

We cannot apply 3SIV to the model directly because the covariance matrix of the errors on all the equations is singular and so would be $\bar{\mathbf{E}}$ as defined in the last section. There are two alternative solutions:

(i) Ignore the identities and estimate by 3SIV the incomplete model $\mathbf{A}_1\mathbf{x}_t = \mathbf{u}_t$.

(ii) Use the second block to eliminate surplus endogenous variables from the first block, i.e.
Partition

$$\mathbf{x}_t = \begin{pmatrix} \mathbf{y}_{1t} \\ \mathbf{x}_{2t} \end{pmatrix}$$

$\mathbf{y}_{1t}$ being the endogenous variables to be eliminated.

Accordingly, partition $\mathbf{A}_1$ and $\mathbf{A}_2$ into $\mathbf{A}_1 = (\mathbf{A}_{21}\mathbf{A}_{22})$. Thus, we can write $\mathbf{A}\mathbf{x}_t = \mathbf{u}_t$ as

$$\mathbf{A}_{11}\mathbf{y}_{1t} + \mathbf{A}_{12}\mathbf{x}_{2t} = \mathbf{u}_t$$

$$\mathbf{A}_{21}\mathbf{y}_{1t} + \mathbf{A}_{22}\mathbf{x}_{2t} = 0.$$

$\mathbf{y}_{1t}$ is chosen such that $\mathbf{A}_{21}$ is square and non-singular. Then

$$\mathbf{y}_{1t} = -\mathbf{A}_{21}^{-1}\mathbf{A}_{22}\mathbf{x}_{2t}.$$

Substituting in the first equation

$$(\mathbf{A}_{12} - \mathbf{A}_{11}\mathbf{A}_{21}^{-1}\mathbf{A}_{22})\mathbf{x}_{2t} = \mathbf{u}_t$$
$$\equiv \mathbf{A}^*\mathbf{x}_{2t} = \mathbf{u}_t$$

and we can estimate this by 3SLS. Notice that $\mathbf{A}_{21}$ and $\mathbf{A}_{22}$ are known and so this is a linear reparameterization of the coefficients.

To see why the estimates of both approaches (i) and (ii) are the same, notice that both are derived from the same criterion function, since the $\mathbf{u}_t$ is the same in both cases and therefore

$$\mathrm{tr}[\hat{\boldsymbol{\Omega}}_{\mathrm{u}}^{-1}\mathbf{U}'\mathbf{Z}(\mathbf{Z}'\mathbf{Z})^{-1}\mathbf{Z}'\mathbf{U}]$$

does not change.

The criterion function for the incomplete model, i.e. ignoring identities is

$$\begin{aligned}\mathbf{C}_1 &= \mathrm{tr}[\hat{\boldsymbol{\Omega}}_{\mathrm{u}}^{-1}\mathbf{U}'\mathbf{Z}(\mathbf{Z}'\mathbf{Z})^{-1}\mathbf{Z}'\mathbf{U}]\\ &= \mathrm{tr}\left[\hat{\boldsymbol{\Omega}}_{\mathrm{u}}^{-1}(\mathbf{A}_{11}\mathbf{A}_{12})\begin{pmatrix}\mathbf{Y}_1'\\ \mathbf{X}_2'\end{pmatrix}\mathbf{Z}(\mathbf{Z}'\mathbf{Z})^{-1}\mathbf{Z}(\mathbf{Y}_1\mathbf{X}_2)\begin{pmatrix}\mathbf{A}_{11}'\\ \mathbf{A}_{12}'\end{pmatrix}\right]\\ &= \mathrm{tr}[\hat{\boldsymbol{\Omega}}_{\mathrm{u}}^{-1}(\mathbf{A}_{11}\mathbf{Y}_1' + \mathbf{A}_{12}\mathbf{X}_2')\mathbf{Z}(\mathbf{Z}'\mathbf{Z})^{-1}\mathbf{Z}'(\mathbf{Y}_1\mathbf{A}_{11}' + \mathbf{X}_2\mathbf{A}_{12}')].\end{aligned}$$

The criterion function for the reparameterized model is

$$\begin{aligned}\mathbf{C}_2 &= [\hat{\boldsymbol{\Omega}}_{\mathrm{u}}^{-1}\mathbf{U}'\mathbf{Z}(\mathbf{Z}'\mathbf{Z})^{-1}\mathbf{Z}'\mathbf{U}]\\ &= \mathrm{tr}[\hat{\boldsymbol{\Omega}}_{\mathrm{u}}^{-1}(\mathbf{A}_{12} - \mathbf{A}_{11}\mathbf{A}_{21}^{-1}\mathbf{A}_{22})\mathbf{X}_2'\mathbf{Z}(\mathbf{Z}'\mathbf{Z})^{-1}\mathbf{Z}'\mathbf{X}_2(\mathbf{A}_{12}' - \mathbf{A}_{22}'\mathbf{A}_{21}'^{-1}\mathbf{A}_{11}')]\\ &= \mathrm{tr}[\hat{\boldsymbol{\Omega}}_{\mathrm{u}}^{-1}(\mathbf{A}_{12}\mathbf{X}_2' + \mathbf{A}_{11}\mathbf{Y}_1')\mathbf{Z}(\mathbf{Z}'\mathbf{Z})^{-1}\mathbf{Z}'(\mathbf{X}_2\mathbf{A}_{12}' + \mathbf{Y}_1\mathbf{A}_{11}')]\\ &= \mathbf{C}_1.\end{aligned}$$

The same arguments apply to the case of the non-linear in parameters model. We forget about identities and work with $\mathbf{A}_1(\boldsymbol{\theta})\mathbf{x}_t = \mathbf{u}_t$ to give a suitable criterion function.

7

Maximum Likelihood Estimation

Part A: Full Information Maximum Likelihood (FIML) Estimation

7.1 The FIML Estimator and its Asymptotic Variance Matrix (AVM)

For the maximum of generality in the exposition we will consider the non-linear in parameter model that can be specialized to the linear case, and to the linear case with geneal linear restrictions very easily.

Let

$$\underset{n\times(n+m)}{\mathbf{A}(\boldsymbol{\theta})} \quad \underset{(n\times m)\times 1}{\mathbf{x}_t} = \underset{(n\times n)(n\times 1)}{\mathbf{B}(\boldsymbol{\theta})\mathbf{y}_t} + \underset{(n\times m)(m\times 1)}{\mathbf{C}(\boldsymbol{\theta})\mathbf{z}_t} = \underset{(n\times 1)}{\mathbf{u}_t}, \quad \mathbf{u}_t \sim \text{NID}(0, \boldsymbol{\Omega}_{\text{u}})$$

be the structural form of a non-linear simultaneous equation model, where $\boldsymbol{\theta}$ is a $(p \times 1)$ vector of unknown coefficients and $\mathbf{A}(\cdot)$, $\mathbf{B}(\cdot)$ and $\mathbf{C}(\cdot)$ are known functions of $\boldsymbol{\theta}$.

The corresponding reduced form (RF) equations are

$$\mathbf{y}_t = \underset{(n\times m)}{\mathbf{P}(\boldsymbol{\theta})} \quad \mathbf{z}_t + \mathbf{v}_t$$

where

$$\mathbf{P}(\boldsymbol{\theta}) = -\mathbf{B}(\boldsymbol{\theta})^{-1}\mathbf{C}(\boldsymbol{\theta})$$

$$\mathbf{v}_t = \mathbf{B}(\boldsymbol{\theta})^{-1}\mathbf{u}_t, \qquad \mathbf{v}_t \sim \text{NID}(0, \boldsymbol{\Omega}_{\text{v}})$$

$$\boldsymbol{\Omega}_{\text{v}} = \mathbf{B}(\boldsymbol{\theta})^{-1}\boldsymbol{\Omega}_{\text{u}}[\mathbf{B}(\boldsymbol{\theta})^{-1}]'$$

and we have assumed that $\mathbf{B}(\boldsymbol{\theta})$ is non-singular in a neighbourhood of the true $\boldsymbol{\theta}$.

The basic assumptions are:

(i) $\mathbf{A}(\cdot)$ and $\mathbf{P}(\cdot)$ are continuously differentiable functions of $\boldsymbol{\theta}$ at $\bar{\boldsymbol{\theta}}$
(ii) $\boldsymbol{\Omega}_{\text{u}}$ (and therefore $\boldsymbol{\Omega}_{\text{v}}$) is a p.d. matrix
(iii) there exist no constraints on $\boldsymbol{\Omega}_{\text{u}}$ (and therefore on $\boldsymbol{\Omega}_{\text{v}}$).

Note that although we use a likelihood function which assumes the errors are normally distributed, it is not necessary to use this assumption in discussing the asymptotic properties of the estimators. For this reason the term quasi-maximum likelihood estimation is sometimes used.

We will derive first the FIML estimator of the RF parameters and then we will obtain from this the FIML estimator of the structural form. We use the differential form approach to develop the appropriate first and second derivatives.

The RF log likelihood function is

$$L[\mathbf{P}(\boldsymbol{\theta}), \boldsymbol{\Omega}_{\text{v}}] = -\frac{Tn}{2}\log 2\pi + \frac{T}{2}\log\det\boldsymbol{\Omega}^* - \frac{1}{2}\text{tr}(\boldsymbol{\Omega}^*\mathbf{V}'\mathbf{V})$$

where

$$\boldsymbol{\Omega}^* = \boldsymbol{\Omega}_{\text{v}}^{-1} \text{ and } \mathbf{V}' = \mathbf{Y}' - \mathbf{P}(\boldsymbol{\theta})\mathbf{Z}'.$$

Let us first concentrate $\boldsymbol{\Omega}_{\text{v}}$ out of the likelihood function. From matrix differentiation algebra we know that for a matrix $\mathbf{A}$

$$\text{d}(\log|\det\mathbf{A}|) = \text{tr}(\mathbf{A}^{-1}\,\text{d}\mathbf{A}). \tag{7.1}$$

By totally differentiating the RF log likelihood function, we obtain therefore (using (7.1) on $\boldsymbol{\Omega}^*$):

$$\begin{aligned}\text{d}L &= \frac{T}{2}\text{tr}(\boldsymbol{\Omega}^{*-1}\,\text{d}\boldsymbol{\Omega}^*) - \frac{1}{2}\text{tr}(\mathbf{V}'\mathbf{V}\,\text{d}\boldsymbol{\Omega}^*)\\ &= \frac{T}{2}\text{tr}\left[\left(\boldsymbol{\Omega}^{*-1} - \frac{\mathbf{V}'\mathbf{V}}{T}\right)\text{d}\boldsymbol{\Omega}^*\right] = 0.\end{aligned}$$

This implies that

$$\hat{\mathbf{\Omega}}^{*-1} - \frac{\mathbf{V}'\mathbf{V}}{T} = 0$$

or

$$\hat{\mathbf{\Omega}}_{\mathrm{v}} = \frac{\mathbf{V}'\mathbf{V}}{T}$$

and so the concentrated likelihood function (LF) is

$$L^*[\mathbf{P}(\boldsymbol{\theta})] = k^* - \frac{T}{2}\log\det\left(\frac{\mathbf{V}'\mathbf{V}}{T}\right)$$

where k^* = constant term.

Notice that maximizing the concentrated LF is therefore equivalent to minimizing the generalized variance

$$\det\left(\frac{\mathbf{V}'\mathbf{V}}{T}\right)$$

(i.e. FIML is a least generalized variance method).

Minimizing with respect to $\boldsymbol{\theta}$ we obtain

$$\mathrm{d}L^* = -\frac{1}{2}T\,\mathrm{tr}\left[\left(\frac{\mathbf{V}'\mathbf{V}}{T}\right)^{-1}\mathrm{d}\frac{\mathbf{V}'\mathbf{V}}{T}\right] \qquad \text{[from (7.1)]}$$

$$= -\frac{1}{2}\mathrm{tr}\left[\left(\frac{\mathbf{V}'\mathbf{V}}{T}\right)^{-1}[(\mathrm{d}\mathbf{V}')\mathbf{V} + \mathbf{V}'(\mathrm{d}\mathbf{V})]\right]$$

$$= -\,\mathrm{tr}\left[\left(\frac{\mathbf{V}'\mathbf{V}}{T}\right)^{-1}\mathbf{V}'\,\mathrm{d}\mathbf{V}\right]$$

using the algebraic properties of the trace operation.

Since $\mathbf{V} = \mathbf{Y} - \mathbf{ZP}'$, then $\mathrm{d}\mathbf{V} = -\mathbf{Z}\,\mathrm{d}\mathbf{P}'$, and substituting in $\mathrm{d}L^*$

$$\mathrm{d}L^* = +\,\mathrm{tr}\left[\hat{\mathbf{\Omega}}_{\mathrm{v}}^{-1}\mathbf{V}'\mathbf{Z}\,\mathrm{d}\mathbf{P}'\right].$$

Since $\mathbf{P}$ is a function of $\boldsymbol{\theta}$, we have

$$\mathrm{d}\mathbf{P} = \sum_{i=1}^{\mathrm{p}}\left(\frac{\partial\mathbf{P}}{\partial\theta_i}\right)\mathrm{d}\theta_i.$$

Thus the differential of L^* with respect to $\boldsymbol{\theta}$ is

$$\mathrm{d}L^* = \sum_{i=1}^{\mathrm{p}}\mathrm{tr}\left[\hat{\mathbf{\Omega}}_{\mathrm{v}}^{-1}\mathbf{V}'\mathbf{Z}\frac{\partial\mathbf{P}'}{\partial\theta_i}\mathrm{d}\theta_i\right]$$

and therefore we need to obtain the second derivatives matrix of L^*

$$\frac{\partial^2 L^*}{\partial\theta_i\partial\theta_j} = -\operatorname{tr}\left[\hat{\mathbf{\Omega}}_{\rm v}^{-1}\,\frac{\partial\mathbf{P}(\boldsymbol{\theta})}{\partial\theta_j}\,(\mathbf{Z}'\mathbf{Z})\,\frac{\partial\mathbf{P}(\boldsymbol{\theta})}{\partial\theta_i}\right]'$$

$$+ \operatorname{tr}\left[\partial\,\frac{(\hat{\mathbf{\Omega}}_{\rm v}^{-1})}{\partial\theta_j}\right]\mathbf{V}'\mathbf{Z}\left[\frac{\partial\mathbf{P}(\boldsymbol{\theta})}{\partial\theta_j}\right]' + \operatorname{tr}\left[\hat{\mathbf{\Omega}}_{\rm v}^{-1}\,(\mathbf{V}'\mathbf{Z})\,\frac{\partial^2\mathbf{P}(\boldsymbol{\theta})'}{\partial\theta_i\partial\theta_j}\right].$$

Using the general result that for a squared matrix $\mathbf{H}$, $\mathrm{d}(\mathbf{H}^{-1}) = -\mathbf{H}^{-1}(\mathrm{d}\mathbf{H})\mathbf{H}^{-1}$, we have

$$\frac{\partial\hat{\mathbf{\Omega}}_{\rm v}^{-1}}{\partial\theta_j} = -\,\hat{\mathbf{\Omega}}_{\rm v}^{-1}\left(\frac{\partial\hat{\mathbf{\Omega}}_{\rm v}}{\partial\theta_j}\right)\hat{\mathbf{\Omega}}_{\rm v}^{-1}.$$

But recall that

$$\hat{\mathbf{\Omega}}_{\rm v} = \frac{\mathbf{V}'\mathbf{V}}{T} \text{ and } \frac{\partial\hat{\mathbf{\Omega}}_{\rm v}}{\partial\theta_j} = \frac{\partial\mathbf{V}'}{\partial\theta_j}\,\frac{\mathbf{V}}{T} + \frac{\mathbf{V}'}{T}\,\frac{\partial\mathbf{V}}{\partial\theta_j}$$

therefore

$$\frac{\partial\hat{\mathbf{\Omega}}_{\rm v}^{-1}}{\partial\theta_j} = -\hat{\mathbf{\Omega}}_{\rm v}^{-1}\left(\frac{\partial\mathbf{V}'}{\partial\theta_j}\right)\frac{\mathbf{V}}{T}\,\hat{\mathbf{\Omega}}_{\rm v}^{-1} - \hat{\mathbf{\Omega}}_{\rm v}^{-1}\,\frac{\mathbf{V}}{T}\left(\frac{\partial\mathbf{V}}{\partial\theta_j}\right)\hat{\mathbf{\Omega}}_{\rm v}^{-1}$$

$$= \hat{\mathbf{\Omega}}_{\rm v}^{-1}\left(\frac{\partial\mathbf{P}(\boldsymbol{\theta})}{\partial\theta_i}\right)\left(\frac{\mathbf{Z}'\mathbf{V}}{T}\right)\hat{\mathbf{\Omega}}_{\rm v}^{-1} + \hat{\mathbf{\Omega}}_{\rm v}^{-1}\,\frac{\mathbf{V}'\mathbf{Z}}{T}\left(\frac{\partial\mathbf{P}(\boldsymbol{\theta})}{\partial\theta_j}\right)'\hat{\mathbf{\Omega}}_{\rm v}^{-1}.$$

Thus

$$\frac{1}{T}\,\frac{\partial^2 L^*}{\partial\theta_i\partial\theta_j} = -\operatorname{tr}\left\{\hat{\mathbf{\Omega}}_{\rm v}^{-1}\left[\frac{\partial\mathbf{P}(\boldsymbol{\theta})}{\partial\theta_j}\right]\frac{\mathbf{Z}'\mathbf{Z}}{T}\left[\frac{\partial\mathbf{P}(\boldsymbol{\theta})}{\partial\theta_i}\right]'\right\}$$

$$+ \operatorname{tr}\left\{\hat{\mathbf{\Omega}}_{\rm v}^{-1}\left[\frac{\partial\mathbf{P}(\boldsymbol{\theta})}{\partial\theta_j}\right]\frac{\mathbf{Z}'\mathbf{V}}{T}\,\hat{\mathbf{\Omega}}_{\rm v}^{-1}\,\frac{\mathbf{V}'\mathbf{Z}}{T}\left[\frac{\partial\mathbf{P}(\boldsymbol{\theta})}{\partial\theta_j}\right]\right\}$$

$$+ \operatorname{tr}\left\{\hat{\mathbf{\Omega}}_{\rm v}^{-1}\,\frac{\mathbf{V}'\mathbf{Z}}{T}\left[\frac{\partial\mathbf{P}(\boldsymbol{\theta})}{\partial\theta_j}\right]'\hat{\mathbf{\Omega}}_{\rm v}^{-1}\,\frac{\mathbf{V}'\mathbf{Z}}{T}\left[\frac{\partial\mathbf{P}(\boldsymbol{\theta})}{\partial\theta_i}\right]'\right\}$$

$$+ \operatorname{tr}\left\{\hat{\mathbf{\Omega}}_{\rm v}^{-1}\,\frac{\mathbf{V}'\mathbf{Z}}{T}\left(\frac{\partial^2\mathbf{P}(\boldsymbol{\theta})}{\partial\theta_i\partial\theta_j}\right)'\right\}.$$

But

$$\operatorname{plim}\frac{\mathbf{V}'\mathbf{Z}}{T} = 0,$$

when $\boldsymbol{\theta} = \bar{\boldsymbol{\theta}}$, or when $\boldsymbol{\theta}$ is such that $\operatorname{plim}\boldsymbol{\theta} = \bar{\boldsymbol{\theta}}$. For then

$$\mathbf{V}'\mathbf{Z} = (\mathbf{Y}' - \mathbf{P}\mathbf{Z}')\mathbf{Z} = (\bar{\mathbf{P}}\mathbf{Z}' + \bar{\mathbf{V}}' - \mathbf{P}\mathbf{Z}')\mathbf{Z}$$

(because $\mathbf{Y}' = \bar{\mathbf{P}}\mathbf{Z}' + \bar{\mathbf{V}}'$)

where $\bar{\mathbf{P}}$ and $\bar{\mathbf{V}}$ denote the true RF parameters and disturbances. Thus

$$\mathbf{V}'\mathbf{Z} = (\bar{\mathbf{P}} - \mathbf{P})\mathbf{Z}'\mathbf{Z} + \bar{\mathbf{V}}'\mathbf{Z}$$

and

$$\operatorname{plim}\frac{\mathbf{V}'\mathbf{Z}}{T} = \operatorname{plim}(\bar{\mathbf{P}} - \mathbf{P})\left(\frac{\mathbf{Z}'\mathbf{Z}}{T}\right) + \operatorname{plim}\frac{\bar{\mathbf{V}}'\mathbf{Z}}{T} = 0$$

since P is the consistent estimator of $\bar{\mathrm{P}}$ and

$$\operatorname{plim}\frac{\bar{\mathbf{V}}'\mathbf{Z}}{T} = 0$$

by assumption of absence of mis-specification. Therefore when taking plim of

$$\frac{1}{T}\,\frac{\partial^2 L^*}{\partial\theta_i\partial\theta_j}$$

the last three elements vanish, and so

$$\operatorname{plim}\frac{1}{T}\,\frac{\partial^2 L^*}{\partial\theta_i\partial\theta_j} = -\operatorname{tr}\left\{\boldsymbol{\Omega}_{\mathrm{v}}^{-1}\,\frac{\partial\mathbf{P}(\boldsymbol{\theta})}{\partial\theta_i}\,\mathbf{M}\left[\frac{\partial\mathbf{P}(\boldsymbol{\theta})}{\partial\theta_j}\right]'\right\}$$

and therefore minus the inverse of this, gives us the *ij*th element of the AVM of $\sqrt{T}(\hat{\boldsymbol{\theta}} - \boldsymbol{\theta})$, i.e.

$$\{\mathrm{AVM}[\sqrt{T}(\hat{\boldsymbol{\theta}} - \boldsymbol{\theta})]\}_{ij} = \operatorname{tr}\left\{\boldsymbol{\Omega}_{\mathrm{v}}^{-1}\left[\frac{\partial\mathbf{P}(\boldsymbol{\theta})}{\partial\theta_i}\right]\mathbf{M}\left[\frac{\partial\mathbf{P}(\boldsymbol{\theta})}{\partial\theta_j}\right]'\right\}^{-1}$$

$$= \left\{\left[\operatorname{vec}\frac{\partial\mathbf{P}(\boldsymbol{\theta})}{\partial\theta_i}\right]'(\boldsymbol{\Omega}_{\mathrm{v}}^{-1}\otimes\mathbf{M})\left[\operatorname{vec}\frac{\partial\mathbf{P}(\boldsymbol{\theta})}{\partial\theta_j}\right]'\right\}^{-1}$$

and therefore the whole matrix is

$$\mathrm{AVM}[\sqrt{T}(\hat{\boldsymbol{\theta}}-\boldsymbol{\theta})] = \left\{\left[\frac{\partial\operatorname{vec}\mathbf{P}(\boldsymbol{\theta})}{\partial\boldsymbol{\theta}'}\right]'(\boldsymbol{\Omega}_{\mathrm{v}}^{-1}\otimes\mathbf{M})\left[\frac{\partial\operatorname{vec}\mathbf{P}(\boldsymbol{\theta})}{\partial\boldsymbol{\theta}'}\right]'\right\}^{-1} \tag{7.4}$$

(End of proof)

For obtaining a consistent estimate of the AVM, we can use the matrix

$$\hat{\mathbf{V}}_\theta = \left\{\left[\frac{\partial\operatorname{vec}\mathbf{P}(\hat{\boldsymbol{\theta}})}{\partial\boldsymbol{\theta}'}\right]\hat{\boldsymbol{\Omega}}_{\mathrm{v}}^{-1}\otimes\frac{\mathbf{Z}'\mathbf{Z}}{T}\left(\frac{\partial\operatorname{vec}\mathbf{P}(\hat{\boldsymbol{\theta}})}{\partial\boldsymbol{\theta}'}\right)'\right\}^{-1}$$

where $\hat{\boldsymbol{\Omega}}_{\mathrm{v}}$ is a consistent estimator of $\boldsymbol{\Omega}_{\mathrm{v}}$.

To get now the AVM of $\sqrt{T}(\hat{\boldsymbol{\theta}} - \boldsymbol{\theta})$, in terms of the structural parameters recall that

$$\frac{\partial \mathbf{P}(\boldsymbol{\theta})}{\partial \theta_i} = -\mathbf{B}(\boldsymbol{\theta})^{-1} \frac{\partial \mathbf{A}(\boldsymbol{\theta})}{\partial \theta_i} \mathbf{Q}$$

and

$$\boldsymbol{\Omega}_{\mathrm{v}}^{-1} = \mathbf{B}'(\boldsymbol{\theta})\boldsymbol{\Omega}_{\mathrm{u}}^{-1}\mathbf{B}(\boldsymbol{\theta}).$$

Therefore, substituting in

$$\frac{1}{T} \frac{\partial^2 L^*}{\partial \theta_i \partial \theta_j}$$

we have

$$\frac{1}{T} \frac{\partial^2 L^*}{\partial \theta_i \partial \theta_j} = -\mathrm{tr}\left\{\hat{\boldsymbol{\Omega}}_{\mathrm{u}}^{-1}\left[\frac{\partial \mathbf{A}(\boldsymbol{\theta})}{\partial \theta_i}\right]\left(\frac{\mathbf{QZ}'\mathbf{ZQ}}{T}\right)\left[\frac{\partial \mathbf{A}(\boldsymbol{\theta})}{\partial \theta_j}\right]'\right\} + \mathrm{O}\left(\frac{1}{\sqrt{T}}\right) \tag{7.4'}$$

where $\mathrm{O}(1/\sqrt{T})$ corresponds to the three terms that vanish asymptotically. Using vec notation we conclude finally after taking the (−plim) of (7.4′) that

$$\mathrm{AVM}[\sqrt{T}(\hat{\boldsymbol{\theta}} - \boldsymbol{\theta})] = \left\{\left[\frac{\partial\, \mathrm{vec}\, \mathbf{A}(\boldsymbol{\theta})}{\partial \boldsymbol{\theta}'}\right] (\boldsymbol{\Omega}_{\mathrm{u}}^{-1} \otimes \mathbf{QMQ}') \left(\frac{\partial\, \mathrm{vec}\, \mathbf{A}(\boldsymbol{\theta})}{\partial \boldsymbol{\theta}'}\right)\right\}^{-1} \tag{7.5}$$

where in this expression $\mathbf{Q} = \mathbf{Q}(\bar{\boldsymbol{\theta}})$.

With (7.3) and (7.5) we can implement a Gauss–Newton iterative procedure, of the form

$$\left\{\left[\frac{\partial\, \mathrm{vec}\, \mathbf{A}(\boldsymbol{\theta})}{\partial \boldsymbol{\theta}'}\right]' (\boldsymbol{\Omega}_{\mathrm{u}}^{-1} \otimes \mathbf{QZ}'\mathbf{ZQ}') \left(\frac{\partial\, \mathrm{vec}\, \mathbf{A}(\boldsymbol{\theta})}{\partial \boldsymbol{\theta}'}\right)\right\}_r (\boldsymbol{\theta}^{r+1} - \boldsymbol{\theta}^r)$$

$$+ \lambda_r \left[\frac{\partial\, \mathrm{vec}\, \mathbf{A}(\boldsymbol{\theta})}{\partial \boldsymbol{\theta}'}\right]'_{\theta r} (\boldsymbol{\Omega}_{\mathrm{u}}^{-1} \otimes \mathbf{QZ}'\mathbf{X})_r\, \mathrm{vec}\, \mathbf{A}(\boldsymbol{\theta}) = 0$$

where at the rth stage $\mathbf{A} = \mathbf{A}(\boldsymbol{\theta}^r)$, $\mathbf{P} = -\mathbf{B}^{-1}\mathbf{C}$, $\boldsymbol{\Omega}_{\mathrm{u}} = \mathbf{A}(\mathbf{X}'\mathbf{X})\mathbf{A}'/T$. Notice that the requirement of the gradient optimization method that the matrix in square brackets be positive definite is guaranteed by the simple product form defining it as a p.d. approximation to the p.d. AVM.

We can alternatively argue that if we started off from consistent estimators, we can keep the Hessian matrix constant, to save computation time, at the value computed from the initial value of the parameters. In practice this saves computer time per iteration, but may require more than a compensating increase in the number of iterations. This general topic of the numerical optimization of the likelihood function is discussed in some detail in Chapter 10.

7.2 A Special Case: General Linear Restrictions

Consider the structural form of a simultaneous equation model

$$\underset{n\times(n+m)}{\mathbf{A}}\ \underset{(n+m)\times T}{\mathbf{X}'} = \underset{n\times T}{\mathbf{U}'}\ ,\quad \mathrm{E}[\mathrm{vec}\,\mathbf{U}'(\mathrm{vec}\,\mathbf{U}')'] = \underset{(n\times n)}{(\boldsymbol{\Omega}_{\mathrm{u}}\otimes\mathbf{I}_T)}$$

subject to a set of $(n-p)$ general linear restrictions which can be parameterized as

$$\mathrm{vec}\,\mathbf{A} = -\,\mathbf{Sa} + \mathbf{s}.$$

In this case, the parameter of relevance is $\mathbf{a}$ instead of $\boldsymbol{\theta}$, and so

$$\left(\frac{\partial\,\mathrm{vec}\,\mathbf{A}(\boldsymbol{\theta})}{\partial\boldsymbol{\theta}'}\right)' \equiv \left(\frac{\partial\mathrm{vec}\,\mathbf{A}}{\partial\mathbf{a}'}\right)' = -\mathbf{S}'.$$

Therefore, the FOCs (7.3) become

$$\frac{\partial L^*}{\partial\mathbf{a}} = \mathbf{S}'(\hat{\boldsymbol{\Omega}}_{\mathrm{u}}^{-1}\otimes\mathbf{QZ}'\mathbf{X})\,\mathrm{vec}\,\mathbf{A} = 0$$

and the AVM (7.5) becomes

$$\mathrm{AVM}[\sqrt{T}(\hat{\mathbf{a}}-\mathbf{a})] = [\mathbf{S}'(\boldsymbol{\Omega}_{\mathrm{u}}^{-1}\otimes\mathbf{QMQ}')\mathbf{S}]^{-1}.$$

Likewise we can construct a Gauss–Newton iterative procedure which, assuming absence of mis-specification (so that the last three terms of

$$\frac{1}{T}\ \frac{\partial^2 L^*}{\partial \mathrm{a}_i\partial \mathrm{a}_j}$$

tend to zero asymptotically), is given by

$$[\mathbf{S}'(\boldsymbol{\Omega}_{\mathrm{u}}^{-1}\otimes\mathbf{QZ}'\mathbf{ZQ}')\mathbf{S}]_r(\boldsymbol{\theta}^{r+1}-\boldsymbol{\theta}^r)$$
$$+\ \lambda_r[\mathbf{S}'(\boldsymbol{\Omega}_{\mathrm{u}}^{-1}\otimes\mathbf{QZ}'\mathbf{X})_r\,\mathrm{vec}\,\mathbf{A}] = 0.$$

7.3 FIML with AR Disturbances

Consider a simultaneous equation model in structural form where the disturbances follow a stationary autoregressive process of order r:

$$\mathbf{A}^*\mathbf{x}_t{}^* = \boldsymbol{\eta}_t \qquad t = 1, \ldots, T$$

$$\underset{n\times 1}{\boldsymbol{\eta}_t} = \underset{(n\times n)}{\mathbf{R}_1}\ \boldsymbol{\eta}_{t-1} + \ldots + \underset{(n\times n)}{\mathbf{R}_r}\ \boldsymbol{\eta}_{t-r} + \underset{(n\times 1)}{\mathbf{u}_t}\ , \quad \mathbf{u}_t \sim \mathrm{NID}(0, \underset{(n\times n)}{\boldsymbol{\Omega}_n}) \qquad (7.6)$$

If there are linear restrictions on $\mathbf{A}^*$, these are reparameterized as

$$\mathrm{vec}\,\mathbf{A}^* = \mathbf{Sa} - \mathbf{s}.$$

Eliminating $\boldsymbol{\eta}_t$ in (7.6) yields

$$\mathbf{A}^*\mathbf{x}_t{}^* - \mathbf{R}_1\mathbf{A}^*\mathbf{x}^*_{t-1} - \ldots - \mathbf{R}_r\mathbf{A}^*\mathbf{x}^*_{t-r} = \mathbf{u}_t$$

and therefore can be written as a non-linear in parameters model

$$\mathbf{A}(\boldsymbol{\theta})\mathbf{x}_t = \mathbf{u}_t$$

where

$$\underset{n\times(r+1)\,(n+m)}{\mathbf{A}(\boldsymbol{\theta})} = \left[\underset{n\times(n+m)}{\mathbf{A}^*} \ \vdots\ \underset{n\times(n+m)}{-\mathbf{R}_1\mathbf{A}^*} \ \vdots \ldots \vdots\ \underset{n\times(n+m)}{-\mathbf{R}_r\mathbf{A}^*}\right]$$

and

$$\underset{[n(n+m)+r_n^2]\times 1}{\boldsymbol{\theta}} = \begin{pmatrix} \mathbf{a} \\ \mathrm{vec}\,\mathbf{R}_1 \\ \vdots \\ \mathrm{vec}\,\mathbf{R}_r \end{pmatrix}; \qquad \mathbf{x}_t = \begin{pmatrix} \mathbf{x}^*_t \\ \mathbf{x}^*_{t-1} \\ \vdots \\ \mathbf{x}^*_{t-r} \end{pmatrix} = \begin{pmatrix} \mathbf{y}_t \\ \mathbf{z}^*_t \\ \mathbf{x}^*_{t-1} \\ \vdots \\ \mathbf{x}^*_{t-r} \end{pmatrix} = \begin{pmatrix} \mathbf{y}_t \\ \mathbf{z}_t \end{pmatrix}$$

$$\mathbf{z}_t = \begin{pmatrix} \mathbf{z}^*_t \\ \mathbf{x}^*_{t-1} \\ \vdots \\ \mathbf{x}^*_{t-r} \end{pmatrix}.$$

The corresponding RF equations are

$$\mathbf{y}_t = \mathbf{P}(\boldsymbol{\theta})\mathbf{z}_t + \mathbf{v}_t$$

(assuming $\mathbf{B}^*$ is non-singular) where $\mathbf{P}(\boldsymbol{\theta})$ is the $n \times [m + r(n + m)]$ matrix

$$\mathbf{P}(\boldsymbol{\theta}) = (-\mathbf{B}^{*-1}\mathbf{C}^* \vdots \mathbf{B}^{*-1}\mathbf{R}_1\mathbf{A}^* \vdots \ldots \vdots \mathbf{B}^{*-1}\mathbf{R}_r\mathbf{A}^*).$$

From (7.3), the FOCs for the non-linear in parameters case are

$$\frac{\partial L^*}{\partial \boldsymbol{\theta}} = -\left(\frac{\partial\,\mathrm{vec}\,\mathbf{A}(\boldsymbol{\theta})}{\partial \boldsymbol{\theta}'}\right)'(\hat{\boldsymbol{\Omega}}_u^{-1} \otimes \mathbf{QZ}'\mathbf{X})\,\mathrm{vec}\,\mathbf{A}(\boldsymbol{\theta}) = 0$$

where **Q** is the $(r + 1)(n + m) \times (m + r)(n + m)$ matrix

$$\mathbf{Q} = \left[\frac{\mathbf{P}(\boldsymbol{\theta})}{\mathbf{I}_{m+r(n+m)}}\right].$$

It is complicated to manipulate this in terms of the vec operator, so we will treat the differential of this system for obtaining the FOCs in terms of the structural parameters, $\mathbf{A}^*, \mathbf{R}_1, \ldots, \mathbf{R}_r$.

Define

$$\underset{T\times(n+m)}{\mathbf{X}_j'} = \begin{pmatrix} \mathbf{x}_{1-j}^{*\prime} \\ \vdots \\ \mathbf{x}_{T-j}^{*\prime} \end{pmatrix} \qquad \underset{(T\times n)}{\boldsymbol{\eta}^*} = \begin{pmatrix} \boldsymbol{\eta}_1' \\ \vdots \\ \boldsymbol{\eta}_T' \end{pmatrix}$$

$$\underset{(T\times n)}{\boldsymbol{\eta}_j^*} = \begin{pmatrix} \boldsymbol{\eta}_{1-j}' \\ \vdots \\ \boldsymbol{\eta}_{T-j}' \end{pmatrix}$$

Theorem 2: The FOCs of the likelihood functions maximization problem in terms of the structural parameters of model (7.6) are

$$\frac{\partial L^*}{\partial \mathbf{R}_j} = \mathbf{A}^*\mathbf{X}_j^{*\prime}\mathbf{X}\mathbf{A}(\boldsymbol{\theta})'\,\hat{\boldsymbol{\Omega}}_{\mathrm{u}}^{-1} = \boldsymbol{\eta}_j^{*\prime}\mathbf{U}\hat{\boldsymbol{\Omega}}_{\mathrm{u}}^{-1} = 0, \qquad j = 1, \ldots, r$$

$$\frac{\partial L^*}{\partial \mathbf{A}^*} = -\hat{\boldsymbol{\Omega}}_{\mathrm{u}}^{-1}\mathbf{U}'\hat{\mathbf{X}}^* + \sum_{j=1}^{r}\mathbf{R}_j'\hat{\boldsymbol{\Omega}}_{\mathrm{u}}^{-1}\mathbf{U}'\hat{\mathbf{X}}_j^* = 0$$

where

$$\hat{\mathbf{X}}^* = (\hat{\mathbf{Y}}\mathbf{Z}^*), \qquad \hat{\mathbf{Y}} = \mathbf{Z}\mathbf{P}'(\boldsymbol{\theta}).$$

Proof: Recall from Section 7.1 that the differential of L^* is

$$\mathrm{d}L^* = -\mathrm{tr}[\hat{\boldsymbol{\Omega}}_{\mathrm{u}}^{-1}\mathbf{A}(\boldsymbol{\theta})\mathbf{X}'\mathbf{Z}\mathbf{Q}'\,\mathrm{d}\mathbf{A}(\boldsymbol{\theta})'].$$

(i) Consider first obtaining

$$\frac{\partial L^*}{\partial \mathbf{R}_j},\ j = 1, \ldots, r.$$

In general

$$\mathbf{Q}'\,\mathrm{d}\mathbf{A}(\boldsymbol{\theta})' = (\mathbf{P}'\mathbf{I}_N)\begin{pmatrix} \mathrm{d}\mathbf{B}^* \\ \mathrm{d}\mathbf{C}^* \\ -\mathbf{A}^{*\prime}\,\mathrm{d}\mathbf{R}_1 - \mathrm{d}\mathbf{A}^{*\prime}\mathbf{R}_1 \\ -\mathbf{A}^{*\prime}\,\mathrm{d}\mathbf{R}_r - \mathrm{d}\mathbf{A}^{*\prime}\mathbf{R}_r \end{pmatrix}$$

where $N = m + r(n + m)$

where $\mathbf{P}'$ multiplies only $\mathrm{d}\mathbf{B}^*$ since it has only n columns.

Therefore, when taking the differential with respect to any $\mathbf{R}_j$ we obtain

$$\mathbf{Q}'\,\mathrm{d}\mathbf{A}(\boldsymbol{\theta})' = \begin{pmatrix} 0 \\ 0 \\ -\mathbf{A}^{*\prime}\,\mathrm{d}\mathbf{R}_j \\ 0 \\ 0 \end{pmatrix}.$$

Hence

$$\mathbf{Z}[\mathbf{Q}'\,\mathrm{d}\mathbf{A}(\boldsymbol{\theta})'] = \begin{pmatrix} \mathbf{z}_0^{*\prime}, & \mathbf{x}_0^{*\prime}, & \ldots, & \mathbf{x}_{1-r}^{*\prime} \\ \ldots & \ldots & \ldots & \ldots \\ \mathbf{z}_T^{*\prime}, & \mathbf{x}_{T-1}^{*\prime}, & \ldots, & \mathbf{x}_{T\,r}^{*\prime} \end{pmatrix} \begin{pmatrix} 0 \\ 0 \\ -\mathbf{A}^{*\prime}\,\mathrm{d}\mathbf{R}_j \\ 0 \\ 0 \end{pmatrix}$$

$$= -\mathbf{X}_j^*\mathbf{A}^{*\prime}\,\mathrm{d}\mathbf{R}_j$$

and $\mathrm{d}L^*$ becomes

$$\mathrm{d}L^* = -\mathrm{tr}[\hat{\boldsymbol{\Omega}}_{\mathrm{u}}^{-1}\mathbf{A}(\boldsymbol{\theta})\mathbf{X}'\mathbf{X}_j^*\mathbf{A}^{*\prime}(-\mathrm{d}\,\mathbf{R}_j)].$$

Therefore

$$\frac{\partial L^*}{\partial \mathbf{R}_j} = \mathbf{A}^*\mathbf{X}_j^{*\prime}\mathbf{X}\mathbf{A}(\boldsymbol{\theta})'\,\hat{\boldsymbol{\Omega}}_{\mathrm{u}}^{-1} = \boldsymbol{\eta}_j^{*\prime}\mathbf{U}\hat{\boldsymbol{\Omega}}_{\mathrm{u}}^{-1}$$

since $\mathbf{A}^*\mathbf{X}_j' = \boldsymbol{\eta}_j^{*\prime}$ and $\mathbf{X}\mathbf{A}(\boldsymbol{\theta})' = \mathbf{U}$.

(ii) Consider now obtaining $\dfrac{\partial L^*}{\partial \mathbf{A}^*}$.

In this case

$$\mathrm{d}\mathbf{A}(\boldsymbol{\theta}) = (\mathrm{d}\mathbf{A}^* - \mathbf{R}_1\,\mathrm{d}\mathbf{A}^* \ldots - \mathbf{R}_r\,\mathrm{d}\mathbf{A}^*)$$

and

$$\begin{aligned} \mathbf{Z}\mathbf{Q}'\,\mathrm{d}\mathbf{A}(\boldsymbol{\theta})' &= \mathbf{Z}(\mathbf{P}'\!:\mathbf{I})\,\mathrm{d}\mathbf{A}(\boldsymbol{\theta})' = (\hat{\mathbf{Y}}\mathbf{Z}^*\mathbf{X}_1^* \ldots \mathbf{X}_r^*)\,\mathrm{d}\mathbf{A}(\boldsymbol{\theta})' \\ &= \hat{\mathbf{X}}^*\,\mathrm{d}\mathbf{A}(\boldsymbol{\theta})' - \mathbf{X}_1^*\,\mathrm{d}\mathbf{A}^{*\prime}\mathbf{R}_1' - \ldots - \mathbf{X}_r^*\,\mathrm{d}\mathbf{A}^{*\prime}\mathbf{R}_r' \\ &= -\sum_{j=0}^{r}\mathbf{X}_j^*\mathrm{d}\mathbf{A}^{*\prime}\mathbf{R}_j', \qquad \text{where } \mathbf{X}_0^* = -\hat{\mathbf{X}}^* \text{ and } \mathbf{R}_0' = \mathbf{I} \end{aligned}$$

$$\mathrm{d}L^* = \mathrm{tr}\left(\sum_{j=0}^{r}\mathbf{R}_j'\,\hat{\boldsymbol{\Omega}}_{\mathrm{u}}^{-1}\mathbf{A}\mathbf{X}'\mathbf{X}_j^*\right)\mathrm{d}\mathbf{A}^{*\prime}$$

and therefore

$$\frac{\mathrm{d}L^*}{\partial \mathbf{A}^*} = \sum_{j=0}^{r}\mathbf{R}_j'\,\hat{\boldsymbol{\Omega}}_{\mathrm{u}}^{-1}\mathbf{A}\mathbf{X}'\mathbf{X}_j^*$$

or

$$\frac{\partial L^*}{\partial \mathbf{A}^*} = -\hat{\boldsymbol{\Omega}}_{\mathrm{u}}^{-1}\mathbf{U}'\hat{\mathbf{X}}^* + \sum_{j=1}^{r} \mathbf{R}_j' \hat{\boldsymbol{\Omega}}_{\mathrm{u}}^{-1}\mathbf{U}'\mathbf{X}_j^*.$$

(End of proof)

In the case of constraints on $\mathbf{A}$ of the form $\mathrm{vec}\,\mathbf{A}^* = -\mathbf{Sa} + \mathbf{s}$, the FOCs with respect to $\mathbf{a}$ are given by

$$\frac{\partial L^*}{\partial \mathbf{a}} = \left(\frac{\partial\, \mathrm{vec}\,\mathbf{A}}{\partial \mathbf{a}}\right)' \mathrm{vec}\left(\frac{\partial L^*}{\partial \mathbf{A}^*}\right) = \mathbf{S}'\,\mathrm{vec}\frac{\partial L}{\partial \mathbf{A}^*} = 0.$$

7.4 Asymptotic Equivalence of FIML and 3SLS Estimators

Theorem 3: Assuming the covariance matrix is unrestricted, the FIML estimator and the 3SLS estimator are asymptotically equivalent in the sense that they differ at the most by a vector of order $(1/\mathbf{T})$, provided that $\mathbf{A}(\boldsymbol{\theta})$ has continuous second derivatives at $\boldsymbol{\theta} = \bar{\boldsymbol{\theta}}$.

Proof: For generality, consider the (non-linear) in parameter model

$$\underset{(N \times n+m)}{\mathbf{A}(\boldsymbol{\theta})} \quad \underset{(n+m \times T)}{\mathbf{X}'} = \underset{(N \times T)}{U'},$$

$$\mathrm{vec}\,\mathbf{U}' \sim \mathrm{NID}(0, \underset{[N \times N]}{\boldsymbol{\Omega}_{\mathrm{u}}} \otimes \mathbf{I}_T)$$

where $\boldsymbol{\theta}$ is a $(p \times 1)$ vector and non-linear function $\mathbf{A}{:}\boldsymbol{\theta} \rightarrow \mathbf{A}(\boldsymbol{\theta})$ is continuous with continuous first derivatives.

Let $\tilde{\boldsymbol{\theta}}$ and $\hat{\boldsymbol{\theta}}$ be the optimal 3SLS and FIML estimators of $\bar{\boldsymbol{\theta}}$ respectively. We want to show that

$$(\tilde{\boldsymbol{\theta}} - \hat{\boldsymbol{\theta}}) = \mathrm{O}(T^{-1})$$

which will ensure that $\sqrt{T}(\tilde{\boldsymbol{\theta}} - \hat{\boldsymbol{\theta}}) = \mathrm{o}(1)$, and so that $\tilde{\boldsymbol{\theta}}$ and $\hat{\boldsymbol{\theta}}$ have the same asymptotic distribution.

The FOCs of 3SLS are

$$\frac{\partial\, \mathrm{vec}\,\mathbf{A}(\tilde{\boldsymbol{\theta}})}{\partial \tilde{\boldsymbol{\theta}}'}\left[\tilde{\boldsymbol{\Omega}}_{\mathrm{u}}^{-1} \otimes \tilde{\mathbf{Q}}\left(\frac{\mathbf{Z}'\mathbf{X}}{T}\right)\right]\mathrm{vec}\,\mathbf{A}(\boldsymbol{\theta}) = 0$$

where $\tilde{\mathbf{Q}} = (\mathbf{X}'\mathbf{Z})\,(\mathbf{Z}'\mathbf{Z})^{-1}$ and $\tilde{\boldsymbol{\Omega}}_{\mathrm{u}}^{-1}$ is obtained from 2SLS residuals (i.e. $\tilde{\boldsymbol{\Omega}}_{\mathrm{u}}^{-1}$ is a consistent estimator of $\boldsymbol{\Omega}_{\mathrm{u}}^{-1}$).

The FOCs of FIML are

$$\left(\frac{\partial \operatorname{vec} \mathbf{A}(\hat{\boldsymbol{\theta}})}{\partial \hat{\boldsymbol{\theta}}'}\right)' \left[\hat{\boldsymbol{\Omega}}_u^{-1} \otimes \hat{\mathbf{Q}}\left(\frac{\mathbf{Z}'\mathbf{X}}{T}\right)\right] \operatorname{vec} \mathbf{A}(\hat{\boldsymbol{\theta}}) = 0$$

where $\hat{\mathbf{Q}} = \begin{pmatrix} \mathbf{P}(\hat{\boldsymbol{\theta}}) \\ \mathbf{I}_m \end{pmatrix}$ and $\hat{\boldsymbol{\Omega}}_u^{-1}$ is also a consistent estimator of $\boldsymbol{\Omega}_u^{-1}$

Now notice that

$$\left(\frac{\partial \operatorname{vec} \mathbf{A}(\boldsymbol{\theta})}{\partial \boldsymbol{\theta}'}\right)_{\tilde{\boldsymbol{\theta}}} - \left(\frac{\partial \operatorname{vec} \mathbf{A}(\boldsymbol{\theta})}{\partial \boldsymbol{\theta}'}\right)_{\boldsymbol{\theta}} = \mathrm{O_p}\left(\frac{1}{\sqrt{T}}\right) \tag{7.7}$$

from the Mean Value Theorem. Equally,

$$(\hat{\mathbf{Q}} - \tilde{\mathbf{Q}}) = \begin{pmatrix} \mathbf{P}(\hat{\boldsymbol{\theta}}) - \tilde{\mathbf{P}} \\ 0 \end{pmatrix} = \mathrm{O_p}\left(\frac{1}{\sqrt{T}}\right) \tag{7.8}$$

since $\mathbf{P}(\hat{\boldsymbol{\theta}}) - \mathbf{P}(\bar{\boldsymbol{\theta}}) = \mathrm{O_p}\left(\frac{1}{\sqrt{T}}\right)$, $\tilde{\mathbf{P}} - \mathbf{P}(\bar{\boldsymbol{\theta}}) = \mathbf{O}_p\left(\frac{1}{\sqrt{T}}\right)$.

Also notice that in the same way that

$$\hat{\boldsymbol{\Omega}}_u - \tilde{\boldsymbol{\Omega}}_u = \mathrm{O_p}\left(\frac{1}{\sqrt{T}}\right) \tag{7.9}$$

so

$$\hat{\boldsymbol{\Omega}}_u^{-1} - \tilde{\boldsymbol{\Omega}}_u^{-1} = \hat{\boldsymbol{\Omega}}_u^{-1}(\tilde{\boldsymbol{\Omega}}_u - \hat{\boldsymbol{\Omega}}_u)\tilde{\boldsymbol{\Omega}}_u^{-1} = \mathrm{O_p}\left(\frac{1}{\sqrt{T}}\right).$$

Now consider the difference

$$\left[\frac{\partial \operatorname{vec} \mathbf{A}(\tilde{\boldsymbol{\theta}})}{\partial \tilde{\boldsymbol{\theta}}'}\right]' \left(\tilde{\boldsymbol{\Omega}}_u^{-1} \otimes \tilde{\mathbf{Q}}\,\frac{\mathbf{Z}'\mathbf{X}}{T}\right) \operatorname{vec}\left[\mathbf{A}(\tilde{\boldsymbol{\theta}}) - \mathbf{A}(\hat{\boldsymbol{\theta}})\right]$$

$$= -\left[\frac{\partial \operatorname{vec} \mathbf{A}(\tilde{\boldsymbol{\theta}})}{\partial \tilde{\boldsymbol{\theta}}'}\right]' \left(\tilde{\boldsymbol{\Omega}}_u^{-1} \otimes \tilde{\mathbf{Q}}\,\frac{\mathbf{Z}'\mathbf{X}}{T}\right) \operatorname{vec} \mathbf{A}(\tilde{\boldsymbol{\theta}}) \text{ (by 3SLSs FOCs)}$$

$$- \left[\frac{\partial \operatorname{vec} \mathbf{A}(\tilde{\boldsymbol{\theta}})}{\partial \tilde{\boldsymbol{\theta}}'}\right]' \left[\tilde{\boldsymbol{\Omega}}_u^{-1} \otimes (\tilde{\mathbf{Q}} - \hat{\mathbf{Q}})\,\frac{\mathbf{Z}'\mathbf{X}}{T}\right] \operatorname{vec} \mathbf{A}(\hat{\boldsymbol{\theta}})$$

$$- \left(\frac{\partial \operatorname{vec} \mathbf{A}(\tilde{\boldsymbol{\theta}})}{\partial \tilde{\boldsymbol{\theta}}'}\right)' \left[\left(\tilde{\boldsymbol{\Omega}}_u^{-1} - \hat{\boldsymbol{\Omega}}_u^{-1}\right) \otimes \hat{\mathbf{Q}}\,\frac{\mathbf{Z}'\mathbf{X}}{T}\right] \operatorname{vec} \mathbf{A}(\hat{\boldsymbol{\theta}})$$

$$- \left\{\left[\frac{\partial \operatorname{vec} \mathbf{A}(\tilde{\boldsymbol{\theta}})}{\partial \tilde{\boldsymbol{\theta}}'}\right] - \left[\frac{\partial \operatorname{vec} \mathbf{A}(\hat{\boldsymbol{\theta}})}{\partial \hat{\boldsymbol{\theta}}'}\right]\right\}' \left(\hat{\boldsymbol{\Omega}}_u^{-1} \otimes \hat{\boldsymbol{\Omega}}\,\frac{\mathbf{Z}'\mathbf{X}}{T}\right) \operatorname{vec} \mathbf{A}(\hat{\boldsymbol{\theta}})$$

$$- \left(\frac{\partial \operatorname{vec} \mathbf{A}(\hat{\boldsymbol{\theta}})}{\partial \hat{\boldsymbol{\theta}}'}\right)' \left(\hat{\boldsymbol{\Omega}}_u^{-1} \otimes \hat{\mathbf{Q}}\,\frac{\mathbf{Z}'\mathbf{X}}{T}\right) \operatorname{vec} \mathbf{A}(\hat{\boldsymbol{\theta}}).$$

The last term vanishes by FIML's FOCs.

Consider now the following part of the remaining three elements

$$\left(\mathbf{I} \otimes \frac{\mathbf{Z}'\mathbf{X}}{T}\right) \operatorname{vec} \mathbf{A}(\hat{\boldsymbol{\theta}}) = \operatorname{vec}\left[\mathbf{A}(\hat{\boldsymbol{\theta}}) \frac{\mathbf{X}'\mathbf{Z}}{T}\right].$$

But

$$\begin{aligned} \mathbf{A}(\hat{\boldsymbol{\theta}}) \frac{\mathbf{X}'\mathbf{Z}}{T} &= [\mathbf{A}(\hat{\boldsymbol{\theta}}) - \mathbf{A}(\bar{\boldsymbol{\theta}})] \frac{\mathbf{X}'\mathbf{Z}}{T} + \mathbf{A}(\bar{\boldsymbol{\theta}}) \frac{\mathbf{X}'\mathbf{Z}}{T} \\ &= [\mathbf{A}(\hat{\boldsymbol{\theta}}) - \mathbf{A}(\bar{\boldsymbol{\theta}})] \frac{\mathbf{X}'\mathbf{Z}}{T} + \frac{\bar{\mathbf{U}}'\mathbf{Z}}{T} \end{aligned}$$

and

$$\mathbf{A}(\hat{\boldsymbol{\theta}}) - \mathbf{A}(\bar{\theta}) = \mathrm{O_p}\left(\frac{1}{\sqrt{T}}\right)$$

from the Mean Value Theorem, and

$$\frac{\bar{\mathbf{U}}'\mathbf{Z}}{T} = \mathrm{O_p}\left(\frac{1}{\sqrt{T}}\right).$$

Hence

$$\mathbf{A}(\hat{\boldsymbol{\theta}}) \frac{\mathbf{X}'\mathbf{Z}}{T} = \mathrm{O_p}\left(\frac{1}{\sqrt{T}}\right).$$

Therefore, from this and (7.7)–(7.9) it follows that

$$\left(\frac{\partial \operatorname{vec} \mathbf{A}(\tilde{\boldsymbol{\theta}})}{\partial \tilde{\boldsymbol{\theta}}'}\right)' \left(\tilde{\boldsymbol{\Omega}}_{\mathrm{u}}^{-1} \otimes \tilde{\mathbf{Q}} \frac{\mathbf{Z}'\mathbf{X}}{T}\right) \operatorname{vec}\left[\mathbf{A}(\tilde{\boldsymbol{\theta}} - \mathbf{A}(\hat{\boldsymbol{\theta}})\right] = \mathrm{O_p}\left(\frac{1}{T}\right)$$

and applying the Mean Value Theorem to $\operatorname{vec} \mathbf{A}(\tilde{\boldsymbol{\theta}})$ and $\operatorname{vec} \mathbf{A}(\hat{\boldsymbol{\theta}})$ we obtain

$$\left\{\left[\frac{\partial \operatorname{vec} \mathbf{A}(\tilde{\boldsymbol{\theta}})}{\partial \boldsymbol{\theta}'}\right]' \left(\tilde{\boldsymbol{\Omega}}_{\mathrm{u}}^{-1} \otimes \tilde{\mathbf{Q}} \frac{\mathbf{Z}'\mathbf{X}}{T}\right) \left[\frac{\partial \operatorname{vec} \mathbf{A}(\boldsymbol{\theta}^{*})}{\partial \boldsymbol{\theta}^{*\prime}}\right]\right\} (\tilde{\boldsymbol{\theta}} - \hat{\boldsymbol{\theta}}) = \mathrm{O_p}\left(\frac{1}{T}\right)$$

where $\boldsymbol{\theta}^{*} = \mathrm{c}\tilde{\boldsymbol{\theta}} + (1 - \mathrm{c})\hat{\boldsymbol{\theta}}$, $0 \leq \mathrm{c} \leq 1$.

The matrix enclosed in the braces has a plim which is a p.d. matrix since the model is identified and therefore its inverse is of $\mathrm{O_p}(1)$.

Therefore

$$(\tilde{\boldsymbol{\theta}} - \hat{\boldsymbol{\theta}}) = \mathrm{O_p}\left(\frac{1}{T}\right)$$

(End of proof)

This theorem shows that

$$\sqrt{T}(\tilde{\boldsymbol{\theta}} - \hat{\boldsymbol{\theta}}) = o_p(1).$$

It follows then that since $\sqrt{T}(\hat{\boldsymbol{\theta}} - \bar{\boldsymbol{\theta}})$ has an asymptotic normal distribution, by the Mann and Wald Approximation Theorem both estimators will have asymptotically the same distribution, i.e.

$$\mathbf{F}_{\tilde{\theta}_T} \xrightarrow{D} \mathbf{F}_{\hat{\theta}_\infty}$$

where $\mathbf{F}_{\hat{\theta}_\infty}$ denotes the asymptotic distribution of the FIML estimator. Therefore, since the FIML estimator is an asymptotically efficient estimator when disturbances are normal, we can say that 3SLS are asymptotically efficient provided the disturbances are normal. Note that previously we proved their asymptotic efficiency in the set of all IV estimators.

7.5 Estimation of the Reduced Form (RF) Coefficients

Consider the non-linear parameters in simultaneous equations model in structural form

$$\mathbf{A}(\boldsymbol{\theta})\mathbf{X}' = \mathbf{B}(\boldsymbol{\theta})\mathbf{Y}' + \mathbf{C}(\boldsymbol{\theta})\mathbf{Z}' = \mathbf{U}'$$

where $\mathbf{B}(\boldsymbol{\theta})$ is assumed to be non-singular in a neighbourhood of the true $\bar{\boldsymbol{\theta}}$ for the $\boldsymbol{\theta}$s that we are interested in. Then the RF parameter matrix has the form

$$\mathbf{P}(\boldsymbol{\theta}) := -\mathbf{B}(\boldsymbol{\theta})^{-1}\mathbf{C}(\boldsymbol{\theta}).$$

If for example we are interested in prediction, we must use the model in RF. So consider the best estimator of the RF parameters and its AVM.

7.5.1 The OLS Estimator

We know that a way of obtaining efficient estimates of **P** if we ignore constraints on **P** is by OLS on the RF since it is equivalent to a maximum likelihood method. This gives

$$\hat{\mathbf{P}} = (\mathbf{Y}'\mathbf{Z})\,(\mathbf{Z}'\mathbf{Z})^{-1}$$

with AVM given by

$$\mathbf{V}_{P,OLS} = (\boldsymbol{\Omega}_v \otimes \mathbf{M}^{-1})$$

where $\mathbf{M} = \text{plim}\,\dfrac{\mathbf{Z'Z}}{T}$.

The question is: if we take account of constraints on the structural form, can we improve on OLS?

7.5.2 The 2SLS Estimator

The question is whether we improve by estimating one structural equation by 2SLS and the rest by OLS, i.e. by taking account only of part of the constraints on the structural form.

Let $\mathbf{P}(\boldsymbol{\theta}) = -\mathbf{B}(\boldsymbol{\theta})^{-1}\mathbf{C}(\boldsymbol{\theta})$, thus

$$\begin{aligned} \mathrm{d}\mathbf{P}(\boldsymbol{\theta}) &= \mathbf{B}(\boldsymbol{\theta})^{-1}\,\mathrm{d}\mathbf{B}(\boldsymbol{\theta})\,\mathbf{B}(\boldsymbol{\theta})^{-1}\,\mathbf{C}(\boldsymbol{\theta}) - \mathbf{B}(\boldsymbol{\theta})^{-1}\,\mathrm{d}\mathbf{C}(\boldsymbol{\theta}) \\ &= \mathbf{B}(\boldsymbol{\theta})^{-1}\,\mathrm{d}\mathbf{A}(\boldsymbol{\theta})\mathbf{Q} \end{aligned}$$

where

$$\mathbf{Q} = \left(\frac{\mathbf{P}}{\mathbf{I}_m}\right).$$

Thus

$$\text{vec}\,\mathrm{d}\mathbf{P}(\boldsymbol{\theta}) = -\,[\mathbf{B}(\boldsymbol{\theta})^{-1} \otimes \mathbf{Q}']\,\text{vec}\,\mathrm{d}\mathbf{A}(\boldsymbol{\theta}). \qquad (7.10)$$

Let $\mathbf{V}_A$ be the covariance matrix of $\text{vec}\,\mathrm{d}\mathbf{A}(\boldsymbol{\theta})$.

The fact that there exists a set of zero–one constraints is going to imply that some of the rows and columns of $\mathbf{V}_A$ will be zero.
From (7.10), the covariance matrix of the reduced form is

$$\mathbf{V}_p = [\mathbf{B}(\boldsymbol{\theta})^{-1} \otimes \mathbf{Q}']\mathbf{V}_A[\mathbf{B}(\boldsymbol{\theta})'^{-1} \otimes \mathbf{Q}]. \qquad (7.11)$$

Where there are constraints in the model, the 2SLS AVM has the form

$$\mathbf{V}_A = \mathbf{S}\{[\mathbf{S}'(\mathbf{I} \otimes \bar{\mathbf{R}})\mathbf{S}]^{-1}\mathbf{S}'(\boldsymbol{\Omega}_u \otimes \bar{\mathbf{R}})\mathbf{S}[\mathbf{S}'(\mathbf{I} \otimes \bar{\mathbf{R}})\mathbf{S}]^{-1}\}^{-1}\mathbf{S}'$$

where $\bar{\mathbf{R}} = \mathbf{QMQ}'$.

Substituting this into (7.11) we obtain $\mathbf{V}_p$ under constraints, which might be expected to be less than the corresponding $\mathbf{V}_{p,OLS} = (\boldsymbol{\Omega}_v \otimes \mathbf{M}^{-1})$, i.e. $\mathbf{V}_p \leqslant (\boldsymbol{\Omega}_v \otimes \mathbf{M}^{-1})$.

This would imply that we improve efficiency by taking into account part of the total number of constraints of the model. However, Dhrymes (1973) has shown that this inequality is not generally true.

Unless we take into account *all* the constraints, that is, unless we use 3SLS estimates to derive the corresponding RF estimates, we cannot prove the inequality. Since 3SLS is asymptotically equivalent to FIML, by substituting $\mathbf{V}_{\mathrm{p,3SLS}} = \mathbf{S}[\mathbf{S}'(\mathbf{\Omega}_{\mathrm{u}}^{-1} \otimes \bar{\mathbf{R}})\mathbf{S}]^{-1}\mathbf{S}'$ into (7.11) we could prove that

$$\mathbf{V}_{\mathrm{p,3SLS}} \leqslant \mathbf{V}_{\mathrm{p,OLS}} = (\mathbf{\Omega}_{\mathrm{v}} \otimes \mathbf{M}^{-1}).$$

Part B: Limited Information Maximum Likelihood (LIML) Estimation

7.6 The LIML Estimator

Consider a set of n simultaneous equations in structural form

$$\underset{n\times(n+m)}{\mathbf{A}} \; \underset{(n+m)\times T}{\mathbf{X}'} = \underset{(n\times m)}{\mathbf{B}} \; \underset{(n\times T)}{\mathbf{Y}'} + \underset{(n\times m)}{\mathbf{C}} \; \underset{(m\times T)}{\mathbf{Z}'} = \mathbf{U}' \tag{7.12}$$

where the matrix $\mathbf{A}$ is subject to the set of linear restrictions

$$\mathbf{Y}\,\mathrm{vec}\,\mathbf{A} = \boldsymbol{\psi}.$$

If we are only interested in a subset of n_1 equations, then (7.12) can be partitioned as

$$\mathbf{A}_1\mathbf{X}' = \mathbf{B}_{11}\mathbf{Y}_1' + \mathbf{B}_{12}\mathbf{Y}_2' + \mathbf{C}_1\mathbf{Z}' = \mathbf{U}_1'. \tag{7.13}$$

$$\mathbf{A}_2\mathbf{X}' = \mathbf{B}_{12}\mathbf{Y}_1' + \mathbf{B}_{22}\mathbf{Y}_2' + \mathbf{C}_2\mathbf{Z}' = \mathbf{U}_2' \tag{7.14}$$

where (7.13) contains the n_1 equations we are interested in and (7.14) contains the remaining $n_2 = n - n_1$ equations. If the constraints on the whole system are separable, i.e. there is no restriction across the two subsets of equations, then the structural equations in (7.13) can be replaced by n_2 reduced form equations

$$\mathbf{Y}_2' = \mathbf{P}_2\mathbf{Z}' + \mathbf{V}_2'. \tag{7.15}$$

In doing this we are ignoring the set of constraints on the second set of equations.

The model consisting of (7.13) and (7.15) can be written as

$$\begin{pmatrix} \mathbf{B}_{11} & \mathbf{B}_{12} & \mathbf{C}_1 \\ \cdots & \cdots & \cdots \\ 0 & \mathbf{I}_{n_2} & -\mathbf{P}_2 \end{pmatrix} \begin{pmatrix} \mathbf{Y}_1' \\ \mathbf{Y}_2' \\ \mathbf{Z}' \end{pmatrix} = \begin{pmatrix} \mathbf{U}_1' \\ \mathbf{V}_2' \end{pmatrix}$$

or compactly as

$$\mathbf{A}^*\mathbf{X}' = \mathbf{B}^*\mathbf{Y}' + \mathbf{C}^*\mathbf{Z}' = \mathbf{U}^{*\prime} \tag{7.16}$$

where

$$\mathbf{B}^* = \begin{pmatrix} \mathbf{B}_{11} & \mathbf{B}_{12} \\ 0 & \mathbf{I}_{n_2} \end{pmatrix} \mathbf{C}^* = \begin{pmatrix} \mathbf{C}_1 \\ -\mathbf{P}_2 \end{pmatrix} \mathbf{U}^{*\prime} = \begin{pmatrix} \mathbf{U}_1' \\ \mathbf{V}_2' \end{pmatrix}.$$

Note that we must partition $\mathbf{y}_t'$ into $(\mathbf{y}_{1t}', \mathbf{y}_{2t}')$ so that $\mathbf{B}_{11}$ is non-singular. We also define

$$\boldsymbol{\Omega} = \mathrm{E}\left(\frac{\mathbf{u}_{1t}\mathbf{u}_{1t}', \mathbf{u}_{1t}\mathbf{v}_{2t}'}{\mathbf{v}_{2t}\mathbf{u}_{1t}', \mathbf{v}_{2t}\mathbf{v}_{2t}'} \right)$$

If the 1st n_1 equations are chosen in such a way that the $(n_1 \times n_1)$ matrix $\mathbf{B}_{11}$ is non-singular, then the system of equations (7.16) can be shown to be identified, provided that the usual conditions for the first block of equations to be identified are satisfied.

Under normal errors the (log) likelihood function for model (7.16) is

$$L(\mathbf{A}^*, \boldsymbol{\Omega}) = -\frac{Tn}{2}\log 2\pi + T\log|\det \mathbf{B}^*| - \frac{T}{2}\log\det\boldsymbol{\Omega} \tag{7.17}$$
$$- \tfrac{1}{2}\mathrm{tr}(\boldsymbol{\Omega}^{-1}\,\mathbf{A}^*\mathbf{X}'\mathbf{X}\mathbf{A}^{*\prime}).$$

The LIML estimator of $\mathbf{A}_1$ will be derived as follows:

(i) First the likelihood function (7.17) will be concentrated with relation to $\mathbf{P}_2$, $\boldsymbol{\Omega}_{12}$, $\boldsymbol{\Omega}_{21}$, $\boldsymbol{\Omega}_{22}$, under the assumption that $\mathbf{P}_2$ and the covariance matrix of the reduced form disturbances are unconstrained. For a general discussion of the concentrated likelihood function, see Section 10.1

(ii) The concentrated likelihood function will then be maximized with relation to $\mathbf{A}_1$ and $\boldsymbol{\Omega}_{11}$.

By the properties of the ML estimation, the resulting LIML estimator of $\mathbf{A}_1$ will be more efficient than any other estimator based on the same information (i.e. ignoring the constraints on the second set of equations). Also the estimates of $\mathbf{P}_2$ will be efficient, taking account of the constraints on the first set of equations, which solves the problem of Section 7.5.

7.6.1 Derivation of the Concentrated Likelihood Function

This section is entirely devoted to the derivation of the likelihood function concentrated with regard to $\mathbf{P}_2$, $\boldsymbol{\Omega}_{12}$, $\boldsymbol{\Omega}_{21}$ and $\boldsymbol{\Omega}_{22}$.

We write the log-likelihood function (7.17) as

$$L(\mathbf{A}^*, \boldsymbol{\Omega}) = \text{const} + T\log|\det \mathbf{B}^*| - \frac{T}{2}\log\det\boldsymbol{\Omega} - \tfrac{1}{2}\text{tr}(\boldsymbol{\Omega}^{-1}\mathbf{U}^{*\prime}\mathbf{U}^*) \quad (7.18)$$

and we define

$$\boldsymbol{\Omega}^{-1} = \begin{pmatrix} \boldsymbol{\Omega}_{11} & \boldsymbol{\Omega}_{12} \\ \boldsymbol{\Omega}_{21} & \boldsymbol{\Omega}_{22} \end{pmatrix}^{-1} = \begin{pmatrix} \mathbf{G}_{11} & \mathbf{G}_{12} \\ \mathbf{G}_{21} & \mathbf{G}_{22} \end{pmatrix}.$$

We first notice that

$$\begin{aligned} \det \mathbf{B}^* &= \det \mathbf{B}_{11} \quad (7.19)\\ \det \boldsymbol{\Omega} &= \det \boldsymbol{\Omega}_{11} \det(\boldsymbol{\Omega}_{22} - \boldsymbol{\Omega}_{21}\boldsymbol{\Omega}_{11}^{-1}\boldsymbol{\Omega}_{12}) \\ &= \det \boldsymbol{\Omega}_{11} \det(\mathbf{G}_{22}^{-1}) \\ &= \det \boldsymbol{\Omega}_{11}/\det \mathbf{G}_{22} \end{aligned}$$

and

$$\begin{aligned} \text{tr}(\boldsymbol{\Omega}^{-1}\mathbf{U}^{*\prime}\mathbf{U}^*) &= \text{tr}\left[\begin{pmatrix} \mathbf{G}_{11} & \mathbf{G}_{12} \\ \mathbf{G}_{21} & \mathbf{G}_{22} \end{pmatrix}\begin{pmatrix} \mathbf{U}_1'\mathbf{U}_1 & \mathbf{U}_1'\mathbf{V}_2 \\ \mathbf{V}_2'\mathbf{U}_1 & \mathbf{V}_2'\mathbf{V}_2 \end{pmatrix}\right] \\ &= \text{tr}(\mathbf{G}_{11}\mathbf{U}_1'\mathbf{U}_1) + 2\,\text{tr}(\mathbf{G}_{12}\mathbf{V}_2'\mathbf{U}_1) + \text{tr}(\mathbf{G}_{22}\mathbf{V}_2'\mathbf{V}_2). \end{aligned} \quad (7.20)$$

By adding and subtracting $\text{tr}(\mathbf{G}_{12}\mathbf{G}_{22}^{-1}\mathbf{G}_{21}\mathbf{U}_1'\mathbf{U}_1)$ to the last expression and by using the fact that $\boldsymbol{\Omega}_{11}^{-1} = \mathbf{G}_{11} - \mathbf{G}_{12}\mathbf{G}_{22}^{-1}\mathbf{G}_{21}$ we obtain

$$\begin{aligned} \text{tr}(\boldsymbol{\Omega}^{-1}\mathbf{U}^{*\prime}\mathbf{U}^*) &= \text{tr}(\boldsymbol{\Omega}_{11}^{-1}\mathbf{U}_1'\mathbf{U}_1) + 2\,\text{tr}(\mathbf{G}_{12}\mathbf{V}_2'\mathbf{U}_1) \\ &\quad + \text{tr}(\mathbf{G}_{22}\mathbf{V}_2'\mathbf{V}_2) + \text{tr}(\mathbf{G}_{12}\mathbf{G}_{22}^{-1}\mathbf{G}_{21}\mathbf{U}_1'\mathbf{U}_1). \end{aligned} \quad (7.21)$$

Now define

$$\mathbf{F}_{12} = \mathbf{G}_{12}\mathbf{G}_{22}^{-1} \qquad \text{and } \mathbf{F}_{21} = \mathbf{F}_{12}' = \mathbf{G}_{22}^{-1}\mathbf{G}_{21}.$$

Substituting (7.19)–(9.21) into (7.18) gives

$$\begin{aligned} L &= \text{const} + T\log|\det \mathbf{B}_{11}| - \frac{T}{2}\log\det\boldsymbol{\Omega}_{11} \quad (7.22)\\ &\quad + \frac{T}{2}\log\det\mathbf{G}_{22} - \tfrac{1}{2}\text{tr}(\boldsymbol{\Omega}_{11}^{-1}\mathbf{U}_1'\mathbf{U}_1) \\ &\quad - \text{tr}(\mathbf{F}_{12}\mathbf{G}_{22}\mathbf{V}_2'\mathbf{U}_1) - \tfrac{1}{2}\text{tr}(\mathbf{G}_{22}\mathbf{V}_2'\mathbf{V}_2) \\ &\quad - \tfrac{1}{2}\text{tr}(\mathbf{F}_{12}\mathbf{G}_{22}\mathbf{F}_{21}\mathbf{U}_1'\mathbf{U}_1). \end{aligned}$$

After replacing $\mathbf{V}_2'$ by $\mathbf{Y}_2' - \mathbf{P}_2\mathbf{Z}'$ we can derive the FOCs for a maximum of (7.22) with regard to $\mathbf{P}_2$

$$\mathbf{G}_{22}\mathbf{F}_{21}\mathbf{U}_1' + \mathbf{G}_{22}\mathbf{V}_2'\mathbf{Z} = 0$$

from which we obtain

$$\mathbf{G}_{22}(\mathbf{F}_{21}\mathbf{U}_1' + \mathbf{Y}_2' - \mathbf{P}_2\mathbf{Z}')\mathbf{Z} = 0$$

i.e.

$$\mathbf{P}_2\mathbf{Z}'\mathbf{Z} = \mathbf{Y}_2'\mathbf{Z} + \mathbf{F}_{21}\mathbf{U}_1'\mathbf{Z}. \tag{7.23}$$

The FOCs for a maximum of (7.22) with regard to $\mathbf{F}_{12}$ are

$$\mathbf{G}_{22}\mathbf{V}_2'\mathbf{U}_1 + \mathbf{G}_{22}\mathbf{F}_{21}\mathbf{U}_1'\mathbf{U}_1 = 0$$

from which we obtain

$$\mathbf{G}_{22}(\mathbf{F}_{21}\mathbf{U}_1' + \mathbf{Y}_2' - \mathbf{P}_2\mathbf{Z}')\mathbf{U}_1 = 0$$

i.e.

$$\mathbf{F}_{21}\mathbf{U}_1'\mathbf{U}_1 + \mathbf{Y}_2'\mathbf{U}_1 - \mathbf{P}_2\mathbf{Z}'\mathbf{U}_1 = 0. \tag{7.24}$$

From (7.23) we have that

$$\mathbf{P}_2 = \mathbf{Y}_2'\mathbf{Z}(\mathbf{Z}'\mathbf{Z})^{-1} + \mathbf{F}_{21}\mathbf{U}_1'\mathbf{Z}(\mathbf{Z}'\mathbf{Z})^{-1}. \tag{7.25}$$

Substituting into (7.24) gives

$$\mathbf{F}_{21}\mathbf{U}_1'[\mathbf{I} - \mathbf{Z}(\mathbf{Z}'\mathbf{Z})^{-1}\mathbf{Z}']\mathbf{U}_1 + \mathbf{Y}_2'[\mathbf{I} - \mathbf{Z}(\mathbf{Z}'\mathbf{Z})^{-1}\mathbf{Z}']\mathbf{U}_1 = 0$$

or

$$-\mathbf{F}_{21}\mathbf{U}_1'\mathbf{\Phi}\mathbf{U}_1 = \mathbf{Y}_2'\mathbf{\Phi}\mathbf{U}_1 \tag{7.26}$$

where

$$\mathbf{\Phi} = \mathbf{I} - \mathbf{Z}(\mathbf{Z}'\mathbf{Z})^{-1}\mathbf{Z}'.$$

Now define

$$\begin{aligned} T\widetilde{\mathbf{G}}_{22}^{-1} &= (\mathbf{V}_2 + \mathbf{U}_1\mathbf{F}_{12})'(\mathbf{V}_2 + \mathbf{U}_1\mathbf{F}_{12}) \\ &= \mathbf{V}_2'\mathbf{V}_2 + \mathbf{F}_{21}\mathbf{U}_1'\mathbf{V}_2 + \mathbf{V}_2'\mathbf{U}_1\mathbf{F}_{12} + \mathbf{F}_{21}\mathbf{U}_1'\mathbf{U}_1\mathbf{F}_{12}. \end{aligned}$$

Then the likelihood function (7.22) becomes

$$\begin{aligned} L = \text{const} &+ T\log|\det \mathbf{B}_{11}| - \frac{T}{2}\log\det \mathbf{\Omega}_{11} \\ &+ \frac{T}{2}\log\det \mathbf{G}_{22} - \frac{1}{2}\text{tr}(\mathbf{\Omega}_{11}^{-1}\mathbf{U}_1'\mathbf{U}_1) \\ &- \frac{T}{2}\text{tr}(\mathbf{G}_{22}\widetilde{\mathbf{G}}_{22}^{-1}) \end{aligned} \tag{7.27}$$

which is maximized with respect to $\mathbf{G}_{22}$ by setting $\mathbf{G}_{22} = \widetilde{\mathbf{G}}_{22}$.

Since $\mathbf{V}_2' = \mathbf{Y}_2' - \mathbf{P}_2\mathbf{Z}'$ we can write

$$\begin{aligned}
\mathbf{T}\widetilde{\mathbf{G}}_{22}^{-1} &= (\mathbf{Y}_2' - \mathbf{P}_2\mathbf{Z}' + \mathbf{F}_{21}\mathbf{U}_1')(\mathbf{Y}_2 - \mathbf{Z}\mathbf{P}_2' - \mathbf{U}_1\mathbf{F}_{22}) \\
&= (\mathbf{Y}_2' - \mathbf{P}_2\mathbf{Z}' + \mathbf{F}_{21}\mathbf{U}_1')\mathbf{Y}_2 \\
&= \mathbf{Y}_2'\mathbf{Y}_2 - \mathbf{P}_2\mathbf{Z}'\mathbf{Y}_2 + \mathbf{F}_{21}\mathbf{U}_1'\mathbf{Y}_2 \\
&= \mathbf{Y}_2'\mathbf{Y}_2 - \mathbf{Y}_2'\mathbf{Z}(\mathbf{Z}'\mathbf{Z})^{-1}\mathbf{Z}'\mathbf{Y}_2 - \mathbf{F}_{21}\mathbf{U}_1'\mathbf{Z}(\mathbf{Z}'\mathbf{Z})^{-1}\mathbf{Z}'\mathbf{Y}_2 \\
&\quad + \mathbf{F}_{21}\mathbf{U}_1'\mathbf{Y}_2
\end{aligned}$$

which by (7.25)

$$= \mathbf{Y}_2' \mathbf{\Phi} \mathbf{Y}_2 + \mathbf{F}_{21}\mathbf{U}_1' \mathbf{\Phi} \mathbf{Y}_2.$$

Notice that by (7.26)

$$\begin{aligned}
\mathbf{F}_{21}\mathbf{U}_1' \mathbf{\Phi} \mathbf{Y}_2 &= \mathbf{F}_{21}(-\mathbf{F}_{21}\mathbf{U}_1' \mathbf{\Phi} \mathbf{U}_1)' = -\mathbf{F}_{21}\mathbf{U}_1' \mathbf{\Phi} \mathbf{U}_1\mathbf{F}_{12} \\
&= -\mathbf{F}_{21}(\mathbf{U}_1' \mathbf{\Phi} \mathbf{U}_1)(\mathbf{U}_1' \mathbf{\Phi} \mathbf{U}_1)^{-1}(\mathbf{U}_1' \mathbf{\Phi} \mathbf{U}_1)\mathbf{F}_{12} \\
&= -\mathbf{Y}_2' \mathbf{\Phi} \mathbf{U}_1(\mathbf{U}_1' \mathbf{\Phi} \mathbf{U}_1)^{-1}\mathbf{U}_1' \mathbf{\Phi} \mathbf{Y}_2.
\end{aligned}$$

Thus

$$\mathbf{T}\widetilde{\mathbf{G}}_{22}^{-1} = \mathbf{Y}_2' \mathbf{\Phi} \mathbf{Y}_2 - \mathbf{Y}_2' \mathbf{\Phi} \mathbf{U}_1(\mathbf{U}_1' \mathbf{\Phi} \mathbf{U}_1)^{-1} \mathbf{U}_1' \mathbf{\Phi} \mathbf{Y}_2.$$

By recalling the formulae for partioned inverses, it follows that

$$\begin{pmatrix} \widetilde{\mathbf{G}}_{11} & \widetilde{\mathbf{G}}_{12} \\ \widetilde{\mathbf{G}}_{21} & \widetilde{\mathbf{G}}_{22} \end{pmatrix}^{-1} = \begin{pmatrix} \mathbf{U}_1' \mathbf{\Phi} \mathbf{U}_1 & \mathbf{U}_1' \mathbf{\Phi} \mathbf{Y}_2 \\ \mathbf{Y}_2' \mathbf{\Phi} \mathbf{U}_1 & \mathbf{Y}_2' \mathbf{\Phi} \mathbf{Y}_2 \end{pmatrix}$$

so that

$$\det \widetilde{\mathbf{G}}_{22} = \frac{\det(\mathbf{U}_1' \mathbf{\Phi} \mathbf{U}_1/T)}{\det\left[\frac{1}{T}\begin{pmatrix} \mathbf{U}_1' \mathbf{\Phi} \mathbf{U}_1 & \mathbf{U}_1' \mathbf{\Phi} \mathbf{Y}_2 \\ \mathbf{Y}_2' \mathbf{\Phi} \mathbf{U}_1 & \mathbf{Y}_2' \mathbf{\Phi} \mathbf{Y}_2 \end{pmatrix}\right]}.$$

Therefore, by setting $\mathbf{G}_{22} = \widetilde{\mathbf{G}}_{22}$, the likelihood function (7.27) becomes

$$\begin{aligned}
L = &+ T\log|\det \mathbf{B}_{11}| - \frac{T}{2}\log\det \mathbf{\Omega}_{11} \\
&+ \frac{T}{2}\log\det \frac{\mathbf{U}_1' \mathbf{\Phi} \mathbf{U}_1}{T} \\
&- \frac{T}{2}\log\det\frac{1}{T}\left[\begin{pmatrix} \mathbf{U}_1' \mathbf{\Phi} \mathbf{U}_1 & \mathbf{U}_1' \mathbf{\Phi} \mathbf{Y}_2 \\ \mathbf{Y}_2' \mathbf{\Phi} \mathbf{U}_1 & \mathbf{Y}_2' \mathbf{\Phi} \mathbf{Y}_2 \end{pmatrix}\right.
\end{aligned}$$

$$-\frac{1}{2}\,\mathrm{tr}(\mathbf{\Omega}_{11}^{-1}\mathbf{U}_1'\mathbf{U}_1). \tag{7.28}$$

Since $\mathbf{BV}' = \mathbf{U}'$ we have that $\mathbf{U}_1' = \mathbf{B}_1\mathbf{V}'$ and so

$$\begin{aligned}
&\mathbf{U}_1'\,\mathbf{\Phi}\,\mathbf{U}_1 = \mathbf{B}_1\mathbf{V}'\,\mathbf{\Phi}\,\mathbf{VB}_1' = \mathbf{B}_1\mathbf{Y}'\,\mathbf{\Phi}\,\mathbf{YB}_1'\\
&\mathbf{Y}_2'\,\mathbf{\Phi}\,\mathbf{Y}_2 = \mathbf{V}_2'\,\mathbf{\Phi}\,\mathbf{V}_2\\
&\mathbf{Y}_2'\,\mathbf{\Phi}\,\mathbf{U}_2 = \mathbf{V}_2'\,\mathbf{\Phi}\,\mathbf{U}_1.
\end{aligned} \tag{7.29}$$

The big determinant in (7.28) therefore becomes

$$\det\left[\frac{1}{T}\begin{pmatrix} \mathbf{U}_1'\,\mathbf{\Phi}\,\mathbf{U}_1 & \mathbf{U}_1'\,\mathbf{\Phi}\,\mathbf{V}_2 \\ \mathbf{V}_2'\,\mathbf{\Phi}\,\mathbf{U}_1' & \mathbf{V}_2'\,\mathbf{\Phi}\,\mathbf{V}_2 \end{pmatrix}\right] =$$

$$= \det\left[\frac{1}{T}\begin{pmatrix} \mathbf{B}_{11}\mathbf{V}_1'\mathbf{\Phi}\mathbf{U}_1+\mathbf{B}_{12}\mathbf{V}_2'\mathbf{\Phi}\mathbf{U}_1 & \mathbf{B}_{11}\mathbf{V}_1'\mathbf{\Phi}\mathbf{V}_2+\mathbf{B}_{12}\mathbf{V}_2'\mathbf{\Phi}\mathbf{V}_2 \\ \mathbf{V}_2'\mathbf{\Phi}\mathbf{U}_1 & \mathbf{V}_2'\mathbf{\Phi}\mathbf{V}_2 \end{pmatrix}\right]$$

(since $\mathbf{U}_1' = \mathbf{B}_{11}\mathbf{V}_1' + \mathbf{B}_{12}\mathbf{V}_2'$)

$$= \det\frac{1}{T}\left[\begin{pmatrix} \mathbf{B}_{11}\mathbf{V}_1'\mathbf{\Phi}\mathbf{U}_1 & \mathbf{B}_{11}\mathbf{V}_1'\mathbf{\Phi}\mathbf{V}_2 \\ \mathbf{V}_2'\mathbf{\Phi}\mathbf{U}_1 & \mathbf{V}_2'\mathbf{\Phi}\mathbf{V}_2 \end{pmatrix}\right]$$

(for the value of a determinant does not change if we add to one of its rows, of columns, a linear combination of other rows, or columns)

$$= \det\left[\frac{1}{T}\begin{pmatrix} \mathbf{B}_{11}\mathbf{V}_1'\mathbf{\Phi}\mathbf{V}_1\mathbf{B}_{11} + \mathbf{B}_{11}'\mathbf{V}_1'\mathbf{\Phi}\mathbf{V}_2\mathbf{B}_{12}' & \mathbf{B}_{11}\mathbf{V}_1'\mathbf{\Phi}\mathbf{V}_2 \\ \mathbf{V}_2'\mathbf{\Phi}\mathbf{V}_1\mathbf{B}_{11}' + \mathbf{V}_2'\mathbf{\Phi}\mathbf{V}_2\mathbf{B}_{12}' & \mathbf{V}_2'\mathbf{\Phi}\mathbf{V}_2 \end{pmatrix}\right]$$

$$= \det\left[\frac{1}{T}\begin{pmatrix} \mathbf{B}_{11}\mathbf{V}_1'\mathbf{\Phi}\mathbf{V}_1\mathbf{B}_{11}' & \mathbf{B}_{11}\mathbf{V}_1'\mathbf{\Phi}\mathbf{V}_2 \\ \mathbf{V}_2'\mathbf{\Phi}\mathbf{V}_1\mathbf{B}_{11}' & \mathbf{V}_2'\mathbf{\Phi}\mathbf{V}_2 \end{pmatrix}\right] \tag{7.30}$$

(for the same reasons as above).

Now consider the 1st and the 4th terms in the right-hand side of (7.28). By (7.30) their sum is equal to

$$
-\frac{T}{2}\log\left\{\frac{\det\left[\frac{1}{T}\left(\begin{array}{c:c} \mathbf{B}_{11}\mathbf{V}_1'\mathbf{\Phi}\mathbf{V}_1\mathbf{B}_{11}' & \mathbf{B}_{11}\mathbf{V}_1'\mathbf{\Phi}\mathbf{V}_2 \\ \hdashline \mathbf{V}_2'\mathbf{\Phi}\mathbf{V}_1\mathbf{B}_{11}' & \mathbf{V}_2'\mathbf{\Phi}\mathbf{V}_2 \end{array}\right)\right]}{|\det\mathbf{B}_{11}|\,|\det\mathbf{B}_{11}|}\right\}
$$

$$
=-\frac{T}{2}\log\det\begin{pmatrix}\mathbf{B}_{11}^{-1} & 0\\ 0 & \mathbf{I}\end{pmatrix}\left[\frac{1}{T}\left(\begin{array}{c:c} \mathbf{B}_{11}\mathbf{V}_1'\mathbf{\Phi}\mathbf{V}_1\mathbf{B}_{11}' & \mathbf{B}_{11}\mathbf{V}_1'\mathbf{\Phi}\mathbf{V}_2 \\ \hdashline \mathbf{V}_2'\mathbf{\Phi}\mathbf{V}_1\mathbf{B}_{11}' & \mathbf{V}_2'\mathbf{\Phi}\mathbf{V}_2 \end{array}\right)\right]\begin{pmatrix}\mathbf{B}_{11}^{-1} & 0\\ 0 & \mathbf{I}\end{pmatrix}
$$

$$
= -\frac{T}{2}\log\det\left[\frac{1}{T}\left(\begin{array}{c:c} \mathbf{V}_1'\mathbf{\Phi}\mathbf{V}_1 & \mathbf{V}_1'\mathbf{\Phi}\mathbf{V}_2 \\ \hdashline \mathbf{V}_2'\mathbf{\Phi}\mathbf{V}_1 & \mathbf{V}_2'\mathbf{\Phi}\mathbf{V}_2 \end{array}\right)\right]
$$

$$
= -\frac{T}{2}\log\det\left(\frac{1}{T}\mathbf{Y}'\,\mathbf{\Phi}\,\mathbf{Y}\right)
$$

$$
= -\frac{T}{2}\log\det\mathbf{W} \tag{7.31}
$$

where

$$
\mathbf{W} = \frac{1}{T}\mathbf{Y}'\,\mathbf{\Phi}\,\mathbf{Y}.
$$

Substituting (7.29) and (7.31) into the likelihood function (7.28) finally gives the desired expression for the concentrated likelihood function

$$
\begin{aligned}
L(\mathbf{A}_1, \mathbf{\Omega}_{11}) = \text{const} &- \frac{T}{2}\log\det\mathbf{\Omega}_{11} + \frac{T}{2}\log\det\mathbf{B}_1\,\mathbf{W}\mathbf{B}_1' \\
&- \frac{T}{2}\log\det\mathbf{W} - \frac{1}{2}\operatorname{tr}(\mathbf{\Omega}_{11}^{-1}\,\mathbf{A}_1\mathbf{X}'\mathbf{X}\mathbf{A}_1').
\end{aligned} \tag{7.32}
$$

Note also equation (7.25) for the optimal estimator of $\mathbf{P}_2$ given the constraints on $\mathbf{A}_1$.

7.6.2 The LIML Estimator as a Least Generalized Variance Ratio Estimator

If the error covariance matrix $\mathbf{\Omega}_{11}$ is unconstrained it can be concentrated out of the likelihood function (7.32). Proceeding in the usual way we obtain the concentrated likelihood function

$$
L^*(\mathbf{A}_1) = \text{const} - \frac{T}{2}\log\det\left(\frac{\mathbf{A}_1\mathbf{X}_1'\mathbf{X}_1\mathbf{A}_1'}{T}\right) + \frac{T}{2}\log\det\mathbf{B}_1\,\mathbf{W}\mathbf{B}_1'
$$

where the term

$$-\frac{T}{2}\log\det \mathbf{W}$$

in (7.32) has been consolidated into the 'const' term.

Now define

$$\widetilde{\mathbf{\Omega}}_1 = \mathbf{B}_1\mathbf{W}\mathbf{B}_1'$$

and

$$\widetilde{\mathbf{\Omega}}_2 = \frac{\mathbf{A}_1\mathbf{X}'\mathbf{X}\mathbf{A}_1'}{T}$$

Notice that both $\widetilde{\mathbf{\Omega}}_1$ and $\widetilde{\mathbf{\Omega}}_2$ are estimates of $\mathbf{\Omega}_{11}$. $\widetilde{\mathbf{\Omega}}_2$ is obtained by maximizing the likelihood function (7.32) with respect to $\mathbf{\Omega}_{11}$. $\widetilde{\mathbf{\Omega}}_2$ is an estimate of $\mathbf{\Omega}_{11}$ based of the regression of $\mathbf{Y}\mathbf{B}_1'$ on $\mathbf{Z}$.

The concentrated likelihood function (7.23) can then be written as

$$L^*(\mathbf{A}_1) = \text{const} - \frac{T}{2}\log\left(\frac{\det \widetilde{\mathbf{\Omega}}_2}{\det \widetilde{\mathbf{\Omega}}_1}\right). \tag{7.33}$$

Maximizing the concentrated likelihood function (7.33) is therefore equivalent to minimizing the ratio of two determinants

$$\frac{T}{2}\log\left(\frac{\det \widetilde{\mathbf{\Omega}}_2}{\det \widetilde{\mathbf{\Omega}}_1}\right).$$

Thus the ML estimator of $\mathbf{A}_1$ can be interpreted as a least generalized variance ratio estimator.

7.7 The Single Equation LIML Estimator

Consider one equation, say the first out of a system of simultaneous equations:

$$\mathbf{X}\mathbf{a}_1 = \mathbf{Y}\mathbf{b}_1 + \mathbf{Z}\mathbf{c}_1 = \mathbf{u}_1, \qquad \mathbf{u}_1 \sim \mathrm{N}(0, \sigma_{11}^2\mathbf{I}_T).$$

By the result in Section 7.6.1 the log likelihood function for the LIML case when $n_1 = 1$ is

$$L(\mathbf{a}_1, \sigma_{11}^2) = \text{const} - \frac{T}{2}\log\sigma_{11}^2 + \frac{T}{2}\log \mathbf{b}_1'\,\mathbf{W}\mathbf{b}_1 - \frac{T}{2}\log\det\mathbf{W} - \frac{1}{2\sigma_{11}^2}\,\mathbf{a}_1'\mathbf{X}'\mathbf{X}\mathbf{a}_1$$

where

$$\mathbf{W} = \frac{1}{T}\mathbf{Y}'[\mathbf{I} - \mathbf{Z}(\mathbf{Z}'\mathbf{Z})^{-1}\mathbf{Z}']\mathbf{Y}.$$

The likelihood function concentrated with respect to σ_{11}^2 is

$$L^*(\mathbf{a}_1) = \text{const} - \frac{T}{2}\log\left(\frac{\mathbf{a}_1'\mathbf{X}'\mathbf{X}\mathbf{a}_1}{T}\right) + \frac{T}{2}\log \mathbf{b}_1'\ \mathbf{W}\mathbf{b}_1$$

$$= \text{const} - \frac{T}{2}\log\frac{1}{T}\left(\frac{\mathbf{a}_1'\mathbf{X}'\mathbf{X}\mathbf{a}_1}{\mathbf{b}_1'\mathbf{W}\mathbf{b}_1}\right). \qquad (7.34)$$

The LIML estimator of $\mathbf{a}_1$ is obtained by maximizing (7.34). This is equivalent to minimizing the ratio of two quadratic forms

$$\frac{1}{T}\ \frac{\mathbf{a}_1'\mathbf{X}'\mathbf{X}\mathbf{a}_1}{\mathbf{b}_1'\mathbf{W}\mathbf{b}_1}.$$

This concentrated likelihood function is perfectly general whatever constraints (linear or non-linear) will be applied at the next stage in minimizing this ratio. If now only zero restrictions are to be used we may consider the variables in the first equation with non-zero coefficients. Let $\mathbf{X}^*$ denote the set of variables included in the first equation and let $\mathbf{a}_1^*$ denote the vector of non-zero coefficients. Correspondingly define $\mathbf{Y}^*$, $\mathbf{Z}^*$, $\mathbf{b}_1^*$ and $\mathbf{c}_1^*$.

The LIML estimator of $\mathbf{a}_1^*$ is then the solution to

$$\text{Min}_{\mathbf{a}_1^*}\ \frac{1}{T}\left(\frac{\mathbf{a}_1^*\mathbf{X}^{*\prime}\mathbf{X}^*\mathbf{a}_1^{*\prime}}{\mathbf{b}_1^{*\prime}\mathbf{W}^*\mathbf{b}_1^*}\right) \qquad (7.35)$$

where $\mathbf{W}^* = \mathbf{Y}^{*\prime}[\mathbf{I} - \mathbf{Z}(\mathbf{Z}'\mathbf{Z})^{-1}\mathbf{Z}']\mathbf{Y}^*/T$.

Theorem 4: The concentrated likelihood function (7.35) is maximized with relation to $\mathbf{a}_1^*$ by taking $(\mathbf{W}^{**} - \lambda\mathbf{W}^*)\mathbf{a}_1^* = 0$ where λ is the minimal latent root of the determinantal equation

$$\det(\mathbf{W}^{**} - \lambda\mathbf{W}^*) = 0$$

where

$$\mathbf{W}^{**} = \frac{1}{T}\mathbf{Y}^{*\prime}[\mathbf{I} - \mathbf{Z}^*(\mathbf{Z}^{*\prime}\mathbf{Z}^*)^{-1}\mathbf{Z}^{*\prime}]\mathbf{Y}^*$$

and

$$\mathbf{W}^* = \frac{1}{T}\mathbf{Y}^{*\prime}[\mathbf{I} - \mathbf{Z}(\mathbf{Z}'\mathbf{Z})^{-1}\mathbf{Z}']\mathbf{Y}^*.$$

Proof: Note that $\mathbf{a}_1^*$ is not determined up to an arbitrary scale factor since (7.35) is zero-order homogeneous in $\mathbf{a}_1^*$. So we may standardize the denominator in (7.35) by setting it equal to unity. Problem (7.35) is then equivalent to the following:

$$\text{Min}_{\mathbf{a}_1^*} \frac{1}{T} \mathbf{a}_1^{*\prime}\mathbf{X}^{*\prime}\mathbf{X}^*\mathbf{a}_1^*$$

subject to

$$\mathbf{b}_1^{*\prime}\mathbf{W}^*\mathbf{b}_1^* = 1.$$

The Lagrangian of this problem is

$$L = \frac{1}{T} \mathbf{a}_1^{*\prime}\mathbf{X}^{*\prime}\mathbf{X}^*\mathbf{a}_1^* - \lambda(\mathbf{b}_1^{*\prime}\mathbf{W}^*\mathbf{b}_1^* - 1)$$

$$= \frac{1}{T} (\mathbf{Y}^*\mathbf{b}_1^* + \mathbf{Z}^*\mathbf{c}_1^*)' \,\mathbf{X}\mathbf{a}_1^* - \lambda\mathbf{b}_1^{*\prime}\mathbf{W}^*\mathbf{b}_1^* + \lambda.$$

The FOCs for **a** maximization are

$$\frac{\partial L}{\partial \mathbf{b}_1^*} = \frac{1}{T} \mathbf{Y}^{*\prime}\mathbf{X}^*\mathbf{a}_1^* - \lambda\mathbf{W}^*\mathbf{b}_1^* = 0 \tag{7.36}$$

$$\frac{\partial L}{\partial \mathbf{c}_1^*} = \frac{1}{T} \mathbf{Z}^{*\prime}\mathbf{X}^*\mathbf{a}_1^* = 0. \tag{7.37}$$

Pre-multiplying (7.36) by $\mathbf{b}_1^{*\prime}$ and (7.37) by $\mathbf{c}_1^{*\prime}$ and then adding the resulting expression gives

$$\frac{1}{T} \mathbf{b}_1^{*\prime}\mathbf{Y}^{*\prime}\mathbf{X}'\mathbf{a}_1^* + \frac{1}{T} \mathbf{c}_1^{*\prime}\mathbf{Z}^{*\prime}\mathbf{X}^*\mathbf{a}_1^* - \lambda\mathbf{b}_1^{*\prime}\mathbf{W}^*\mathbf{b}_1^* = 0$$

from which we obtain

$$\frac{1}{T} \mathbf{a}_1^{*\prime}\mathbf{X}^{*\prime}\mathbf{X}^*\mathbf{a}_1^* - \lambda\mathbf{b}_1^{*\prime}\mathbf{W}^*\mathbf{b}_1^* = 0$$

i.e.

$$\lambda = \frac{1}{T} \left(\frac{\mathbf{a}_1^{*\prime}\mathbf{X}^{*\prime}\mathbf{X}^*\mathbf{a}_1^*}{\mathbf{b}_1^{*\prime}\mathbf{W}^*\mathbf{b}_1^*} \right). \tag{7.38}$$

Now rewrite condition (7.37) as

$$\mathbf{Z}^{*\prime}(\mathbf{Y}^*\mathbf{b}_1 + \mathbf{Z}^*\mathbf{c}_1^*) = 0.$$

Then

$$\mathbf{c}_1^* = -(\mathbf{Z}^{*\prime}\mathbf{Z}^*)^{-1}\mathbf{Z}^{*\prime}\mathbf{Y}^*\mathbf{b}_1^*.$$

Substituting into (7.36) gives

$$\frac{1}{T} \mathbf{Y}^{*\prime}\mathbf{Y}^*\mathbf{b}_1^* - \frac{1}{T} \mathbf{Y}^{*\prime}\mathbf{Z}^*(\mathbf{Z}^{*\prime}\mathbf{Z}^*)^{-1}\mathbf{Z}^{*\prime}\mathbf{Y}^*\mathbf{b}_1^* - \lambda\mathbf{W}^*\mathbf{b}_1^* = 0$$

from which we have

$$(\mathbf{W}^{**} - \lambda\mathbf{W}^*)\mathbf{b}_1^* = 0 \qquad (7.39)$$

where

$$\mathbf{W}^{**} = \frac{1}{T}\mathbf{Y}^{*\prime}[\mathbf{I} - \mathbf{Z}(\mathbf{Z}^{*\prime}\mathbf{Z}^*)^{-1}\mathbf{Z}^{*\prime}]\mathbf{Y}^*.$$

Since $\mathbf{b}_1^* \neq 0$, equation (7.39) is satisfied only if

$$\det(\mathbf{W}^{**} - \lambda\mathbf{W}^*) = 0. \qquad (7.40)$$

In view of (7.38) the LIML estimator of $\mathbf{a}_1^*$ is then obtained by taking the smallest latent root of the determinantal equation (7.40).

7.8 The LIML Estimator with Linear Restrictions

Consider the system of n simultaneous equations introduced in Section 7.6.

$$\mathbf{AX}' = \mathbf{BY}' + \mathbf{CZ}' = \mathbf{U}'.$$

We have assumed in Section 7.6 that the parameter matrix $\mathbf{A}$ is subject to a set of linear restrictions of the form $\mathbf{\Phi}\,\text{vec}\,\mathbf{A} = \boldsymbol{\phi}$, and that

$$\mathbf{\Phi} = \begin{pmatrix} \mathbf{\Phi}_1 & 0 \\ 0 & \mathbf{\Phi}_2 \end{pmatrix}$$

i.e. the restrictions are separable with reference to the two subsets of n_1 and $n_2 = n - n_1$ equations respectively in which model (7.1) has been partitioned.

We now assume that the set of linear restrictions on the first subset of n_1 equations i.e., $\mathbf{\Phi}_1\,\text{vec}\,\mathbf{A}_1 = \boldsymbol{\phi}_1$, can be parameterized as

$$\text{vec}\,\mathbf{B}_1 = \mathbf{S}_1\,\boldsymbol{\beta} - \mathbf{s}_1$$

$$\text{vec}\,\mathbf{C}_1 = \mathbf{S}_2\,\boldsymbol{\gamma} - \mathbf{s}_2$$

or

$$\text{vec}\,\mathbf{A}_1 = \mathbf{S}\,\boldsymbol{\alpha} - \mathbf{s} \qquad (7.41)$$

where

$$\boldsymbol{\alpha} = (\boldsymbol{\beta}', \boldsymbol{\gamma}')' \text{ and } \mathbf{S} = \begin{pmatrix} \mathbf{S}_1 & 0 \\ 0 & \mathbf{S}_2 \end{pmatrix}.$$

This is assuming that the two sets of constraints on $\mathbf{B}_1$ and $\mathbf{C}_1$ are separable.

We want to derive the FOCs for a maximization of the concentrated log likelihood function

$$L^*(\mathbf{A}_1) = \text{const} - \frac{T}{2}\log\det\left(\frac{\mathbf{A}_1\mathbf{X}_1'\mathbf{X}_1\mathbf{A}_1'}{T}\right) + \frac{T}{2}\log\det\mathbf{B}_1\ \mathbf{W}\mathbf{B}_1' \tag{7.42}$$

in terms of $\boldsymbol{\beta}$ and $\boldsymbol{\gamma}$.

Consider first the differential of the 2nd term in (7.42)

$$\mathrm{d}\left[\frac{T}{2}\log\det\left(\frac{\mathbf{A}_1\mathbf{X}_1'\mathbf{X}_1\mathbf{A}_1'}{T}\right)\right] \tag{7.43}$$

$$= \frac{1}{2}\mathrm{tr}\left[\left(\frac{\mathbf{A}_1\mathbf{X}_1'\mathbf{X}_1\mathbf{A}_1'}{T}\right)^{-1}\ \mathrm{d}(\mathbf{A}_1\mathbf{X}_1'\mathbf{X}_1\mathbf{A}_1')\right]$$

$$= \frac{1}{2}\mathrm{tr}[\widetilde{\boldsymbol{\Omega}}_2^{-1}\ \mathrm{d}(\mathbf{A}_1\mathbf{X}_1'\mathbf{X}_1\mathbf{A}_1')]$$

where by (7.41)

$$\widetilde{\boldsymbol{\Omega}}_2 = (\mathbf{A}_1\mathbf{X}_1'\mathbf{X}_1\mathbf{A}_1'/T),$$

$$= \frac{1}{2}\mathrm{tr}[\widetilde{\boldsymbol{\Omega}}_2^{-1}\ \mathrm{d}\mathbf{A}_1(\mathbf{X}_1'\mathbf{X}_1\mathbf{A}_1')] + \frac{1}{2}\mathrm{tr}[\widetilde{\boldsymbol{\Omega}}_2^{-1}(\mathbf{A}_1\mathbf{X}_1'\mathbf{X}_1)\ \mathrm{d}\mathbf{A}_1']$$

$$= \mathrm{tr}[\widetilde{\boldsymbol{\Omega}}_2^{-1}\ \mathbf{A}_1\mathbf{X}_1'\mathbf{X}_1\mathrm{d}\mathbf{A}_1']$$

$$= (\mathrm{vec}\,\mathrm{d}\mathbf{A}_1')'\ \mathrm{vec}(\widetilde{\boldsymbol{\Omega}}_2^{-1}\ \mathbf{A}_1\mathbf{X}_1'\mathbf{X}_1)$$

$$= (\mathrm{vec}\,\mathrm{d}\mathbf{A}_1)'\ \mathrm{vec}(\widetilde{\boldsymbol{\Omega}}_2^{-1} \otimes \mathbf{X}_1'\mathbf{X}_1)\,\mathrm{vec}\,\mathbf{A}_1$$

$$= (\mathbf{S}\,\mathrm{d}\boldsymbol{\alpha})'\ (\widetilde{\boldsymbol{\Omega}}_2^{-1} \otimes \mathbf{X}_1'\mathbf{X}_1)\,\mathrm{vec}\,\mathbf{A}_1$$

Notice that

$$(\mathrm{d}\boldsymbol{\alpha}')\mathbf{S}' = (\mathrm{d}\boldsymbol{\beta}' \vdots \mathrm{d}\boldsymbol{\gamma}')\begin{pmatrix} \mathbf{S}_1' & 0 \\ 0 & \mathbf{S}_2' \end{pmatrix} = [(\mathrm{d}\boldsymbol{\beta}')\mathbf{S}_1' \vdots (\mathrm{d}\boldsymbol{\gamma}')\mathbf{S}_2']$$

We now introduce the permutation matrix $\boldsymbol{\Pi}$ with the property that if

$$\boldsymbol{\alpha} = \begin{pmatrix} \boldsymbol{\alpha}_1 \\ \boldsymbol{\alpha}_2 \\ \vdots \end{pmatrix} = \begin{pmatrix} \boldsymbol{\beta}_1 \\ \boldsymbol{\gamma}_1 \\ \boldsymbol{\beta}_2 \\ \boldsymbol{\gamma}_2 \\ \vdots \end{pmatrix}$$

then

$$\boldsymbol{\Pi\alpha} = \begin{pmatrix} \boldsymbol{\beta}_1 \\ \boldsymbol{\beta}_2 \\ \vdots \\ \boldsymbol{\gamma}_1 \\ \boldsymbol{\gamma}_2 \\ \vdots \end{pmatrix}$$

Using the permutation matrix we obtain

$$\boldsymbol{\Pi}(\widetilde{\boldsymbol{\Omega}}_2^{-1} \otimes \mathbf{X}_1'\mathbf{X}_1)\,\text{vec}\,\mathbf{A}_1 = \begin{pmatrix} \widetilde{\boldsymbol{\Omega}}_2^{-1} \otimes \mathbf{Y}_1'\mathbf{X}_1 \\ \widetilde{\boldsymbol{\Omega}}_2^{-1} \otimes \mathbf{Z}_1'\mathbf{X}_1 \end{pmatrix} \text{vec}\,\mathbf{A}_1$$

from which the differential (7.43) becomes

$$(\mathrm{d}\boldsymbol{\beta}')\mathbf{S}_1'(\widetilde{\boldsymbol{\Omega}}_2^{-1} \otimes \mathbf{Y}_1'\mathbf{X}_1)\,\text{vec}\,\mathbf{A}_1 + (\mathrm{d}\boldsymbol{\gamma}')\mathbf{S}_2'(\widetilde{\boldsymbol{\Omega}}_2^{-1} \otimes \mathbf{Z}_1'\mathbf{X}_1)\,\text{vec}\,\mathbf{A}_1.$$

Proceeding in an analogous way with the differential of the 3rd term in (7.42) we obtain

$$\mathrm{d}\left[\frac{T}{2}\log\det \mathbf{B}_1\mathbf{W}\mathbf{B}_1'\right] = T(\mathrm{d}\boldsymbol{\beta}')\mathbf{S}_1'(\widetilde{\boldsymbol{\Omega}}_1^{-1} \otimes \mathbf{W})\,\text{vec}\,\mathbf{B}_1$$

where $\widetilde{\boldsymbol{\Omega}}_1 = \mathbf{B}_1\mathbf{W}\mathbf{B}_1'$.

Then the FOCs for a maximization of the concentrated likelihood function (7.42) with reference to $\boldsymbol{\beta}$ and $\boldsymbol{\gamma}$ are respectively,

$$\begin{aligned} \frac{\partial L^*}{\partial \boldsymbol{\beta}} &= -\,\mathbf{S}_1'(\widetilde{\boldsymbol{\Omega}}_2^{-1} \otimes \mathbf{Y}_1'\mathbf{X}_1)\,\text{vec}\,\mathbf{A}_1 \\ &\quad + T\mathbf{S}_1'(\widetilde{\boldsymbol{\Omega}}_1^{-1} \otimes \mathbf{W})\,\text{vec}\,\mathbf{B}_1 = 0 \\ \frac{\partial L^*}{\partial \boldsymbol{\gamma}} &= -\,\mathbf{S}_2'(\widetilde{\boldsymbol{\Omega}}_2^{-1} \otimes \mathbf{Z}_1'\mathbf{X}_1)\,\text{vec}\,\mathbf{A}_1 = 0. \end{aligned}$$

More generally we can write

$$\begin{aligned} \frac{\partial L^*}{\partial \boldsymbol{\alpha}} &= -\,T\mathbf{S}'\left[\widetilde{\boldsymbol{\Omega}}_2^{-1} \otimes (\mathbf{X}_1'\mathbf{X}_1)/T - \widetilde{\boldsymbol{\Omega}}^{-1} \otimes \begin{pmatrix} \mathbf{W} & 0 \\ 0 & 0 \end{pmatrix}\right] \text{vec}\,\mathbf{A}_1 \\ &= 0. \end{aligned}$$

7.9 Relationship between LIML and 3SLS

Consider a subset of n_1 equations out of a simultaneous equation system.

$$\mathbf{A}_1\mathbf{X}' = \mathbf{U}_1', \qquad \text{vec}\,\mathbf{U}_1 \sim \mathrm{N}(0, \boldsymbol{\Omega}_{11} \otimes \mathbf{I}) \tag{7.44}$$

where the parameter matrix $\mathbf{A}_1$ is subject to a set of general linear restrictions of the form

$$\operatorname{vec}\mathbf{A}_1 = \mathbf{S}\,\boldsymbol{\alpha} - \mathbf{s}.$$

Theorem 5: The LIML estimator of $\boldsymbol{\alpha}$ and its 3SLS estimator are asymptotically equivalent in the sense that their difference is at most of the order of T^{-1}, if there is no constraint on $\boldsymbol{\Omega}_u$.

Proof: Consider the concentrated likelihood function

$$L^*(\mathbf{A}_1) = \text{const} - \frac{T}{2}\log\left(\frac{\det\widetilde{\boldsymbol{\Omega}}_2}{\det\widetilde{\boldsymbol{\Omega}}_1}\right)$$

(where $\widetilde{\boldsymbol{\Omega}}_2 = \mathbf{A}_1\mathbf{X}'\mathbf{X}'\mathbf{A}_1'/T$ and $\widetilde{\boldsymbol{\Omega}}_1 = \mathbf{B}_1\mathbf{W}\mathbf{B}_1'$

$$= \text{const} - \frac{T}{2}\log\det(\widetilde{\boldsymbol{\Omega}}_1^{-1}\,\widetilde{\boldsymbol{\Omega}}_2)$$

$$= \text{const} - \frac{T}{2}\log\det[\mathbf{I} + \widetilde{\boldsymbol{\Omega}}_1^{-1}(\widetilde{\boldsymbol{\Omega}}_1 - \widetilde{\boldsymbol{\Omega}}_2)]. \tag{7.45}$$

First notice that

$$\widetilde{\boldsymbol{\Omega}}_2 - \widetilde{\boldsymbol{\Omega}}_1 = \frac{1}{T}\mathbf{A}_1\mathbf{X}'\mathbf{X}\mathbf{A}_1' - \mathbf{B}_1\mathbf{W}\mathbf{B}_1'$$

$$= \frac{1}{T}\mathbf{A}_1\mathbf{X}'\mathbf{X}\mathbf{A}_1' - (\mathbf{B}_1\mathbf{C}_1)\begin{pmatrix}\mathbf{W} & 0\\ 0 & 0\end{pmatrix}\begin{pmatrix}\mathbf{B}_1'\\ \hline \mathbf{C}_1'\end{pmatrix}$$

$$= \mathbf{A}_1\left[\frac{\mathbf{X}'\mathbf{X}}{T} - \begin{pmatrix}\mathbf{W} & 0\\ 0 & 0\end{pmatrix}\right]\mathbf{A}_1'$$

$$= \mathbf{A}_1\mathbf{R}\mathbf{A}_1/T$$

where

$$\mathbf{R}:= \left(\begin{array}{cc}\mathbf{Y}'\mathbf{Y} & \mathbf{Y}'\mathbf{Z}\\ \hline \mathbf{Z}'\mathbf{Y} & \mathbf{Z}'\mathbf{Z}\end{array}\right) - \left(\begin{array}{cc}\mathbf{Y}'\mathbf{Y} - \mathbf{Y}'\mathbf{Z}(\mathbf{Z}'\mathbf{Z})^{-1}\mathbf{Z}'\mathbf{Y} & 0\\ \hline 0 & 0\end{array}\right)$$

$$= \left(\begin{array}{cc}\mathbf{Y}'\mathbf{Z}(\mathbf{Z}'\mathbf{Z})^{-1}\mathbf{Z}'\mathbf{Y} & \mathbf{Y}'\mathbf{Z}\\ \hline \mathbf{Z}'\mathbf{Y} & \mathbf{Z}'\mathbf{Z}\end{array}\right) = \mathbf{X}'\mathbf{Z}(\mathbf{Z}'\mathbf{Z})^{-1}\mathbf{Z}'\mathbf{X}.$$

Thus (7.45) becomes

$$L^*(\mathbf{A}_1) = \text{const} - \frac{T}{2}\log\det\left[\mathbf{I} + \widetilde{\boldsymbol{\Omega}}_1^{-1}\left(\frac{\mathbf{A}_1\mathbf{R}\mathbf{A}_1'}{T}\right)\right].$$

Totally differentiating gives

$$dL^* = -\frac{T}{2}\text{tr}\left\{\left[\mathbf{I} + \widetilde{\boldsymbol{\Omega}}_1^{-1}\left(\frac{\mathbf{A}_1\mathbf{R}\mathbf{A}_1'}{T}\right)\right]^{-1} \text{d}\left[\mathbf{I} + \widetilde{\boldsymbol{\Omega}}_1^{-1}\left(\frac{\mathbf{A}_1\mathbf{R}\mathbf{A}_1'}{T}\right)\right]\right\}$$

$$= -\frac{T}{2}\text{tr}\{(\widetilde{\boldsymbol{\Omega}}_1^{-1}\widetilde{\boldsymbol{\Omega}}_2)^{-1}\left[\text{d}\widetilde{\boldsymbol{\Omega}}_1^{-1}\left(\frac{\mathbf{A}_1\mathbf{R}\mathbf{A}_1'}{T}\right) + \widetilde{\boldsymbol{\Omega}}_1^{-1}\,\text{d}\left(\frac{\mathbf{A}_1\mathbf{R}\mathbf{A}_1'}{T}\right)\right]\right\}$$

$$= -\frac{T}{2}\text{tr}\left\{(\widetilde{\boldsymbol{\Omega}}_1^{-1}\widetilde{\boldsymbol{\Omega}}_2)^{-1}\,\text{d}\widetilde{\boldsymbol{\Omega}}_1^{-1}\left(\frac{\mathbf{A}_1\mathbf{R}\mathbf{A}_1'}{T}\right)\right\} \tag{7.46}$$

$$-\frac{T}{2}\text{tr}\left\{\widetilde{\boldsymbol{\Omega}}_2^{-1}\,\text{d}\left(\frac{\mathbf{A}_1\mathbf{R}\mathbf{A}_1'}{T}\right)\right\}.$$

The 1st term in (7.46) is negligible since

$$\frac{\mathbf{A}_1\mathbf{R}\mathbf{A}_1'}{T} = \frac{1}{T}\mathbf{A}_1\mathbf{X}'\mathbf{Z}(\mathbf{Z}'\mathbf{Z})^{-1}\mathbf{Z}'\mathbf{X}\mathbf{A}_1'$$

$$= \frac{1}{T}\frac{\mathbf{U}_1'\mathbf{Z}}{\sqrt{T}}\left(\frac{\mathbf{Z}'\mathbf{Z}}{T}\right)^{-1}\left(\frac{\mathbf{Z}'\mathbf{U}_1}{\sqrt{T}}\right) = \text{O}\left(\frac{1}{T}\right).$$

Thus consider the 2nd term in (7.46)

$$-\frac{T}{2}\text{tr}\left[\widetilde{\boldsymbol{\Omega}}_2^{-1}\,\text{d}\left(\frac{\mathbf{A}_1\mathbf{R}\mathbf{A}_1'}{T}\right)\right] = -\frac{1}{2}\text{tr}\{\widetilde{\boldsymbol{\Omega}}_2^{-1}[\text{d}\mathbf{A}_1(\mathbf{R}\mathbf{A}_1') + (\mathbf{A}_1\mathbf{R})\,\text{d}\mathbf{A}_1']\}$$

$$= -\,\text{tr}[\widetilde{\boldsymbol{\Omega}}_2^{-1}\,\mathbf{R}\mathbf{A}_1(\text{d}\mathbf{A}_1')]$$

$$= -\,(\text{vec}\,\widetilde{\boldsymbol{\Omega}}_2^{-1}\,\mathbf{A}_1\mathbf{R})'\,\text{vec}\,\text{d}\mathbf{A}_1'$$

$$= -\,(\text{vec}\,\mathbf{A}_1)'\,(\widetilde{\boldsymbol{\Omega}}_2^{-1}\otimes\mathbf{R})\,\text{vec}\,\text{d}\mathbf{A}_1',$$

where $\text{vec}\,\mathbf{A}_1 = \mathbf{S}\,\boldsymbol{\alpha} - \mathbf{s}$.

The FOCs for a maximization with reference to $\boldsymbol{\alpha}$ are therefore

$$\frac{\partial L^*}{\partial\boldsymbol{\alpha}} = -\,\mathbf{S}'(\widetilde{\boldsymbol{\Omega}}_2^{-1}\otimes\mathbf{R})\,\text{vec}\,\mathbf{A}_1 = \text{O}(1/T)$$

from which we obtain the expression defining the LIML estimator of $\boldsymbol{\alpha}$

$$\mathbf{S}'(\widetilde{\boldsymbol{\Omega}}_2^{-1}\otimes\mathbf{R})\,\text{vec}\,\mathbf{A}_1 = \text{O}(1/T). \tag{7.47}$$

Expression (7.47) is similar to the one derived in Section 7.1 for the 3SLS estimator of $\boldsymbol{\alpha}$.

It can be shown that

$$\widetilde{\boldsymbol{\Omega}}_2 - \hat{\boldsymbol{\Omega}} = O\left(\frac{1}{\sqrt{T}}\right)$$

where $\widetilde{\boldsymbol{\Omega}}_2$ is the (consistent) estimate of $\boldsymbol{\Omega}_{11}$ used in the derivation of the 3SLS estimator. The remainder of the proof is simply an adaptation of the argument in the previous theorem for the complete model (Section 7.4).
(End of proof)

7.10 Estimation of the Reduced Form (RF) Coefficients

Consider the model (7.16) in Section 7.6

$$\mathbf{A}^*\mathbf{X}' = \mathbf{U}^{*\prime}$$

or

$$\begin{aligned} \mathbf{B}_{11}\mathbf{Y}_1' + \mathbf{B}_{12}\mathbf{Y}_2' + \mathbf{C}_1\mathbf{Z}' &= \mathbf{U}_1' \\ \mathbf{Y}_2' - \mathbf{P}_2\mathbf{Z}' &= \mathbf{U}_2'. \end{aligned}$$

The complete matrix of reduced form coefficients is given by

$$\mathbf{P} = \begin{pmatrix} \mathbf{B}_{11} & \mathbf{B}_{12} \\ 0 & \mathbf{I} \end{pmatrix}^{-1} \begin{pmatrix} \mathbf{C}_1 \\ \mathbf{P}_2 \end{pmatrix}. \tag{7.48}$$

Once $\mathbf{B}_{11}$, $\mathbf{B}_{12}$, $\mathbf{C}_1$ and $\mathbf{P}_2$ have been estimated by LIML, it is possible to obtain estimates of the whole set of reduced form coefficients by using (7.48).

The LIML estimator of $\mathbf{P}$ can be shown to possess finite moments up to the $(T - n - m)$th moment. This property is not shared by the corresponding estimator obtained from the 3SLS estimator of $\mathbf{B}_{11}$, $\mathbf{B}_{12}$ and $\mathbf{C}_1$ and the OLS estimator of $\mathbf{P}_2$, for, if $\hat{\mathbf{P}}_2$ denotes the 3SLS estimator of $\mathbf{P}_2$, it can be shown that

$$\Pr(|\hat{\mathbf{P}}_2| > \mathbf{P}_2) \propto \frac{1}{\mathbf{P}_2}$$

and no moment will exist since the infinite integral defining the 1st moment does not converge. In other words, the 3SLS estimator of the reduced form parameters has very big tails which implies very large errors have a much higher probability than for a normal distribution with the same interquartile distance.

7.11 The Non-Linear LIML

Consider a set of n_1 non-linear in parameter equations, out of a simultaneous equations system.

$$\mathbf{A}_1(\boldsymbol{\theta})\mathbf{X}' = \mathbf{B}_1(\boldsymbol{\theta})\mathbf{Y}' + \mathbf{C}_1(\boldsymbol{\theta})\mathbf{Z}' = \mathbf{U}_1', \quad \operatorname{vec}\mathbf{U}_1' \sim \mathrm{N}(0, \boldsymbol{\Omega}_{11} \otimes \mathbf{I})$$

where $\boldsymbol{\theta}$ is a $(p \times 1)$ vector of unknown parameters.

By proceeding in the same way as in Section 7.6 it is possible to show that the non-linear LIML estimator of $\boldsymbol{\theta}$ is obtained by maximizing with reference to $\boldsymbol{\theta}$ the concentrated (log) likelihood function

$$L^*(\boldsymbol{\theta}) = \text{const} - \frac{T}{2}\log\det\left[\frac{\mathbf{A}_1(\boldsymbol{\theta})\mathbf{X}'\mathbf{X}\mathbf{A}_1(\boldsymbol{\theta})'}{T}\right] + \frac{T}{2}\log\det\mathbf{B}_1(\boldsymbol{\theta})\mathbf{W}\mathbf{B}_1(\boldsymbol{\theta})'$$

where

$$\mathbf{W} = \mathbf{Y}'[\mathbf{I} - \mathbf{Z}(\mathbf{Z}'\mathbf{Z})^{-1}\mathbf{Z}']\mathbf{Y}/T.$$

Furthermore, by proceeding in the same way as in Section 7.8 it is possible to show that the non-linear LIML estimator of $\boldsymbol{\theta}$ and the non-linear 3SLS estimator are asymptotically equivalent in the sense that their difference is at most of the order of T^{-1}.

8

Testing Equations for Mis-specification

8.1 Introduction

We will start with the simplest case, which contains nevertheless all the main features involved in these tests, and generalize it later. There are two main approaches to mis-specification testing for single equations in SEM which depend closely on the estimation procedure used in computing the parameters of that equation. Consider the single equation without normalization:

$$\mathbf{y} = \mathbf{X}\mathbf{a} + \mathbf{u} \equiv \mathbf{Y}\mathbf{b} + \mathbf{Z}\mathbf{c} + \mathbf{u}, \qquad \mathrm{E}(u_t^2) = \sigma^2. \tag{8.1}$$

This can be estimated by either an IV or LIML single equation.

8.1.1 IV Approach to Mis-specification Testing

In this approach we may be interested in two different types of mis-specification.

(i) We may want to compare (8.1) against

$$\mathbf{y} = \mathbf{X}\mathbf{a} + \mathbf{X}^+\mathbf{a}^+ + \mathbf{u},$$

i.e. to test for mis-specification in the regressors, we add a set of new variables. $\mathbf{X}^+$ and test for $\mathbf{H}_0 : \mathbf{a}^+ = 0$. Notice that in this case therefore, we are dealing with zero–one restrictions and so to test mis-specification is equivalent to testing the over-identifying restrictions.

(ii) Alternatively, since we are considering IV estimation, we are using a set of instrumental variables **Z**. We may be interested in testing for correct specification of **Z**, i.e. whether the matrix of IV, **Z**, contains correct instruments.

8.1.2 Single Equation LIML Approach to Mis-specification Testing

In this case it is difficult to check whether variables are really predetermined, and therefore we only consider mis-specification of type (i), asking whether the constraints that we impose are correct or not. But we should not forget that we may reject the null hypothesis because of (ii).

We examine closely these two approaches, starting with the latter.

8.2 The LIML Approach: The LR Test

The LIML is based on the LR test, comparing the maximum of the LF of the just identified model against the maximum of the LF of the over-identified model, to test whether those over-identifying restrictions are correct or not.

Obviously we cannot compare the maximum likelihood function of the over-identifying model with the maximum likelihood function of the initial totally unconstrained model, since the latter is unidentified and therefore has no finite asymptotic error variance matrix which is required for the proof of the asymptotic distribution of the test. Hence the first set of restrictions (up to obtaining the just identified model) are not testable, and we can only test the 'over'-identifying restrictions.

Recall from Chapter 7 that the concentrated LF for the LIML estimator has the form

$$L^* = k - \tfrac{1}{2}T\log\det\Omega_{11} - \tfrac{1}{2}\mathrm{tr}(\Omega_{11}^{-1}\mathbf{A}_1'\mathbf{X}'\mathbf{X}\mathbf{A}_1) + \tfrac{1}{2}T\log\det\mathbf{B}_1\mathbf{W}\mathbf{B}_1' \tag{8.2}$$

which, for a single equation like (8.1) becomes

$$L^* = k - T\log\sigma - \tfrac{1}{2}\frac{\mathbf{a}_1^{*\prime}\mathbf{X}^{*\prime}\mathbf{X}^*\mathbf{a}_1^*}{\sigma^2} + \tfrac{1}{2}T\log\mathbf{b}_1^{*\prime}\mathbf{W}^*\mathbf{b}_1^*$$

where $\mathbf{W}^* = T^{-1}\mathbf{Y}'[\mathbf{I} - \mathbf{Z}(\mathbf{Z}'\mathbf{Z})^{-1}\mathbf{Z}']\mathbf{Y}$.

Concentrating σ^2 out gives

$$\sigma^2 = \frac{\mathbf{a}_1^{*\prime}\mathbf{X}^{*\prime}\mathbf{X}^*\mathbf{a}_1^*}{T},$$

and substituting in L^* yields

$$\begin{aligned} L^* &= k^* + \tfrac{1}{2}T\log \mathbf{b}_1^{*\prime}\mathbf{W}^*\mathbf{b}_1^* - \tfrac{1}{2}T\log\left(\frac{\mathbf{a}_1^{*\prime}\mathbf{X}^{*\prime}\mathbf{X}^*\mathbf{a}_1^*}{T}\right) \\ &= k^* - \tfrac{1}{2}T\log\left[\frac{\left(\dfrac{\mathbf{a}_1^{*\prime}\mathbf{X}'\mathbf{X}\mathbf{a}_1^*}{T}\right)}{\mathbf{b}_1^{*\prime}\mathbf{W}^*\mathbf{b}_1^*}\right]. \end{aligned} \tag{8.3}$$

We must consider now the maximization of L^* for the just identified case and for the over-identified case.

For the just identified case we are going to show that $\lambda = 1$, and so the maximum of L^* is just k^*. We have

$$L^* = k^* - \tfrac{1}{2}T\log\lambda = k^* + \tfrac{1}{2}T\log\frac{1}{\lambda}$$

where

$$\begin{aligned} \frac{1}{\lambda} &= \frac{\mathbf{b}_1^{*\prime}\mathbf{W}^*\mathbf{b}_1^*}{\left(\dfrac{\mathbf{a}_1^{*\prime}\mathbf{X}^{*\prime}\mathbf{X}^*\mathbf{a}_1^*}{\mathrm{T}}\right)} \\ &= 1 + \frac{1}{\mathbf{a}_1^{*\prime}\left(\dfrac{\mathbf{X}^{*\prime}\mathbf{X}^*}{T}\right)\mathbf{a}_1^*}\left[\mathbf{b}_1^{*\prime}\mathbf{W}^*\mathbf{b}_1 - \mathbf{a}_1^{*\prime}\left(\frac{\mathbf{X}^{*\prime}\mathbf{X}^*}{T}\right)\mathbf{a}_1^*\right]. \end{aligned} \tag{8.4}$$

This is the notation of Section 7.2. To simplify it we drop the asterisks on all the coefficients and variables, and use a suffix '1', primarily to distinguish between $\mathbf{Z}$ and $\mathbf{Z}_1$. Developing the term in brackets yields

$$\begin{aligned} \mathbf{b}_1'\mathbf{W}_1\mathbf{b}_1 - \mathbf{a}_1'\left(\frac{\mathbf{X}_1'\mathbf{X}_1}{T}\right)\mathbf{a}_1 &= \left[\mathbf{a}_1'\begin{pmatrix}\mathbf{W}_1 & 0\\ 0 & 0\end{pmatrix}\mathbf{a}_1 - \mathbf{a}_1'\left(\frac{\mathbf{X}_1'\mathbf{X}_1}{T}\right)\mathbf{a}_1\right] \\ &= T^{-1}\mathbf{a}_1'\left[\begin{pmatrix}\mathbf{Y}_1'\mathbf{Y}_1 - \mathbf{Y}_1'\mathbf{Z}(\mathbf{Z}'\mathbf{Z})^{-1}\mathbf{Z}'\mathbf{Y}_1 & 0\\ 0 & 0\end{pmatrix} - \begin{pmatrix}\mathbf{Y}_1'\mathbf{Y}_1 & \mathbf{Y}_1'\mathbf{Z}_1\\ \mathbf{Z}_1'\mathbf{Y}_1 & \mathbf{Z}_1'\mathbf{Z}_1\end{pmatrix}\right]\mathbf{a}_1 \\ &= T^{-1}\mathbf{a}_1'\begin{pmatrix}-\mathbf{Y}_1'\mathbf{Z}(\mathbf{Z}'\mathbf{Z})^{-1}\mathbf{Z}'\mathbf{Y}_1 & -\mathbf{Y}_1'\mathbf{Z}_1\\ -\mathbf{Z}_1'\mathbf{Y}_1 & -\mathbf{Z}_1'\mathbf{Z}_1\end{pmatrix}\mathbf{a}_1 \\ &= -T^{-1}\mathbf{a}_1'\mathbf{X}_1'\mathbf{Z}(\mathbf{Z}'\mathbf{Z})^{-1}\mathbf{Z}'\mathbf{X}_1\mathbf{a}_1\left[\text{since } \mathbf{Z}_1'\mathbf{Z}(\mathbf{Z}'\mathbf{Z})^{-1} = \begin{pmatrix}\mathbf{I}_{n_1} & 0\end{pmatrix}\right] \end{aligned}$$

$$= -T^{-1}\mathbf{a}_1'\mathbf{R}\mathbf{a}_1 \qquad \text{where } \mathbf{R} = \mathbf{X}_1'\mathbf{Z}(\mathbf{Z}'\mathbf{Z})^{-1}\mathbf{Z}'\mathbf{X}_1$$

and L^* becomes

$$L^* = k^* + \tfrac{1}{2}T\log\left[1 - \frac{\mathbf{a}_1'\left(\dfrac{\mathbf{R}}{T}\right)\mathbf{a}_1}{\mathbf{a}_1'\left(\dfrac{\mathbf{X}_1'\mathbf{X}_1}{T}\right)\mathbf{a}_1}\right]. \tag{8.5}$$

The maximum therefore will be obtained when

$$\frac{\mathbf{a}_1'\mathbf{R}\mathbf{a}_1'}{T} = 0,$$

i.e. when $\mathbf{a}_1'\mathbf{X}_1'\mathbf{Z}(\mathbf{Z}'\mathbf{Z})^{-1}\mathbf{Z}'\mathbf{X}_1\mathbf{a}_1 = 0$. But since $(\mathbf{Z}'\mathbf{Z})^{-1}$ is a p.d. matrix, this will happen when $\mathbf{Z}'\mathbf{X}_1\mathbf{a}_1 = 0$. Recall that we have not normalized the equation yet so normalizing we have

$$\mathbf{a}_1 = \begin{pmatrix} \mathbf{a}_1^* \\ -1 \end{pmatrix}, \qquad \mathbf{X}_1 = (\mathbf{X}_1^*, \mathbf{y}_1).$$

Thus, $$\mathbf{Z}'\mathbf{X}_1\mathbf{a}_1 = (\mathbf{Z}'\mathbf{X}_1^*\mathbf{y}_1)\begin{pmatrix} \mathbf{a}_1^* \\ -1 \end{pmatrix} = 0 \rightarrow \mathbf{Z}'\mathbf{X}_1^*\mathbf{a}_1^* - \mathbf{Z}'\mathbf{y}_1 = 0 \tag{8.6}$$

or

$$\mathbf{Z}'\mathbf{X}_1^*\tilde{\mathbf{a}}_1^* = \mathbf{Z}'\mathbf{y}_1. \tag{8.7}$$

Equation (8.7) is simply the IV estimator for a just identified equation, i.e. the 2SLS for a just identified equation. Therefore, for the just identified case we have the result that 2SLS is identical to LIML, since $\tilde{\mathbf{a}}_1^*$ makes L^* take its maximum value:

$$L^* = k^* + \tfrac{1}{2}T\log\left(1 - \frac{0}{\mathbf{a}_1\left(\dfrac{\mathbf{X}_1'\mathbf{X}_1}{T}\right)\mathbf{a}_1}\right) = k^*.$$

For the over-identified case however, $\mathbf{a}_1'\mathbf{R}\mathbf{a}_1$ is no longer 0, and the maximum L^* will be given in (8.4) by the smallest λ, i.e. the smallest latent root for the ratio of quadratic forms,

$$\max L^* = k^* - \tfrac{1}{2}T\log\lambda^*$$

where λ^* is the smallest latent root.

We can therefore now construct a LR test. We know that under $\mathbf{H}_0$, $2\log \mathrm{LR} \underset{a}{\sim} \chi_d^2$, where d = number of over-identifying restrictions. In our case

$$2\log\mathrm{LR} = k^* - (k^* - \tfrac{1}{2}T\log\lambda^*) = \tfrac{1}{2}T\log\lambda^*$$

Hence

$$\log \mathrm{LR} = T \log \lambda^* \underset{\mathrm{a}}{\sim} \chi^2_d. \tag{8.8}$$

The order condition for identification of one equation tells us that the number of endogenous variables present in the equation minus one (from normalization) must be less or equal to the number of exogenous variables not present in the equation, since the latter are to be used as instruments of the former. If the number of unknown coefficients in the first equation is $n_1 + m_1^{-1}$, the order condition becomes

$$m - m_1 \geq n_1^{-1}$$

i.e. $m - (m_1 + n_1 - 1) = d =$ number of over-identifying restrictions.

For local alternatives $\mathbf{H}_0$, the likelihood ratio will be asymptotically distributed as non-central χ^2. An alternative test procedure is as follows. Define

$$\boldsymbol{\mu} = \frac{\mathbf{a}_1'\left(\dfrac{\mathbf{R}}{T}\right)\mathbf{a}_1}{\mathbf{a}_1'\left(\dfrac{\mathbf{X}_1'\mathbf{X}}{T}\right)\mathbf{a}_1}$$

where $\mathbf{a}_1$ is the LIML estimator.

Notice that $\mu = 1 - \dfrac{1}{\lambda^*}$.

We can write λ^* using (8.8) as

$$\lambda^* = \exp\left(\frac{Z}{T}\right),$$

where $Z = T \log \lambda^*$. By using the Mean Value Theorem we obtain

$$\begin{aligned}\lambda^* = \exp(Z/T) &= \exp(0) + \frac{Z}{T}\exp\left(\theta\frac{Z}{T}\right)\\ &= 1 + \frac{Z}{T}\exp\left(\theta\frac{Z}{T}\right)\end{aligned}$$

where θ is a scalar such that $0 \leq \theta \leq 1$.

Therefore,

$$T(\lambda^* - 1) = Z\exp\left(\theta\frac{Z}{T}\right) \equiv Z + Z\left[\exp\left(\theta\frac{Z}{T}\right) - 1\right].$$

We know from (8.18) that $Z = \mathrm{O}(1)$ since it has an asymptotic χ^2 distribution, therefore

$$\frac{Z}{T} = O\left(\frac{1}{T}\right).$$

So

$$\text{plim}\left(\theta\frac{Z}{T}\right) = 0.$$

Given that the exponential function is continuous everywhere, we can apply the Slutsky Theorem to obtain

$$\text{plim}\left[\exp\left(\theta\,\frac{Z}{T}\right) - 1\right] = 0.$$

Therefore

$$T(\lambda^* - 1) = Z + o(1).$$

Since $Z \underset{a}{\sim} \chi^2_d$ we can therefore apply the Mann and Wald Approximation Theorem to obtain

$$T(\lambda^* - 1) \underset{a}{\sim} \chi^2_d$$

Since

$$\mu = 1 - \frac{1}{\lambda^*} = 1 - \exp\left(-\frac{Z}{T}\right),$$

repeating the same argument (Mean Value Theorem, plim, the Slutsky Theorem) we find that

$$T\mu = T\left[1 - \exp\left(-\theta\,\frac{Z}{T}\right)\right] = Z = o(1)$$

and so

$$T\mu \underset{a}{\sim} \chi^2_d.$$

We are interested in μ because it is easier to compute and easier to relate to a χ^2 test for IV as we shall see in the next section. Notice that defining μ as

$$\mu = \frac{\mathbf{a}_1'\mathbf{R}\mathbf{a}_1}{s^2},$$

where s^2 is the estimator of σ^2 we obtain the LR test asymptotically since s^2 is a consistent estimator of σ^2.

8.3 The IV Approach

Consider a single equation out of a set of simultaneous equations

$$\mathbf{y} = \mathbf{X}\mathbf{a} + \mathbf{u}$$

and let **Z** be the matrix of IV of order $(T \times m)$.

We saw in the IV estimation chapter for single equations that

$$\mathbf{w} = \frac{Z'\mathbf{u}}{\sqrt{T}} \underset{a}{\sim} \mathrm{N}(0, \sigma^2\mathbf{M}),$$

where

$$M = \mathrm{plim}\frac{\mathbf{Z}'\mathbf{Z}}{T}.$$

However, if the model is mis-specified this asymptotic distribution is not correct. It is only when **a** is known, that we can know **w** exactly. Also recall that if $\xi \underset{a}{\sim} \mathrm{N}(0, \boldsymbol{\Omega})$ then $\xi'\boldsymbol{\Omega}^{-1}\xi \underset{a}{\sim} \chi^2_m$, where m is the rank of $\boldsymbol{\Omega}$. In this case we would therefore use the criterion function

$$\frac{\mathbf{w}'\left(\frac{\mathbf{Z}'\mathbf{Z}^{-1}}{T}\right)\mathbf{w}}{\sigma^2}$$

which has a χ^2_m distribution asymptotically. But in practice **a** is not known, so we must consider $\mathbf{y} = \mathbf{X}\hat{\mathbf{a}} + \hat{u}$, where $\hat{\mathbf{a}}$ is the IV estimator, and

$$\hat{\mathbf{w}} = \frac{\mathbf{Z}'\hat{\mathbf{u}}}{\sqrt{T}},$$

and

$$s^2 = \frac{\hat{\mathbf{u}}'\hat{\mathbf{u}}}{T}$$ and the criterion function becomes

$$\frac{\hat{\mathbf{u}}'\mathbf{Z}(\mathbf{Z}'\mathbf{Z})^{-1}\mathbf{Z}'\hat{\mathbf{u}}}{\hat{\mathbf{u}}'\hat{\mathbf{u}}/T} \tag{8.9}$$

which is very similar to the ratio

$$\frac{\mathbf{a}_1'\mathbf{R}\mathbf{a}_1}{\mathbf{a}_1'\left(\frac{\mathbf{X}_1'\mathbf{X}_1}{T}\right)\hat{\mathbf{a}}_1'}$$

that occurred in the last section, since

$$\mathbf{X}_1 = \quad (\mathbf{y} \vdots \mathbf{X})$$

$$\mathbf{a}_1 = \quad \begin{pmatrix} -1 \\ \mathbf{a} \end{pmatrix}$$

and so

$$\mathbf{a}_1'\mathbf{R}\mathbf{a}_1 = (\mathbf{y}'\mathbf{Z})(\mathbf{Z}'\mathbf{Z})^{-1}(\mathbf{Z}'\mathbf{y}) - 2\mathbf{y}'\mathbf{Z}(\mathbf{Z}'\mathbf{Z})^{-1}\mathbf{Z}'\mathbf{X}\mathbf{a} + \mathbf{a}'\mathbf{X}'\mathbf{Z}(\mathbf{Z}'\mathbf{Z})^{-1}\mathbf{Z}'\mathbf{X}\mathbf{a}.$$

To avoid confusion denote

$$\mathbf{R}^* = T^{-1}(\mathbf{X}'\mathbf{Z})(\mathbf{Z}'\mathbf{Z})^{-1}(\mathbf{Z}'\mathbf{X})$$

then

$$\hat{\mathbf{a}} = \mathbf{R}^{*-1}(\mathbf{X}'\mathbf{Z})(\mathbf{Z}'\mathbf{Z})^{-1}\left(\frac{\mathbf{Z}'\mathbf{y}}{T}\right)$$

and so

$$\sqrt{T}(\hat{\mathbf{a}} - \mathbf{a}) = \mathbf{R}^{*-1}(\mathbf{X}'\mathbf{Z})(\mathbf{Z}'\mathbf{Z})^{-1}\frac{\mathbf{Z}'\mathbf{u}}{\sqrt{T}}.$$

It will be shown that the criterion function (8.9) has a χ_d^2 asymptotic distribution, where $d = m - n$, n being the total number of unknown coefficients in the equation, i.e. $n \neq m_1 + n_1 - 1$. To do this we just need to show that

$$\hat{\mathbf{u}}'\mathbf{Z}(\mathbf{Z}'\mathbf{Z})^{-1}\mathbf{Z}'\hat{\mathbf{u}} \;\widetilde{a}\; \sigma^2\chi_d^2$$

since

$$\text{plim}\frac{\hat{\mathbf{u}}'\hat{\mathbf{u}}}{T} = \sigma^2$$

and therefore we can apply the Cramer Linear Transformation Theorem to (8.9) to show that (8.9) has the same asymptotic χ_d^2 distribution. First notice that we can write

$$\hat{\mathbf{u}} = \mathbf{y} - \mathbf{X}\hat{\mathbf{a}} = \mathbf{X}\mathbf{a} + \mathbf{u} - \mathbf{X}\hat{\mathbf{a}} = \mathbf{u} - \mathbf{X}(\hat{\mathbf{a}} - \mathbf{a}).$$

Then

$$\mathbf{Z}'\hat{\mathbf{u}} = \mathbf{Z}'\mathbf{u} - \mathbf{Z}'\mathbf{X}(\hat{\mathbf{a}} - \mathbf{a}) = \mathbf{Z}'\mathbf{u} - \mathbf{Z}'\mathbf{X}\mathbf{R}^{*-1}(\mathbf{X}'\mathbf{Z})(\mathbf{Z}'\mathbf{Z})^{-1}\frac{\mathbf{Z}'\mathbf{u}}{T}.$$

Denote

$$\mathbf{w}^* = (\mathbf{Z}'\mathbf{Z})^{-1/2}\mathbf{Z}'\mathbf{u}$$

$$\mathbf{Q}^* = \left(\frac{\mathbf{Z}'\mathbf{Z}}{T}\right)^{-1/2}\frac{\mathbf{Z}'\mathbf{X}}{T}\mathbf{R}^{*-1}\left(\frac{\mathbf{X}'\mathbf{Z}}{T}\right)\left(\frac{\mathbf{Z}'\mathbf{Z}'}{T}\right)^{-1/2}$$

where $\mathbf{Q}^*\mathbf{Q}^* = \mathbf{Q}^*$, i.e. $\mathbf{Q}^*$ is idempotent and symmetric of order n (the trace of $\mathbf{Q}^*$).

Then

$$(\mathbf{Z}'\mathbf{Z})^{-1/2}\mathbf{Z}'\hat{\mathbf{u}} = (\mathbf{Z}'\mathbf{Z})^{-1/2}\mathbf{Z}'\mathbf{u}$$
$$-(\mathbf{Z}'\mathbf{Z})^{-1/2}\mathbf{Z}'\mathbf{X}\mathbf{R}^{*-1}(\mathbf{X}'\mathbf{Z})(\mathbf{Z}'\mathbf{Z})^{-1}\frac{\mathbf{Z}'\mathbf{u}}{T}$$
$$= \mathbf{w}^* - \mathbf{Q}^*\mathbf{w}^* = (\mathbf{I}_m - \mathbf{Q}^*)\mathbf{w}^*.$$

The matrix $(\mathbf{I}_m - \mathbf{Q}^*)$ is idempotent also, or order $(m - n)$.

Hence

$$\hat{\mathbf{u}}'\mathbf{Z}(\mathbf{Z}'\mathbf{Z})^{-1}\mathbf{Z}'\hat{\mathbf{u}} = \mathbf{w}^{*\prime}(\mathbf{I}_m - \mathbf{Q}^*)\mathbf{w}^*$$

To obtain the asymptotic distribution, notice that

$$\mathbf{w}^* = \left(\frac{\mathbf{Z}'\mathbf{Z}}{T}\right)^{-1/2}\frac{\mathbf{Z}'\mathbf{u}}{\sqrt{T}} = \left(\frac{\mathbf{Z}'\mathbf{Z}}{T}\right)^{-1/2}\mathbf{w}.$$

By the Slutsky Theorem

$$\text{plim}\left(\frac{\mathbf{Z}'\mathbf{Z}}{T}\right)^{-1/2} = \mathbf{M}^{-1/2}$$

and by Central Limit Theorem, $\mathbf{w} \underset{a}{\sim} N(0, \sigma^2\mathbf{M})$. Therefore applying the Cramer Linear Transformation Theorem,

$$\mathbf{w}^* \underset{a}{\sim} N(0, \sigma^2\mathbf{I}_m)$$

and so we conclude that

$$\hat{\mathbf{u}}'\mathbf{Z}(\mathbf{Z}'\mathbf{Z})^{-1}\mathbf{Z}'\hat{\mathbf{u}} = \mathbf{w}^*(\mathbf{I}_m - \mathbf{Q}^*)\mathbf{w}^* \underset{a}{\sim} \sigma^2\chi^2_{m-n}.$$

A simpler proof uses the result that any idempotent matrix like $\mathbf{I}_m - \mathbf{Q}^*$ can be decomposed in a product of two rectangular matrices, of full rank, i.e.

$$\mathbf{I}_\mathrm{m} - \mathbf{Q}^* = \mathbf{H}'\mathbf{H}$$

such that $\mathbf{H}\mathbf{H}' = \mathbf{I}$, where $\mathbf{H}$ is an $(m - n) \times m$ matrix of rank $m - n$, and defined in such a way that its plim exists.

Then

$$\mathbf{w}^{*\prime}(\mathbf{I}_\mathrm{m} - \mathbf{Q}^*)\mathbf{w}^* = (\mathbf{w}^{*\prime}\mathbf{H}')(\mathbf{H}\mathbf{w}^*)$$

and since

$$\mathbf{H}\mathbf{w}^* \underset{a}{\sim} N(0, \sigma^2\mathbf{I}_{m-n})$$

we obtain again that

$$(\mathbf{w}^{*\prime}\mathbf{H}')(\mathbf{H}\mathbf{w}^{*}) \;\tilde{a}\; \sigma^2\chi^2_{m-n}.$$

A heuristic interpretation of the criterion function (8.9) is as follows: Write (8.9) as

$$\frac{T\left(\dfrac{\hat{\mathbf{u}}'\mathbf{Z}}{T}\right)\left(\dfrac{\mathbf{Z}'\mathbf{Z}}{T}\right)\left(\dfrac{\mathbf{Z}'\hat{\mathbf{u}}}{T}\right)}{s^2}.$$

If the equation is correctly specified, and $\mathbf{Z}$ is a set of valid instruments, we require that $\hat{\mathbf{u}}$ is independent of $\mathbf{Z}$. In case of correct specification, we know that

$$\frac{\mathbf{Z}'\hat{\mathbf{u}}}{T} = \mathrm{O}(1/\sqrt{T}),$$

and so

$$\frac{\hat{\mathbf{u}}'\mathbf{Z}}{T}\left(\frac{\mathbf{Z}'\mathbf{Z}}{T}\right)^{-1}\frac{\mathbf{Z}'\hat{\mathbf{u}}}{T} = \mathrm{O}\left(\frac{1}{T}\right)$$

thus

$$\frac{T\left(\dfrac{\hat{\mathbf{u}}'\mathbf{Z}}{T}\right)\left(\dfrac{\mathbf{Z}'\mathbf{Z}}{T}\right)^{-1}\left(\dfrac{\mathbf{Z}'\hat{\mathbf{u}}}{T}\right)}{s^2} = \mathrm{O}(1).$$

In case of either equation mis-specification or mis-specification of the set of IV $\mathbf{Z}$ (i.e. when we classify as predetermined a variable which is endogenous) this result no longer holds since $\hat{\mathbf{u}}$ and $\mathbf{Z}$ are not independent any longer. Therefore this is a powerful test against these two types of mis-specification. However note that the form of the asymptotic distribution on the null hypothesis depends on the complete specification of the model, and in particular on the assumption that the errors are serially uncorrelated. Thus if the test statistic is significant, it needs to be considered whether this might be due to serial correlation. Note that as a test of serial independence of the disturbances it is quite a strong test, since when the errors are serially correlated then

$$\frac{\mathbf{Z}'\hat{\mathbf{u}}}{T} = \mathrm{O}(1)$$

if there are lagged endogenous variables included in $\mathbf{Z}$ and the estimates will be generally inconsistent. One strategy to consider this possibility is to include all the variables lagged in the equation and then to use a suitable (COMFAC) test to consider whether the result may be due to autoregressive errors (see Sargan, 1980).

8.4 Asymptotic Equivalence of the LIML and 2SLS Approaches

When the IV test is used with a 2SLS estimator it is asymptotically equivalent to the LR test.

The difference between (8.9) and

$$T\mu = \frac{\mathbf{a}_1'\mathbf{R}\mathbf{a}_1}{\mathbf{a}_1'\left(\frac{\mathbf{X}_1'\mathbf{X}_1}{T}\right)\mathbf{a}_1}$$

is just a difference between the estimators of $\mathbf{a}_1$, the one involved in (8.9) being the 2SLS estimator whereas $T\mu$ uses the LIML estimator. Denote

$$\tilde{\mathbf{a}}_1 = \text{LIML estimator}$$

$$\hat{\mathbf{a}}_1 = \text{2SLS estimator}$$

and consider the difference between the two criterion functions.

$$\frac{\tilde{\mathbf{a}}_1'\mathbf{R}\tilde{\mathbf{a}}_1}{\tilde{s}^2} - \frac{\hat{\mathbf{a}}_1'\mathbf{R}\hat{\mathbf{a}}_1}{\hat{s}^2}.$$

Using the argument in Section 9.3, that LIML and 3SLS are asymptotically equivalent we can infer that for the single equation case LIML and 2SLS are asymptotically equivalent, i.e.

$$\tilde{\mathbf{a}}_1 - \hat{\mathbf{a}}_1 = O\left(\frac{1}{T}\right)$$

and therefore, since

$$\tilde{s}^2 - \hat{s}^2 = 0\left(\frac{1}{T}\right)$$

and

$$\frac{\mathbf{Z}'\mathbf{X}_1}{T}\tilde{\mathbf{a}}_1 = O\left(\frac{1}{\sqrt{T}}\right),$$

we conclude that

$$T\left(\frac{\tilde{\mathbf{a}}_1'\mathbf{R}\tilde{\mathbf{a}}_1}{\tilde{s}^2} - \frac{\hat{\mathbf{a}}_1'\mathbf{R}\hat{\mathbf{a}}_1}{\hat{s}^2}\right) = 0\left(\frac{1}{\sqrt{T}}\right)$$

and so the 2SLS criterion is asymptotically equivalent to the LR test.

8.5 More General Results

Suppose now that instead of a single equation, we are considering a system of n_1^* equations initially over-identified from which we remove restrictions until the system is just identified. In this case the LR is

$$\tfrac{1}{2}T\left[\log\det \mathbf{B}_1\mathbf{W}\mathbf{B}_1' - \log\det\left(\frac{\mathbf{A}_1'\mathbf{X}'\mathbf{X}\mathbf{A}_1}{T}\right)\right].$$

If we let N be the number of coefficients to be estimated in the over-identified case, in the just identified case we have mn_1^* parameters, and therefore the degrees of freedom of the χ^2 are $d = mn_1^* - N$. Thus

$$T\left[\log\det\left(\frac{\mathbf{A}_1'\mathbf{X}'\mathbf{X}\mathbf{A}_1}{T}\right) - \log\det \mathbf{B}_1\mathbf{W}\mathbf{B}_1'\right] \underset{\text{a}}{\sim} \chi_d^2. \qquad (8.10)$$

If we consider a set of *nested hypotheses*, then we can construct successive $\chi^2_{d_i}$, and to compare the nested hypotheses we compare the difference between the successive χ^2s corresponding to successively more constrained hypotheses. From the general properties of MLE, the χ^2s are independent of each other asymptotically. Finally for the FIML case, the expression is identical to (8.10) with only the difference that now $\mathbf{B}_1$ and $\mathbf{W}$ are square matrices and thus

$$\log\det \mathbf{B}_1\mathbf{W}\mathbf{B}_1' = 2\log\det \mathbf{B}_1 + \log\det \mathbf{W}$$

8.5.1 The Non-Linear in Parameters Case

In this case (8.10) becomes

$$T\left[\log\det\left(\frac{\mathbf{A}_1(\hat{\boldsymbol{\theta}})'\mathbf{X}'\mathbf{X}\mathbf{A}(\hat{\boldsymbol{\theta}})}{T}\right) - \log\det \mathbf{B}_1(\hat{\boldsymbol{\theta}})\mathbf{W}\mathbf{B}_1(\hat{\boldsymbol{\theta}})'\right] \underset{\text{a}}{\sim} \chi^2_{d^*}$$

where $d^* = mn_1^* - p$, and p is the number of parameters in the vector $\boldsymbol{\theta}$. For the single equation case the likelihood function is

$$L^* = k^* + \tfrac{1}{2}T\log\left[\frac{b_1(\boldsymbol{\theta})'\mathbf{W}_1\mathbf{b}_1(\boldsymbol{\theta})}{\mathbf{a}_1(\boldsymbol{\theta})'\left(\frac{\mathbf{X}_1'\mathbf{X}_1}{T}\right)\mathbf{a}_1(\boldsymbol{\theta})}\right].$$

Therefore the LR test becomes

$$T\log\left[\frac{\mathbf{a}_1(\hat{\boldsymbol{\theta}})'\mathbf{X}_1'\mathbf{X}_1\mathbf{a}_1(\hat{\boldsymbol{\theta}})}{\mathbf{b}_1(\hat{\boldsymbol{\theta}})'\mathbf{W}_1\mathbf{b}_1(\hat{\boldsymbol{\theta}})}\right] \underset{\text{a}}{\sim} \chi^2_d, \qquad d = m - p.$$

In the IV case also nothing substantial changes, the test criterion being

$$T\left[\frac{\left(\frac{\hat{\mathbf{u}}'\mathbf{Z}}{T}\right)\left(\frac{\mathbf{Z}'\mathbf{Z}}{T}\right)^{-1}\left(\frac{\mathbf{Z}'\hat{\mathbf{u}}}{T}\right)}{s^2}\right] \underset{\mathrm{a}}{\sim} \chi^2_{m-p}$$

where $\hat{\mathbf{u}} = \mathbf{y} - \mathbf{Xa}(\hat{\boldsymbol{\theta}})$.

Again it is not difficult to show that LR and 2SLS test statistics are asymptotically equivalent.

8.6 3SIV Test for a Subset of Equations

3SIV can be considered also the same way as the IV single equation. The criterion in this case as we saw in Chapter 6 is

$$\mathrm{tr}[\hat{\boldsymbol{\Omega}}_{\mathrm{u}}^{-1}\mathbf{AX}'\mathbf{Z}(\mathbf{Z}'\mathbf{Z})^{-1}\mathbf{Z}'\mathbf{XA}'] \tag{8.11}$$

where $\mathbf{AX}' = \mathbf{U}'$, and $\hat{\boldsymbol{\Omega}}_{\mathrm{u}}$ is a consistent estimate of $\boldsymbol{\Omega}_{\mathrm{u}}$. We can also introduce a set of constraints, which for the non-linear case gives $\mathbf{A} = \mathbf{A}(\boldsymbol{\theta})$, where $\boldsymbol{\theta}$ is a $(p \times 1)$ vector of parameters.

Suppose we end up with estimates $\hat{\mathbf{A}}$ or $\mathbf{A}(\hat{\boldsymbol{\theta}})$ in the non-linear case then under $\mathbf{H}_0$ again the criterion function (8.11) is asymptotically distributed as a χ^2_d, where

$$d = mn_1^* - N \text{ in the linear case}$$

$$= mn_1^* - p \text{ in the non-linear case}$$

where N is the total number of unconstrained coefficients in the linear case, or p is the number of parameters $\boldsymbol{\theta}$ in the non-linear case. It is possible to show the asymptotic equivalence between (8.11) and (8.10), i.e. between the IV and the LIML approaches, when 3SLS includes all the predetermined variables as instruments. The above criterion (8.11) can be used in the same way as described before to test a set of nested hypotheses, by looking to the different $\chi^2_{d_i}$ starting with the least constrained. However for computation (estimation) of either ML or 3SLS estimates it is usually easier to start with the *most* constrained, and to use the values obtained at one stage as starting values for the estimation of the next stage. Otherwise we may find ourselves in a situation where the maximum of the constrained LF is higher that that of the unconstrained, since the LF may have multiple optima and if we begin from the least constrained we may go to a local optimum which is not the global optimum. This would produce a negative value of the test criterion.

9

Alternative Significance Tests

9.1 The Likelihood Ratio (LR) Test

We saw an application of the LR test in Section 8.1. Let us now briefly consider its general theory.

Consider a set of parameters

$$\boldsymbol{\theta} = \begin{pmatrix} \boldsymbol{\theta}_1 \\ \boldsymbol{\theta}_2 \end{pmatrix}$$

and suppose we want to test the set of restrictions $\mathbf{H}_0 : \boldsymbol{\theta}_2 = 0$. Equivalently we can consider more general restrictions $\boldsymbol{\phi}(\boldsymbol{\theta}) = 0$, where $\boldsymbol{\phi}(\cdot)$ is a continuous function, but since this can be reparameterized as zero restrictions (see Wald Test, Section 9.2.3) we need only consider the former type of zero restrictions,

We are going to construct the LR statistic in terms of the concentrated log likelihood function.

Let $\hat{\boldsymbol{\theta}}$ be the unconstrained maximum likelihood (ML) estimate, and $\tilde{\boldsymbol{\theta}}$ the constrained one, i.e.

$$\tilde{\boldsymbol{\theta}} = \begin{pmatrix} \tilde{\boldsymbol{\theta}}_1 \\ 0 \end{pmatrix}.$$

Define the concentrated log likelihood function as

$$L^*(\boldsymbol{\theta}_2) = \max_{\boldsymbol{\theta}_1} L(\boldsymbol{\theta}_1, \boldsymbol{\theta}_2)$$

and

$$L^*(0) = L(\tilde{\boldsymbol{\theta}}).$$

Defining $\hat{\boldsymbol{\theta}}_2$ as the maximum of L^* and satisfying the first-order conditions

$$\frac{\partial L^*(\boldsymbol{\theta}_2)}{\partial \boldsymbol{\theta}_2} = 0,$$

we can write $L^*(\hat{\boldsymbol{\theta}}_2) = L(\hat{\boldsymbol{\theta}})$.

Making a Taylor Series Expansion around $\hat{\boldsymbol{\theta}}_2$ of $L^*(0)$ we obtain

$$L^*(0) = L(\hat{\boldsymbol{\theta}}_2) + \left(\frac{\partial L^*}{\partial \boldsymbol{\theta}_2}\right)'_{\hat{\boldsymbol{\theta}}_2}(0 - \hat{\boldsymbol{\theta}}_2)$$
$$+ \tfrac{1}{2}(0 - \hat{\boldsymbol{\theta}}_2)'\left(\frac{\partial^2 L^*}{\partial \boldsymbol{\theta}_2 \partial \boldsymbol{\theta}_2'}\right)_{\hat{\boldsymbol{\theta}}_2}(0 - \hat{\boldsymbol{\theta}}_2), \tag{9.1}$$

where $\boldsymbol{\theta}_2^*$ is some point between 0 and $\hat{\boldsymbol{\theta}}_2$.

From (9.1) the LR statistic is

$$-2[L^*(0) - L(\hat{\boldsymbol{\theta}}_2)] = \left[\sqrt{T}\hat{\boldsymbol{\theta}}_2'\left(-\frac{1}{T}\frac{\partial^2 L^*}{\partial \boldsymbol{\theta}_2 \partial \boldsymbol{\theta}_2'}\right)_{\hat{\boldsymbol{\theta}}_2}\sqrt{T}\hat{\boldsymbol{\theta}}_2\right] \tag{9.2}$$

since

$$\left(\frac{\partial L^*}{\partial \boldsymbol{\theta}_2}\right)_{\hat{\boldsymbol{\theta}}_2}$$

in (9.1) is zero from the FOC for a maximum of the likelihood function.

If $\mathbf{V}_{\theta_2}$ is the AVM of $\sqrt{T}(\hat{\boldsymbol{\theta}}_2 - \boldsymbol{\theta}_2)$, then from the properties of the concentrated likelihood function

$$\mathbf{V}_{\theta_2}^{-1} = \text{plim}\left[-\frac{1}{T}\left(\frac{\partial^2 L^*}{\partial \boldsymbol{\theta}_2 \partial \boldsymbol{\theta}_2'}\right)_{\hat{\boldsymbol{\theta}}_2}\right]. \tag{9.3}$$

If the log likelihood function has continuous second derivatives, and the general model is identified, $\hat{\boldsymbol{\theta}}_2$ is asymptotically normal, and after dividing by T the Hessian matrix has a non-singular limit, i.e. $\mathbf{V}_{\theta_2}$ is well defined. Then using the limit distribution theorem of Chapter 1 the right-hand side of (9.2) has the limit distribution of a standard quadratic form asymptotically distributed as a $\chi^2_{p_2}$ where p_2 is the number of restrictions, i.e. the number of elements of $\boldsymbol{\theta}_2$. To see this, recall that if a variable $\boldsymbol{\xi}$ has $\boldsymbol{\xi} \underset{a}{\sim} \text{N}(0, \boldsymbol{\Omega})$ then $\boldsymbol{\xi}'\boldsymbol{\Omega}^{-1}\boldsymbol{\xi} \underset{a}{\sim} \chi^2_m$ where $\boldsymbol{\Omega}$ is a $m \times m$ p.d. matrix. As a last remark, notice that if the information matrix ($\mathbf{V}_{\theta_2}$) is non-singular, the model is identified.

9.2 The Wald Test Statistic

9.2.1 Derivation

Let $\boldsymbol{\theta}$ be a $(p \times 1)$ vector of parameters. Consider a set of r constraints to be tested of the form $\boldsymbol{\phi}(\bar{\boldsymbol{\theta}}) = 0$, i.e., $\mathbf{H}_0 : \boldsymbol{\phi}(\bar{\boldsymbol{\theta}}) = 0$.

Let $\hat{\boldsymbol{\theta}}$ be some consistent asymptotically normal estimate of $\boldsymbol{\theta}$ (not necessarily the ML estimate), which satisfies

$$\sqrt{T}(\hat{\boldsymbol{\theta}} - \bar{\boldsymbol{\theta}}) \;\tilde{a}\; \mathrm{N}(0, \mathbf{V}_\theta) \tag{9.4}$$

where $\bar{\boldsymbol{\theta}}$ is the true parameter set.

Let $\hat{\mathbf{V}}_\theta$ be an estimate of $\mathbf{V}_\theta$ such that

$$\mathrm{plim}\hat{\mathbf{V}}_\theta = \mathbf{V}_\theta. \tag{9.5}$$

The Wald test statistic is based on the estimation of the *unconstrained* model. It tests whether the unconstrained estimate $\hat{\boldsymbol{\theta}}$ satisfies the constraints, by means of a quadratic form in $\boldsymbol{\phi}(\boldsymbol{\theta})$. We start from a relatively unconstrained model and we consider whether additional constraints can be added to it.

Notice how the fact of being based only on estimates of the unconstrained model gives the Wald test an advantage over the LR test that needs both constrained and unconstrained estimates, especially if a sequence of nested hypotheses is to be tested. The basic idea is to find the asymptotic distribution of $\boldsymbol{\phi}(\hat{\boldsymbol{\theta}}) - \boldsymbol{\phi}(\bar{\boldsymbol{\theta}})$. Assume that:

Assumption 9.1(A9.1): The function $\boldsymbol{\phi}(\cdot)$ has continuous first derivatives at $\boldsymbol{\theta} = \bar{\boldsymbol{\theta}}$

Assumption 9.2(A9.2): rank $\left(\dfrac{\partial \boldsymbol{\phi}}{\partial \boldsymbol{\theta}'}\right)_{\bar{\theta}} = r$ where $\left(\dfrac{\partial \boldsymbol{\phi}}{\partial \boldsymbol{\theta}'}\right)$ is an $(r \times p)$ matrix.

By the Mean Value Theorem applied to $\boldsymbol{\phi}(\boldsymbol{\theta})$ around $\bar{\boldsymbol{\theta}}$, we obtain

$$\boldsymbol{\phi}(\hat{\boldsymbol{\theta}}) = \boldsymbol{\phi}(\bar{\boldsymbol{\theta}}) + \left(\frac{\partial \boldsymbol{\phi}}{\partial \boldsymbol{\theta}'}\right)_{\boldsymbol{\theta}^*} (\hat{\boldsymbol{\theta}} - \bar{\boldsymbol{\theta}}) \tag{9.6}$$

for $\boldsymbol{\theta}^* = c\hat{\boldsymbol{\theta}} + (1 - c)\bar{\boldsymbol{\theta}}, 0 \leq c \leq 1$.

A9.1 and A9.2 ensure that rank $\left(\dfrac{\partial \boldsymbol{\phi}}{\partial \boldsymbol{\theta}'}\right)_{\boldsymbol{\theta}^*} = r$ for $\boldsymbol{\theta}^*$ belonging to a neighbourhood of $\bar{\boldsymbol{\theta}}_T$.

By the Slutsky Theorem

$$\text{plim}\left(\frac{\partial \boldsymbol{\phi}}{\partial \boldsymbol{\theta}}\right)_{\boldsymbol{\theta}^*} = \left(\frac{\partial \boldsymbol{\phi}}{\partial \boldsymbol{\theta}}\right)_{\bar{\boldsymbol{\theta}}}.$$

Then applying the Cramer Linear Transformation to (9.6) after rescaling and recalling (9.5)

$$\sqrt{T}[\boldsymbol{\phi}(\hat{\boldsymbol{\theta}}) - \boldsymbol{\phi}(\bar{\boldsymbol{\theta}}) \mathrel{\tilde{a}} \text{N}\left[0, \left(\frac{\partial \boldsymbol{\phi}}{\partial \boldsymbol{\theta}'}\right)_{\bar{\boldsymbol{\theta}}} \mathbf{V}_{\theta}\left(\frac{\partial \boldsymbol{\phi}}{\partial \boldsymbol{\theta}'}\right)'_{\bar{\boldsymbol{\theta}}}\right] = \text{N}(0, \mathbf{V}_{\phi}) \qquad (9.7)$$

where we have defined

$$\mathbf{V}_{\phi} = \left[\left(\frac{\partial \boldsymbol{\phi}}{\partial \boldsymbol{\theta}'}\right)_{\bar{\boldsymbol{\theta}}} \mathbf{V}_{\theta}\left(\frac{\partial \boldsymbol{\phi}}{\partial \boldsymbol{\theta}'}\right)'_{\bar{\boldsymbol{\theta}}}\right].$$

Under H_0: $\boldsymbol{\phi}(\bar{\boldsymbol{\theta}}) = 0$, (9.7) becomes

$$\sqrt{T}\boldsymbol{\phi}(\hat{\boldsymbol{\theta}}) \mathrel{\tilde{a}} \text{N}(0, \mathbf{V}_{\phi}). \qquad (9.8)$$

To find the distribution under the alternative hypothesis, we obtain it by means of a *sequence of local alternatives*

$$\boldsymbol{\phi}(\bar{\boldsymbol{\theta}}_{\text{T}}) = \frac{\boldsymbol{\alpha}}{\sqrt{T}}$$

such that $\bar{\boldsymbol{\theta}}_T \to \bar{\boldsymbol{\theta}}$ as $T \to \infty$ where $\boldsymbol{\alpha}$ = a constant vector. N.B. for $\mathbf{H}_0 : \boldsymbol{\theta} = \bar{\boldsymbol{\theta}}, \boldsymbol{\alpha} = 0$.

Then (9.7) under the alternatives becomes

$$\sqrt{T}\boldsymbol{\phi}(\hat{\boldsymbol{\theta}}) \mathrel{\tilde{a}} \text{N}(\boldsymbol{\alpha}, \mathbf{V}_{\phi}). \qquad (9.9)$$

Introducing this local alternative we can study the asymptotic power of the test, since the asymptotic power λ is clearly a function only of $\boldsymbol{\alpha}$ and $\mathbf{V}_{\phi}$. The tests whose asymptotic power we can calculate are given by $\mathbf{H}_0 : \boldsymbol{\alpha} = 0$ and $\mathbf{H}_1 : \boldsymbol{\alpha} \neq 0$ but constant.

From (9.8) and (9.9) we can now easily construct a statistic that on the null hypothesis has a χ^2 as asymptotic distribution: Let $\sqrt{(T)}\boldsymbol{\phi}(\hat{\boldsymbol{\theta}}) = \mathbf{w}_{\phi}$.

Since $\mathbf{w}_{\phi} \mathrel{\tilde{a}} \text{N}(0, \mathbf{V}_{\phi})$ then *under the null*

$$\mathbf{w}'_{\phi}\mathbf{V}_{\phi}^{-1}\mathbf{w}_{\phi} \mathrel{\tilde{a}} \chi^2_{r}. \qquad (9.10)$$

Let now $\mathbf{H}$ be a matrix such that

$$\mathbf{HH}' = \mathbf{V}_{\phi}^{-1}$$

and thus $\mathbf{H}'\mathbf{V}_{\phi}\mathbf{H} = \mathbf{I}$.

Define $\mathbf{w}^* = \mathbf{H}'\mathbf{w}_{\phi}$ then from (9.9) on the alternative hypothesis

$$\mathbf{w}^* = \sqrt{T}\mathbf{H}'\boldsymbol{\phi}(\hat{\boldsymbol{\theta}}) \ \tilde{\text{a}}\ \text{N}(\mathbf{H}'\boldsymbol{\alpha}, \mathbf{I})$$

and so

$$\mathbf{w}^{*\prime}\mathbf{w}^* = \mathbf{w}'_\phi\mathbf{V}_\phi^{-1}\mathbf{w}_\phi \ \tilde{\text{a}}\ \chi^2(r, \lambda) \tag{9.11}$$

i.e. a χ^2 with non-centrality $\lambda = \boldsymbol{\alpha}'\mathbf{HH}'\boldsymbol{\alpha} = \boldsymbol{\alpha}'\mathbf{V}_\phi^{-1}\boldsymbol{\alpha}$.

9.2.2 Feasible Wald Test Statistic

Since $\mathbf{V}_\phi$ is unknown, we must consider $\hat{\mathbf{V}}_\phi$, defined as

$$\hat{\mathbf{V}}_\phi = \left[\left(\frac{\partial\phi}{\partial\boldsymbol{\theta}'}\right)\hat{\mathbf{V}}_\theta\left(\frac{\partial\boldsymbol{\phi}}{\partial\boldsymbol{\theta}'}\right)'\right]_{\hat{\boldsymbol{\theta}}}$$

where $\hat{\mathbf{V}}_\theta$ satisfies (9.5).

In this case we must consider the statistic

$$\mathbf{w}'_\phi\hat{\mathbf{V}}_\phi^{-1}\mathbf{w}_\phi = T\boldsymbol{\phi}(\hat{\boldsymbol{\theta}})\hat{\mathbf{V}}_\phi^{-1}\boldsymbol{\phi}(\hat{\boldsymbol{\theta}}). \tag{9.12}$$

To work out the asymptotic distribution of (9.12), by the Slutsky Theorem

$$\text{plim}\hat{\mathbf{V}}_\phi^{-1} = \mathbf{V}_\phi^{-1},$$

i.e.

$$\hat{\mathbf{V}}_\phi^{-1} - \mathbf{V}_\phi^{-1} = \text{o}(1).$$

On the other hand, from (9.8) we know that $\boldsymbol{\phi}(\hat{\boldsymbol{\theta}}) = \text{O}(T^{-1/2})$, hence

$$T\boldsymbol{\phi}(\hat{\boldsymbol{\theta}})'(\hat{\mathbf{V}}_\phi^{-1} - \mathbf{V}_\phi^{-1})\boldsymbol{\phi}(\hat{\boldsymbol{\theta}}) = T\cdot\text{O}(T^{-1/2})\text{o}(1)\text{O}(T^{-1/2}) = \text{o}(1)$$

and therefore the difference between the feasible statistic (9.12) and the theoretical ones is of o(1), i.e. has plim zero.

Then applying the Mann and Wald Approximation Theorem, both feasible and theoretical statistics will have the same asymptotic distribution, i.e.

$$\mathbf{w}'_\phi\hat{\mathbf{V}}_\phi^{-1}\mathbf{w}_\phi \ \tilde{\text{a}}\ \chi^2_r \quad \text{under } \mathbf{H}_0,$$

$$\mathbf{w}'_\phi\hat{\mathbf{V}}_\phi^{-1}\mathbf{w}_{\phi\text{a}} \ \tilde{\text{a}}\ \chi^2(r, \lambda) \qquad \text{under the alternative } \mathbf{H}_1.$$

In actual estimation $\boldsymbol{\alpha}$ is not known, but it is occasionally useful to have a rough approximation to the power of the test for hypothetical values of $\bar{\boldsymbol{\theta}}$, such that $\boldsymbol{\phi}(\bar{\boldsymbol{\theta}}) \neq 0$ by computing $\hat{\lambda} = \boldsymbol{\alpha}'\hat{\mathbf{V}}_\phi^{-1}\boldsymbol{\alpha}$, and using this to compute the probability of the test statistic being outside a given central χ^2 confidence limit. The efficiency of the Wald test depends on the efficiency of the estimate $\hat{\boldsymbol{\theta}}$. The more efficient $\hat{\boldsymbol{\theta}}$ (i.e. the smaller $\mathbf{V}_\phi$), the higher the value of λ since $\hat{\lambda} = \boldsymbol{\alpha}'\mathbf{V}_\phi^{-1}\boldsymbol{\alpha}$, and the higher λ the more powerful the test since the probability of type II error diminishes.

9.2.3 Equivalence of Wald Test and LR Test

It is a matter of convenience in later algebra to express the general restrictions in a simpler form by reparameterizing the model. Consider the log likelihood function $L(\boldsymbol{\theta})$ where $\boldsymbol{\theta}$ is a $(p \times l)$ vector of parameters and consider r independent restrictions of the form,

$$\boldsymbol{\phi}(\boldsymbol{\theta}) = 0,$$

where we use 'independent' to mean that

$$\text{rank}\left(\frac{\partial \boldsymbol{\phi}}{\partial \boldsymbol{\theta}'}\right)_{\bar{\boldsymbol{\theta}}} = r.$$

Reorder the parameters if necessary and partition

$$\boldsymbol{\theta} = \begin{pmatrix} \boldsymbol{\theta}_1 \\ \boldsymbol{\theta}_2 \end{pmatrix} \text{ where } \boldsymbol{\theta}_2 \text{ is an } (r \times l) \text{ vector such that}$$

$$\text{rank}\left(\frac{\partial \boldsymbol{\phi}}{\partial \boldsymbol{\theta}_2'}\right)_{\bar{\boldsymbol{\theta}}} = r.$$

Consider a transformation to new parameters $\boldsymbol{\psi}$

$$\boldsymbol{\psi}(\boldsymbol{\theta}) = \begin{pmatrix} \boldsymbol{\theta}_1 \\ \boldsymbol{\phi}(\boldsymbol{\theta}) \end{pmatrix}$$

This transformation is invertible in a neighbourhood of $\bar{\boldsymbol{\theta}}$ since

$$\text{rank}\left\{\frac{\partial[\boldsymbol{\psi}(\boldsymbol{\theta})]}{\partial \boldsymbol{\theta}'}\right\}_{\bar{\boldsymbol{\theta}}} = \text{rank}\begin{pmatrix} \mathbf{I} & 0 \\ \dfrac{\partial \boldsymbol{\phi}}{\partial \boldsymbol{\theta}_1'} & \dfrac{\partial \boldsymbol{\phi}}{\partial \boldsymbol{\theta}_2'} \end{pmatrix}, = (p - r) + r = p.$$

Thus we can write

$$\boldsymbol{\theta} = \mathbf{g}(\boldsymbol{\psi})$$

where $\mathbf{g}(\cdot)$ is a one-to-one function in the neighbourhood of $\bar{\boldsymbol{\theta}}$.

Thus we can define

$$L^*(\boldsymbol{\psi}) = L[\mathbf{g}(\boldsymbol{\psi})] = L(\boldsymbol{\theta})$$

if

$$\boldsymbol{\theta} = \mathbf{g}(\boldsymbol{\psi}),$$

and the restrictions $\boldsymbol{\phi}(\boldsymbol{\theta}) = 0$ are equivalent to $\boldsymbol{\psi}_2 = 0$. Also from the invariance of the ML estimates with respect to changes in parameters, the unconstrained estimator of $\boldsymbol{\psi}$ will be such that $\hat{\boldsymbol{\psi}}_1 = \hat{\boldsymbol{\theta}}_1$, $\hat{\boldsymbol{\psi}}_2 = \boldsymbol{\phi}(\hat{\boldsymbol{\theta}})$, and the constrained and unconstrained maxima of the likelihood function will be unchanged. So the LR test is also unchanged by the reparameterization.

For the Wald test note that

$$\left[\frac{\partial^2 L^*}{\partial \boldsymbol{\psi} \partial \boldsymbol{\psi}'}\right]_{\hat{\psi}} = \frac{\partial^2}{\partial \boldsymbol{\psi} \partial \boldsymbol{\psi}'}\{L[\mathbf{g}(\boldsymbol{\psi})]\}_{\hat{\psi}}$$

$$= \left[\left(\frac{\partial \mathbf{g}'}{\partial \boldsymbol{\psi}}\right)\frac{\partial^2 L}{\partial \boldsymbol{\theta} \partial \boldsymbol{\theta}'}\left(\frac{\partial \mathbf{g}}{\partial \boldsymbol{\psi}'}\right)\right]_{\hat{\boldsymbol{\theta}}}$$

where use is made of $\left(\dfrac{\partial L}{\partial \boldsymbol{\theta}}\right)_{\hat{\boldsymbol{\theta}}} = 0.$

Thus

$$\hat{\mathbf{V}}_{\psi} = \left(\frac{\partial \boldsymbol{\psi}'}{\partial \boldsymbol{\theta}}\right)_{\hat{\boldsymbol{\theta}}} \hat{\mathbf{V}}_{\theta}\left(\frac{\partial \boldsymbol{\psi}}{\partial \boldsymbol{\theta}'}\right)_{\hat{\boldsymbol{\theta}}}$$

and so

$$(\hat{\mathbf{V}}_{\psi})_{22} = \hat{\mathbf{V}}_{\phi}$$

where $(\hat{\mathbf{V}}_{\psi})_{22}$ is the principal (diagonal) submatrix of $\hat{\mathbf{V}}_{\psi}$ corresponding to the ψ_2 parameters, and $\hat{\mathbf{V}}_{\psi}$ is the above estimate of the AVM of $\sqrt{T}(\hat{\boldsymbol{\psi}} - \boldsymbol{\psi})$. So we can always transform our parameters so that the constraints are simple zero constraints.

We now consider the case where $\boldsymbol{\theta}_2 = 0$ is the set of restrictions, and from equation (9.2) of this chapter the LR test statistic can be written

$$L^*(\hat{\boldsymbol{\theta}}_2) - L^*(0) = -\tfrac{1}{2}\hat{\boldsymbol{\theta}}_2'\left(\frac{\partial^2 L}{\partial \boldsymbol{\theta}_2 \partial \boldsymbol{\theta}_2'}\right)_{\boldsymbol{\theta}_2^*}\hat{\boldsymbol{\theta}}_2. \tag{9.13}$$

From the properties of the concentrated likelihood function, we know that

$$-\text{plim}\,\frac{1}{T}\left(\frac{\partial^2 L^*}{\partial \hat{\boldsymbol{\theta}}_2 \partial \hat{\boldsymbol{\theta}}_2'}\right) = \mathbf{V}_{\theta_2}^{-1}$$

where $\mathbf{V}_{\theta_2}^{-1}$ is the AVM of $\sqrt{T}(\hat{\boldsymbol{\theta}}_2 - \bar{\boldsymbol{\theta}}_2)$. Since the Hessian is a negative definite matrix, then $\mathbf{V}_{\theta_2}^{-1}$ is a positive definite matrix. Rescaling (9.13), the LR test statistic is

$$\sqrt{T}\hat{\boldsymbol{\theta}}_2'\left(\frac{1}{T}\frac{\partial^2 L^*}{\partial\boldsymbol{\theta}_2\partial\boldsymbol{\theta}_2'}\right)_{\boldsymbol{\theta}_2^*}\hat{\boldsymbol{\theta}}_2\sqrt{T}. \tag{9.14}$$

But (9.14) has the same expression as the Wald test statistic (9.10) where $\boldsymbol{\phi}(\boldsymbol{\theta}) = 0$ is specialized to $\boldsymbol{\theta}_2 = 0$. The only difference between both LR test and Wald test statistics is that $\mathbf{V}_2^{-1}$ is estimated at different points, $\hat{\boldsymbol{\theta}}_2$ in the Wald test and $\boldsymbol{\theta}_2^*$ in the LR test. But because of the definition of $\hat{\boldsymbol{\theta}}_2$ and $\boldsymbol{\theta}_2^*$, this makes no difference asymptotically, i.e.

$$\begin{aligned}\text{W} - \text{LR} &= T\hat{\boldsymbol{\theta}}_2'(\hat{\mathbf{V}}_{\theta_2}^{-1})\hat{\boldsymbol{\theta}}_2 - T\hat{\boldsymbol{\theta}}_2'(\tilde{\mathbf{V}}_{\theta_2}^{-1})\hat{\boldsymbol{\theta}}_2\\ &= \sqrt{T}\hat{\boldsymbol{\theta}}_2'(\hat{\mathbf{V}}_{\theta_2}^{-1} - \tilde{\mathbf{V}}_{\theta_2}^{-1})\hat{\boldsymbol{\theta}}_2\sqrt{T} = \text{O}(T^{-1/2}),\end{aligned}$$

since $\boldsymbol{\theta}_2^* \underset{T\to\infty}{\to} \hat{\boldsymbol{\theta}}_2$ and $\sqrt{T}\hat{\boldsymbol{\theta}}_2' = \text{O}(1)$ and $\hat{\mathbf{V}}_{\theta_2}^{-1} - \tilde{\mathbf{V}}_{\theta_2}^{-1} = \text{O}(T^{-1/2})$.

So from the Mann and Wald Approximation Theorem the LR test statistic is asymptotically distributed like the Wald test statistic, i.e. as χ_r^2. By the same argument, we can also show that under a sequence of local alternatives $\boldsymbol{\theta}_2 = \dfrac{\boldsymbol{\alpha}}{\sqrt{T}}$ the asymptotic distribution of both tests is a $\chi_{r,\lambda}^2$ where $\lambda = (\boldsymbol{\alpha}'\mathbf{V}_{\theta_2}^{-1}\boldsymbol{\alpha})$ is the non-centrality parameter.

9.3 The Lagrange Multiplier (LM) Test Statistic

9.3.1 Derivation

As with the Wald test, the LM test criteria only requires computation of one model, but contrary to the Wald test, the computation is now of the constrained model. This test can be interpreted as the comparison of the first-order conditions (FOC) of the log likelihood function of the unconstrained model worked out at the maximum subject to the constraints. If the constraints are correct, the unconstrained FOC will be $\text{O}(T^{-1/2})$ at the constrained estimate of $\boldsymbol{\theta}$.

The test was based originally on ML estimates but it can be based upon IV estimates.

Consider the constrained maximization problem

$$\max_{\boldsymbol{\theta}} l(\boldsymbol{\theta})$$

subject to

$$\boldsymbol{\phi}(\boldsymbol{\theta}) = 0$$

where $\boldsymbol{\theta}$ is a $(p \times 1)$ vector of parameters, and the constraints are $r \leq p$.

To obtain the FOCs consider the Lagrangian maximization

$$\max_{\boldsymbol{\theta}} l(\boldsymbol{\theta}) = L(\boldsymbol{\theta}) - \sqrt{T}\boldsymbol{\lambda}'\boldsymbol{\phi}(\boldsymbol{\theta}) \tag{9.15}$$

where $\boldsymbol{\lambda}$ is a vector of Lagrange multipliers with as many elements as constraints considered, i.e. an $(r \times 1)$ vector.

The FOCs for the maximum are:

$$\frac{1}{\sqrt{T}}\left(\frac{\partial L}{\partial \boldsymbol{\theta}'}\right)'_{\tilde{\boldsymbol{\theta}}} - \left(\frac{\partial \boldsymbol{\phi}}{\partial \boldsymbol{\phi}'}\right)'_{\tilde{\boldsymbol{\theta}}} \boldsymbol{\lambda} = 0. \tag{9.16}$$

We assume that the global constrained maximum of $L(\boldsymbol{\theta})$ gives us a consistent estimate in the neighbourhood of the true value $\bar{\boldsymbol{\theta}}$. We also assume that the Hessian is continuous at $\bar{\boldsymbol{\theta}}$, which ensures that there are continuous first derivatives in that neighbourhood.

Let the score be denoted by

$$L_\theta = \frac{1}{\sqrt{T}}\left(\frac{\partial L}{\partial \boldsymbol{\theta}'}\right)'_{\boldsymbol{\theta}=\bar{\boldsymbol{\theta}}}$$

where

$$L\,\theta \tilde{a}\ \mathrm{N}(0, \mathbf{V}_\theta) \tag{9.17}$$

(by applying the suitable Central Limit Theorem, since in a wide class of models L_θ is a sum of iid random variables), as discussed in Chapter 6.

The variance $\mathbf{V}_\theta$ can be derived assuming regularity conditions as

$$\mathbf{V}_\theta = \lim_{T\to\infty} \frac{1}{T}\mathrm{E}\left(\frac{\partial L}{\partial \boldsymbol{\theta}}\frac{\partial L}{\partial \boldsymbol{\theta}'}\right)_{\bar{\boldsymbol{\theta}}} \tag{9.18}$$

$$\operatorname{plim} \frac{1}{T}\left(\frac{\partial L}{\partial \boldsymbol{\theta}}\frac{\partial L}{\partial \boldsymbol{\theta}'}\right)_{\tilde{\boldsymbol{\theta}}} = -\operatorname{plim} \frac{1}{T}\left(\frac{\partial^2 L}{\partial \boldsymbol{\theta}\partial \boldsymbol{\theta}'}\right)_{\tilde{\boldsymbol{\theta}}}.$$

Making a first-order Taylor Series expansion of

$$\left(\frac{\partial L}{\partial \boldsymbol{\theta}'}\right)_{\tilde{\boldsymbol{\theta}}}$$

around $\bar{\boldsymbol{\theta}}$ yields

$$\frac{1}{\sqrt{T}}\left(\frac{\partial L}{\partial \boldsymbol{\theta}'}\right)'_{\tilde{\boldsymbol{\theta}}} = \frac{1}{\sqrt{T}}\left(\frac{\partial L}{\partial \boldsymbol{\theta}}\right)'_{\bar{\boldsymbol{\theta}}} + \frac{1}{\sqrt{T}}\left(\frac{\partial^2 L}{\partial \boldsymbol{\theta}\partial \boldsymbol{\theta}'}\right)_{\boldsymbol{\theta}^*} \sqrt{T}(\tilde{\boldsymbol{\theta}} - \bar{\boldsymbol{\theta}}) \tag{9.19}$$

where $\boldsymbol{\theta}^* = c\tilde{\boldsymbol{\theta}} + (1-c)\bar{\boldsymbol{\theta}}, 0 \leq c \leq 1$.

Substituting (9.19) into the FOCs (9.16) gives the $(p \times 1)$ vector

$$\frac{1}{T}\left(\frac{\partial^2 L}{\partial\boldsymbol{\theta}\partial\boldsymbol{\theta}'}\right)_{\boldsymbol{\theta}^*}\sqrt{T}(\tilde{\boldsymbol{\theta}} - \bar{\boldsymbol{\theta}}) - \left(\frac{\partial\boldsymbol{\phi}(\boldsymbol{\theta})}{\partial\boldsymbol{\theta}'}\right)'_{\tilde{\boldsymbol{\theta}}}\boldsymbol{\lambda} = -L_\theta. \tag{9.20}$$

Expanding also $\sqrt{T}\boldsymbol{\phi}(\boldsymbol{\theta}) = 0$ around $\bar{\boldsymbol{\theta}}$, gives the $(r \times 1)$ vector

$$\begin{aligned}\sqrt{T}\boldsymbol{\phi}(\tilde{\boldsymbol{\theta}}) = 0 &= \sqrt{T}\boldsymbol{\phi}(\bar{\boldsymbol{\theta}}) + \sqrt{T}\left(\frac{\partial\boldsymbol{\phi}}{\partial\boldsymbol{\theta}'}\right)'_{\boldsymbol{\theta}^+}(\tilde{\boldsymbol{\theta}} - \bar{\boldsymbol{\theta}})\\ &= \sqrt{T}\left(\frac{\partial\boldsymbol{\phi}}{\partial\boldsymbol{\theta}'}\right)'_{\boldsymbol{\theta}^+}(\tilde{\boldsymbol{\theta}} - \bar{\boldsymbol{\theta}})\end{aligned} \tag{9.21}$$

since $\boldsymbol{\phi}(\bar{\boldsymbol{\theta}}) = 0$, where $\boldsymbol{\theta}^+ = d\tilde{\boldsymbol{\theta}} + (1-d)\bar{\boldsymbol{\theta}}, 0 \leq d \leq 1$.

Hence we have $(p + r)$ equations linear in L_θ determining $(p + r)$ elements, p of $(\tilde{\boldsymbol{\theta}} - \bar{\boldsymbol{\theta}})$ and r of $\boldsymbol{\lambda}$.

Since our test is a quadratic form in the $\boldsymbol{\lambda}$s we need their asymptotic distribution. From (9.20)

$$\sqrt{T}(\tilde{\boldsymbol{\theta}} - \bar{\boldsymbol{\theta}}) = -\mathbf{V}_{\theta^*}^{-1}\left(\frac{\partial\boldsymbol{\phi}}{\partial\boldsymbol{\theta}'}\right)'_{\tilde{\boldsymbol{\theta}}}\boldsymbol{\lambda} + \mathbf{V}_{\theta^*}^{-1}L_\theta \tag{9.22}$$

where

$$\mathbf{V}_{\theta^*} = -\frac{1}{T}\left(\frac{\partial^2 L}{\partial\boldsymbol{\theta}\partial\boldsymbol{\theta}'}\right)_{\boldsymbol{\theta}^*}.$$

Multiplying (9.22) by

$$\sqrt{T}\left(\frac{\partial L}{\partial\boldsymbol{\theta}'}\right)_{\boldsymbol{\theta}^+}$$

and by noticing the relation (9.21)

$$\left(\frac{\partial\boldsymbol{\phi}}{\partial\boldsymbol{\theta}'}\right)_{\boldsymbol{\theta}^+}\mathbf{V}_{\theta^*}^{-1}\left(\frac{\partial\boldsymbol{\phi}'}{\partial\boldsymbol{\theta}^{*\prime}}\right)'_{\tilde{\boldsymbol{\theta}}}\boldsymbol{\lambda} = \left(\frac{\partial\boldsymbol{\phi}}{\partial\boldsymbol{\theta}'}\right)_{\boldsymbol{\theta}^+}\mathbf{V}_{\theta^*}^{-1}L_\theta. \tag{9.23}$$

Notice that

$$\frac{\partial\boldsymbol{\phi}}{\partial\boldsymbol{\theta}'}$$

is evaluated at different points, but asymptotically, these are equivalent.

Applying the Cramer Linear Transformation Theorem to (9.23) notice that $\text{plim}\mathbf{V}_{\theta^*} = \mathbf{V}_\theta$ and the asymptotic distribution given by (9.17)

$$\boldsymbol{\lambda} \ \tilde{\text{a}} \ \text{N}\left(0, \left[\left(\frac{\partial \boldsymbol{\phi}}{\partial \boldsymbol{\theta}'}\right)\mathbf{V}_{\theta}^{-1}\left(\frac{\partial \boldsymbol{\phi}}{\partial \boldsymbol{\theta}'}\right)\right]^{-1}\right) \tag{9.24}$$

on the null.

To obtain the asymptotic distribution of $\sqrt{T}(\tilde{\boldsymbol{\theta}} - \bar{\boldsymbol{\theta}})$, we substitute the expression of $\boldsymbol{\lambda}$ (9.23) into (9.22), which gives

$$\sqrt{T}(\tilde{\boldsymbol{\theta}} - \bar{\boldsymbol{\theta}})$$

$$= \mathbf{V}_{\theta^*}^{-1}L_\theta - \mathbf{V}_{\theta^*}^{-1}\left(\frac{\partial \boldsymbol{\phi}}{\partial \boldsymbol{\theta}'}\right)'_{\tilde{\boldsymbol{\theta}}}\left[\left(\frac{\partial \boldsymbol{\phi}}{\partial \boldsymbol{\theta}'}\right)_{\boldsymbol{\theta}^+}\mathbf{V}_{\theta^*}^{-1}\left(\frac{\partial \boldsymbol{\phi}}{\partial \boldsymbol{\theta}'}\right)'_{\tilde{\boldsymbol{\theta}}}\right]^{-1}\left(\frac{\partial \boldsymbol{\phi}}{\partial \boldsymbol{\theta}'}\right)_{\boldsymbol{\theta}^+}\mathbf{V}_{\theta^*}^{-1}L_\theta$$

$$= \left[\mathbf{V}_{\theta^*}^{-1} - \mathbf{V}_{\theta^*}^{-1}\left(\frac{\partial \boldsymbol{\phi}}{\partial \boldsymbol{\theta}'}\right)_{\tilde{\boldsymbol{\theta}}}\left[\left(\frac{\partial \boldsymbol{\phi}}{\partial \boldsymbol{\theta}'}\right)_{\boldsymbol{\theta}^+}\mathbf{V}_{\theta^*}^{-1}\left(\frac{\partial \boldsymbol{\phi}}{\partial \boldsymbol{\theta}'}\right)'_{\tilde{\boldsymbol{\theta}}}\right]^{-1}\left(\frac{\partial \boldsymbol{\phi}}{\partial \boldsymbol{\theta}'}\right)_{\boldsymbol{\theta}^+}\mathbf{V}_{\theta^*}^{-1}\right]L_\theta$$

and applying the Cramer Linear Transformation Theorem

$$\sqrt{T}(\tilde{\boldsymbol{\theta}}-\bar{\boldsymbol{\theta}}) \ \tilde{\text{a}} \ \text{N}\left(0,\left[\mathbf{V}_{\theta}^{-1}-\mathbf{V}_{\theta}^{-1}\left(\frac{\partial \boldsymbol{\phi}}{\partial \boldsymbol{\theta}'}\right)\left[\left(\frac{\partial \boldsymbol{\phi}}{\partial \boldsymbol{\theta}'}\right)\mathbf{V}_{\theta}^{-1}\left(\frac{\partial \boldsymbol{\phi}}{\partial \boldsymbol{\theta}'}\right)'\right]^{-1}\left(\frac{\partial \boldsymbol{\phi}}{\partial \boldsymbol{\theta}'}\right)\mathbf{V}_{\theta}^{-1}\right]\right).$$

If we had reparameterized the constraints in order to get zero–one restrictions by $\boldsymbol{\theta} = \mathbf{g}(\boldsymbol{\psi})$, then by maximizing $L[\mathbf{g}(\boldsymbol{\psi})]$ with respect to $\boldsymbol{\psi}_1$ setting $\boldsymbol{\psi}_2 = 0$ we will obtain the same maximum as if we had used $L(\boldsymbol{\theta})$ and $\boldsymbol{\phi}(\boldsymbol{\theta}) = 0$.

As before define $L[\mathbf{g}(\boldsymbol{\psi})] = L^*(\boldsymbol{\psi})$. The Hessian associated with L^* will give an estimate of the AVM for the constrained estimates

$$\mathbf{H}^* = \text{plim}\left[-\frac{1}{T}\left(\frac{\partial^2 L}{\partial \boldsymbol{\psi}_1 \partial \boldsymbol{\psi}'_1}\right)_{\tilde{\psi}}\right]^{-1}$$

which is somewhat simpler than the last variance matrix formula.

To obtain the AVM $\sqrt{T}(\tilde{\boldsymbol{\theta}} - \bar{\boldsymbol{\theta}})$ take a Taylor Series expansion of $\tilde{\boldsymbol{\theta}}$ around $\bar{\boldsymbol{\theta}}$

$$\tilde{\boldsymbol{\theta}} - \bar{\boldsymbol{\theta}} = \left(\frac{\partial \mathbf{g}}{\partial \boldsymbol{\psi}'_1}\right)(\tilde{\boldsymbol{\psi}}_1 - \boldsymbol{\psi}_1)$$

and applying the Cramer Linear Transformation Theorem

$$\text{AVM}\sqrt{T}(\tilde{\boldsymbol{\theta}} - \bar{\boldsymbol{\theta}}) = \left(\frac{\partial \mathbf{g}}{\partial \boldsymbol{\psi}'_1}\right)\mathbf{H}^*\left(\frac{\partial \mathbf{g}}{\partial \boldsymbol{\psi}'_1}\right)$$

Since $\boldsymbol{\psi}$ is of dimension $(p - r)$ and $\mathbf{H}^*$ is a $(p - r) \times (p - r)$ matrix, then the rank of AVM $\sqrt{T}(\tilde{\boldsymbol{\theta}} - \bar{\boldsymbol{\theta}})$ is $(p - r)$ provided $\mathbf{H}^*$ is of full rank. The equivalence of this reparameterization method to the original one can be demonstrated, and it is worth working with the reparameterization approach because it reduces computing problems for the numerical optimization.

From (9.24) we can state that on the null

$$\boldsymbol{\lambda}'(\mathbf{V}_{\lambda}^{-1})\boldsymbol{\lambda} \;\tilde{\text{a}}\; \chi_r^2 \tag{9.25}$$

where

$$\mathbf{V}_{\lambda}^{-1} = \left[\left(\frac{\partial \boldsymbol{\phi}}{\partial \boldsymbol{\theta}'}\right)\mathbf{V}_{\theta}^{-1}\left(\frac{\partial \boldsymbol{\phi}}{\partial \boldsymbol{\theta}'}\right)'\right]$$

which is the *LM test statistic*.

The *feasible LM test* is obtained by using an estimate of the AVM of $\boldsymbol{\lambda}$, i.e.

$$\hat{\mathbf{V}}_{\lambda}^{-1} = \left(\frac{\partial \boldsymbol{\phi}}{\partial \boldsymbol{\theta}'}\right)_{\tilde{\boldsymbol{\theta}}} \tilde{\mathbf{V}}_{\theta}^{-1}\left(\frac{\partial \boldsymbol{\phi}}{\partial \boldsymbol{\theta}'}\right)_{\tilde{\boldsymbol{\theta}}}'$$

and substituting in (9.25)

$$\boldsymbol{\lambda}'\hat{\mathbf{V}}_{\lambda}^{-1}\boldsymbol{\lambda} \;\tilde{\text{a}}\; \chi_r^2 \tag{9.26}$$

on the null.

Expression $\boldsymbol{\lambda}'\hat{\mathbf{V}}_{\lambda}^{-1}$ can be written as

$$\boldsymbol{\lambda}'\left(\frac{\partial \boldsymbol{\phi}}{\partial \boldsymbol{\theta}'}\right)_{\tilde{\boldsymbol{\theta}}} \tilde{\mathbf{V}}_{\theta}^{-1}\left(\frac{\partial \boldsymbol{\phi}}{\partial \boldsymbol{\theta}'}\right)_{\tilde{\boldsymbol{\theta}}}' \boldsymbol{\lambda}.$$

But from (9.16)

$$\boldsymbol{\lambda}'\left(\frac{\partial \boldsymbol{\phi}}{\partial \boldsymbol{\theta}'}\right)_{\tilde{\boldsymbol{\theta}}} \boldsymbol{\lambda} = \frac{1}{\sqrt{T}}\left(\frac{\partial L}{\partial \boldsymbol{\theta}'}\right)_{\tilde{\boldsymbol{\theta}}}.$$

Hence using (9.18) and (9.16), we can write (9.26) as

$$\frac{1}{T}\left(\frac{\partial L}{\partial \boldsymbol{\theta}'}\right)\tilde{\mathbf{V}}_{\theta}^{-1}\left(\frac{\partial L}{\partial \boldsymbol{\theta}'}\right)' = \left(\frac{\partial L}{\partial \boldsymbol{\theta}'}\right)\left(\frac{\partial^2 L}{\partial \boldsymbol{\theta}\partial \boldsymbol{\theta}'}\right)_{\tilde{\boldsymbol{\theta}}}^{-1}\left(\frac{\partial L}{\partial \boldsymbol{\theta}'}\right)' \;\tilde{\text{a}}\; \chi_r^2 \tag{9.27}$$

which is also called the *score test*.

The LM test is a kind of diagnostic test since we use the constrained estimates. For instance, if we run a regression by least squares and we test the constraints that the coefficients of the autoregressive structure of the errors are zero, we are making a post-diagnostic test. The disadvantage is that it is not very useful if we start with considerable doubt about what the final form of our model should be, i.e. what constraints can be expected to be statistically acceptable.

9.3.2 Equivalence between the Wald Test and the LM Test

Consider again equation (9.23), i.e.

$$\left(\frac{\partial \boldsymbol{\phi}}{\partial \boldsymbol{\theta}'}\right)_{\boldsymbol{\theta}^+} \mathbf{V}_{\theta^*}^{-1} \left(\frac{\partial \boldsymbol{\phi}}{\partial \boldsymbol{\theta}'}\right)'_{\tilde{\boldsymbol{\theta}}} \boldsymbol{\lambda} = \left(\frac{\partial \boldsymbol{\phi}}{\partial \boldsymbol{\theta}'}\right)_{\boldsymbol{\theta}^+} \mathbf{V}_{\theta^*}^{-1} L_{\theta}.$$

We know that the FOC defining $\hat{\boldsymbol{\theta}}$ are

$$\left(\frac{\partial L}{\partial \boldsymbol{\theta}}\right)_{\hat{\boldsymbol{\theta}}} = 0.$$

Doing a Taylor Series expansion of this around $\bar{\boldsymbol{\theta}}$ we obtain,

$$-\frac{1}{T}\left(\frac{\partial^2 L}{\partial \boldsymbol{\theta} \partial \boldsymbol{\theta}'}\right)_{\boldsymbol{\theta}^0} \sqrt{T}(\hat{\boldsymbol{\theta}} - \bar{\boldsymbol{\theta}}) = L_{\theta} \tag{9.28}$$

where $\boldsymbol{\theta}^0 = b\hat{\boldsymbol{\theta}} + (1-b)\bar{\boldsymbol{\theta}}$, $0 \leq b \leq 1$, and L_θ is the score defined already in (9.17) as

$$L_\theta = \frac{1}{\sqrt{T}}\left(\frac{\partial L}{\partial \boldsymbol{\theta}'}\right)_{\bar{\boldsymbol{\theta}}}.$$

Substituting (9.28) into (9.23) we have

$$\left(\frac{\partial \boldsymbol{\phi}}{\partial \boldsymbol{\theta}'}\right)_{\boldsymbol{\theta}^+} \mathbf{V}_{\theta^*}^{-1} \left(\frac{\partial \boldsymbol{\phi}}{\partial \boldsymbol{\theta}'}\right)'_{\tilde{\boldsymbol{\theta}}} \boldsymbol{\lambda} = \left(\frac{\partial \boldsymbol{\phi}}{\partial \boldsymbol{\theta}'}\right)'_{\boldsymbol{\theta}^+} \mathbf{V}_{\theta^*}^{-1} \left(-\frac{1}{T}\frac{\partial^2 L}{\partial \boldsymbol{\theta} \partial \boldsymbol{\theta}'}\right)_{\boldsymbol{\theta}^0} \sqrt{T}(\hat{\boldsymbol{\theta}} - \bar{\boldsymbol{\theta}}). \tag{9.29}$$

Notice that $\mathbf{V}_{\theta^*}$ and

$$-\left(\frac{1}{T}\frac{\partial^2 L}{\partial \boldsymbol{\theta} \partial \boldsymbol{\theta}'}\right)_{\boldsymbol{\theta}^0}$$

are the same Hessian matrix worked out at different points in the neighbourhood of $\bar{\boldsymbol{\theta}}$. Assuming continuity, the product

$$\mathbf{V}_{\theta^*}^{-1}\left(-\frac{1}{T}\frac{\partial^2 L}{\partial \boldsymbol{\theta} \partial \boldsymbol{\theta}'}\right)_{\boldsymbol{\theta}^0} = \mathbf{I} + \mathrm{O}(1/\sqrt{T})$$

where $\mathbf{I}$ is the identity matrix. Therefore the right-hand side of (9.29) is just

$$\left(\frac{\partial \boldsymbol{\phi}}{\partial \boldsymbol{\theta}'}\right)_{\boldsymbol{\theta}^+} \sqrt{T}(\hat{\boldsymbol{\theta}} - \bar{\boldsymbol{\theta}}) + \mathrm{O}(1/\sqrt{T})$$

or

$$\left(\frac{\partial \boldsymbol{\phi}}{\partial \boldsymbol{\theta}'}\right)_{\bar{\boldsymbol{\theta}}} \sqrt{T}(\hat{\boldsymbol{\theta}} - \bar{\boldsymbol{\theta}}) + \mathrm{O}(1/\sqrt{T})$$

and this is just the first-order Taylor Series expansion of $\sqrt{T}\boldsymbol{\phi}(\hat{\boldsymbol{\theta}})$ around $\bar{\boldsymbol{\theta}}$.

Hence we can write (9.29) as

$$\left(\frac{\partial \boldsymbol{\phi}}{\partial \boldsymbol{\theta}'}\right)_{\boldsymbol{\theta}^+} \mathbf{V}_{\theta^*}^{-1}\left(\frac{\partial \boldsymbol{\phi}}{\partial \boldsymbol{\theta}'}\right)'_{\tilde{\boldsymbol{\theta}}} \boldsymbol{\lambda} = \sqrt{T}\boldsymbol{\phi}(\hat{\boldsymbol{\theta}}) + \mathrm{O}\left(\frac{1}{\sqrt{T}}\right). \tag{9.30}$$

Notice how (9.30) is going to give us the relation of asymptotic equivalence between both tests.

Consider the expressions of both tests:

The quadratic form of the LM test is, from (9.26)

$$\boldsymbol{\lambda}'\hat{\mathbf{V}}_{\lambda}^{-1}\boldsymbol{\lambda} = \boldsymbol{\lambda}'\left(\frac{\partial \boldsymbol{\phi}}{\partial \boldsymbol{\theta}'}\right)_{\tilde{\boldsymbol{\theta}}} \mathbf{V}_{\boldsymbol{\theta}}^{-1}\left(\frac{\partial \boldsymbol{\phi}}{\partial \boldsymbol{\theta}'}\right)' \boldsymbol{\lambda}.$$

The quadratic form of the Wald test is from (9.10)

$$\sqrt{T}\boldsymbol{\phi}(\hat{\boldsymbol{\theta}})'\left[\left(\frac{\partial \boldsymbol{\phi}}{\partial \boldsymbol{\theta}'}\right)_{\hat{\boldsymbol{\theta}}} \hat{\mathbf{V}}_{\theta}^{-1}\left(\frac{\partial \boldsymbol{\phi}}{\partial \boldsymbol{\theta}'}\right)'_{\hat{\boldsymbol{\theta}}}\right]^{-1} \sqrt{T}\boldsymbol{\phi}(\hat{\boldsymbol{\theta}}).$$

Denote

$$\hat{\mathbf{V}}_{\theta}^{-1} = \left[\left(\frac{\partial \boldsymbol{\phi}}{\partial \boldsymbol{\theta}'}\right)_{\hat{\boldsymbol{\theta}}} \hat{\mathbf{V}}_{\theta}^{-1}\left(\frac{\partial \boldsymbol{\phi}}{\partial \boldsymbol{\theta}'}\right)'_{\hat{\boldsymbol{\theta}}}\right]^{-1}$$

for simplicity of notation.

Let us compare the two test statistics

$$\mathrm{LM} - \mathrm{W} = \boldsymbol{\lambda}\hat{\mathbf{V}}_{\lambda}^{-1}\boldsymbol{\lambda} - \sqrt{T}\boldsymbol{\phi}(\hat{\boldsymbol{\theta}})'\hat{\mathbf{V}}_{\phi}^{-1}\sqrt{T}\boldsymbol{\phi}(\hat{\boldsymbol{\theta}}). \tag{9.31}$$

From (9.30) taking plim we can see that

$$\sqrt{T}\boldsymbol{\phi}(\hat{\boldsymbol{\theta}})' = \boldsymbol{\lambda}'\hat{\mathbf{V}}_{\lambda}^{-1} + \mathrm{O}(T^{-1/2}).$$

Therefore (9.31) becomes

$$\boldsymbol{\lambda}'[\hat{\mathbf{V}}_{\lambda}^{-1} - \hat{\mathbf{V}}_{\lambda}^{-1}\mathbf{V}_{\phi}^{-1}\hat{\mathbf{V}}_{\lambda}^{-1}]\boldsymbol{\lambda} + \mathrm{O}(T^{-1/2})$$

and since $\operatorname{plim}\hat{\mathbf{V}}_{\lambda}^{-1} = \operatorname{plim}\mathbf{V}_{\phi}^{-1} = \bar{\mathbf{V}}_{\lambda}^{-1}$ this can be expressed as

$$\boldsymbol{\lambda}'(\bar{\mathbf{V}}_{\lambda}^{-1} - \bar{\mathbf{V}}_{\lambda}^{-1}\bar{\mathbf{V}}_{\lambda}\bar{\mathbf{V}}_{\lambda}^{-1})\boldsymbol{\lambda} + \mathrm{O}\left(\frac{1}{\sqrt{T}}\right)$$

and therefore

$$\mathrm{LM} - \mathrm{W} = \mathrm{O}\left(\frac{1}{\sqrt{T}}\right)$$

and hence is asymptotically negligible.

By applying the Mann and Wald Approximation Theorem, we can conclude that both test statistics have the same asymptotic distribution. This equivalence can be easily extended to the LR test since as we saw in section 1.2.3. it is equivalent asymptotically to the Wald test. Finally it is possible to show that the LR test can be developed from a concentrated likelihood function provided that the test constraints are functions only of the parameters contained in the concentrated likelihood function.

9.3.3 Special Case: LM Test for Single Equations

For generality consider the non-linear in parameters single equation

$$\mathbf{y} = \mathbf{X}\mathbf{a}(\boldsymbol{\theta}) + \mathbf{u}, \quad \mathbf{u} \sim \mathrm{N}(0, \sigma^2 \mathbf{I}_T)$$

where $\boldsymbol{\theta}$ is a $(p \times 1)$ vector of parameters, and let us split $\boldsymbol{\theta}$ into

$$\boldsymbol{\theta} = \begin{pmatrix} \boldsymbol{\theta}_1 \\ \boldsymbol{\theta}_2 \end{pmatrix}$$

where $\boldsymbol{\theta}_2$ is an $(r \times 1)$ vector.

The log likelihood function for a single equation of this type is

$$L = k - \tfrac{1}{2} T \log \sigma^2 - \tfrac{1}{2} \frac{\mathbf{u}'\mathbf{u}}{\sigma^2}$$

where $\mathbf{u} = \mathbf{y} - \mathbf{X}\mathbf{a}(\boldsymbol{\theta})$.

We want to consider constraints of the type $\boldsymbol{\theta}_2 = 0$. Denote by $\hat{\boldsymbol{\theta}}$ the LM estimates of the constrained set of parameters, i.e.

$$\hat{\boldsymbol{\theta}} = \begin{pmatrix} \hat{\boldsymbol{\theta}}_1 \\ \mathbf{O} \end{pmatrix}.$$

Instead of forming the Lagrangian, introduce directly the constraints into the likelihood maximization problem.

Consider

$$L = k - \tfrac{1}{2} T \log \hat{\sigma}^2 - \frac{1}{2} \frac{\hat{\mathbf{u}}'\hat{\mathbf{u}}}{\hat{\sigma}^2}$$

where $\hat{\mathbf{u}} = \mathbf{y} - \mathbf{X}\mathbf{a}(\hat{\boldsymbol{\theta}})$ and

$$\hat{\sigma}^2 = \frac{\hat{\mathbf{u}}'\hat{\mathbf{u}}}{T}.$$

Concentrating with respect to $\hat{\sigma}^2$ we obtain

$$L^* = k^* - \tfrac{1}{2}T\log\frac{\hat{\mathbf{u}}'\hat{\mathbf{u}}}{T}.$$

To form the LM test statistic, recall from (9.27) that we need the first and second derivatives of the constrained log likelihood function.

Then

$$\left(\frac{\partial L^*}{\partial \boldsymbol{\theta}'}\right)' = \frac{1}{\hat{\sigma}^2}\left(\frac{\partial \mathbf{a}(\boldsymbol{\theta})}{\partial \boldsymbol{\theta}'}\right)'_{\hat{\boldsymbol{\theta}}}\mathbf{X}'\hat{\mathbf{u}} \tag{9.32}$$

and

$$\frac{1}{T}\frac{\partial^2 L^*}{\partial \boldsymbol{\theta}\partial \boldsymbol{\theta}'} = -\frac{1}{\hat{\sigma}^2}\left(\frac{\partial \mathbf{a}(\boldsymbol{\theta})}{\partial \boldsymbol{\theta}'}\right)'_{\hat{\boldsymbol{\theta}}}\frac{\mathbf{X}'\mathbf{X}}{T}\left(\frac{\partial \mathbf{a}(\boldsymbol{\theta})}{\partial \boldsymbol{\theta}'}\right)_{\hat{\boldsymbol{\theta}}}$$
$$+\frac{1}{\hat{\sigma}^2}\frac{\partial^2}{\partial \boldsymbol{\theta}\partial \boldsymbol{\theta}'}\left(\mathbf{a}(\boldsymbol{\theta})'\frac{\mathbf{X}'\mathbf{u}}{T}\right) + \frac{1}{\hat{\sigma}^4}\left[\left(\frac{\partial \mathbf{a}(\boldsymbol{\theta})}{\partial \boldsymbol{\theta}'}\right)'_{\hat{\boldsymbol{\theta}}}\mathbf{X}'\hat{\mathbf{u}}\right]^2 \tag{9.33}$$

and the last two terms can be shown to be $O(T^{-1/2})$.

Substituting (9.32) and (9.33) into the usual LM statistic (9.27) we have

$$\left(\frac{\partial L^*}{\partial \boldsymbol{\theta}'}\right)\left(-\frac{\partial^2 L^*}{\partial \boldsymbol{\theta}\partial \boldsymbol{\theta}'}\right)^{-1}\left(\frac{\partial L^*}{\partial \boldsymbol{\theta}}\right)$$
$$= \frac{1}{\hat{\sigma}^2}\hat{\mathbf{u}}'\mathbf{X}\left[\frac{\partial \mathbf{a}(\boldsymbol{\theta})}{\partial \boldsymbol{\theta}'}\right]_{\hat{\boldsymbol{\theta}}}\left\{\left[\frac{\partial \mathbf{a}(\boldsymbol{\theta})}{\partial \boldsymbol{\theta}'}\right]'_{\hat{\boldsymbol{\theta}}}\mathbf{X}'\mathbf{X}\left[\frac{\partial \mathbf{a}(\boldsymbol{\theta})}{\partial \boldsymbol{\theta}'}\right]_{\hat{\boldsymbol{\theta}}}\right\}^{-1}\left[\frac{\partial \mathbf{a}(\boldsymbol{\theta})}{\partial \boldsymbol{\theta}'}\right]'_{\hat{\boldsymbol{\theta}}}\mathbf{X}'\hat{\mathbf{u}}$$
$$+ O(T^{-1/2})$$

or letting

$$\mathbf{X}^* = \mathbf{X}\left[\frac{\partial \mathbf{a}(\boldsymbol{\theta})}{\partial \boldsymbol{\theta}'}\right]_{\hat{\boldsymbol{\theta}}}$$
$$= \frac{1}{\hat{\sigma}^2}\hat{\mathbf{u}}'\mathbf{X}^*(\mathbf{X}^{*\prime}\mathbf{X}^*)^{-1}\mathbf{X}^{*\prime}\hat{\mathbf{u}}. \tag{9.34}$$

We can think of this as running a regression of $\hat{\mathbf{u}}$ on $\mathbf{X}^*$. Let

$$\hat{\mathbf{u}} = \mathbf{X}^*\boldsymbol{\beta} + \mathbf{u}^*.$$

The regression coefficient will be

$$\boldsymbol{\beta}^* = (\mathbf{X}^{*\prime}\mathbf{X}^*)^{-1}\mathbf{X}^{*\prime}\hat{\mathbf{u}}$$

and the residuals are

$$\tilde{\mathbf{u}}^{+} = \hat{\mathbf{u}} - \mathbf{X}^{*}\boldsymbol{\beta}^{*}. \tag{9.35}$$

Thus

$$\tilde{\mathbf{u}}^{+\prime}\tilde{\mathbf{u}}^{+} = \hat{\mathbf{u}}'\hat{\mathbf{u}} - \hat{\mathbf{u}}'\mathbf{X}^{*}(\mathbf{X}^{*\prime}\mathbf{X}^{*})^{-1}\mathbf{X}^{*\prime}\hat{\mathbf{u}}$$

and therefore the LM statistic (9.34) can be written as

$$\frac{1}{\hat{\sigma}^2}(\hat{\mathbf{u}}'\hat{\mathbf{u}} - \tilde{\mathbf{u}}^{+\prime}\tilde{\mathbf{u}}^{+}) = T\left[\frac{\hat{\mathbf{u}}'\hat{\mathbf{u}} - \tilde{\mathbf{u}}^{+\prime}\tilde{\mathbf{u}}^{+}}{\hat{\mathbf{u}}'\hat{\mathbf{u}}}\right]. \tag{9.36}$$

Notice that the term in brackets has a formal expression similar to that of a coefficient of determination since $\hat{\mathbf{u}}$ is the dependent variable in (9.35) and $\tilde{\mathbf{u}}^{+}$ the residual estimate. The fact that it is not an exact R^2 is due to not having taken deviations from the mean in defining $\hat{\mathbf{u}}^{+}$.

Expression (9.36) indicates how LM = TR^2. Notice that (9.36) is an F-test statistic except for the constant factor r. Also notice that since we dropped the $O(T^{-1/2})$ terms in (9.33) when substituting in (9.27) what we have obtained is not an *exact* LM test.

9.4 Small Sample Comparisons

We have seen how asymptotically the three test statistic procedures that we have considered, LR test, W test and LM test have the same asymptotic distribution, and how they differ basically in the point at which $\mathbf{V}_{\theta}^{-1}$ is estimated. We will for the important constrained regression model now prove that the inequality

$$W > LR > LM$$

holds in every sample.

Consider a set of linear constraints in a linear regression model (this proof can be extended to non-linear restrictions also). We look to the concentrated likelihood function of the basic model using the reduced form,

$$\mathbf{Y}' = \mathbf{P}\mathbf{Z}' + \mathbf{V}' \tag{9.37}$$

and consider a set of constraints on (9.37)

$$\boldsymbol{\Phi}\,\mathrm{vec}\,\mathbf{P} = \boldsymbol{\phi}. \tag{9.38}$$

We will denote the constrained estimates (which here means constrained ML estimates) by '~' and the unconstrained (which here means OLS) by '^'.

The concentrated likelihood function has the form

$$L^* = k^* - \frac{T}{2}\log\det\left[\frac{(\mathbf{Y}' - \mathbf{PZ}')(\mathbf{Y} - \mathbf{ZP}')}{T}\right]$$

and we maximize L^* subject to the constraints. The Lagrangian will be

$$C = k^* - \frac{T}{2}\log\det\left[\frac{(\mathbf{Y}' - \mathbf{PZ}')(\mathbf{Y} - \mathbf{ZP}')}{T}\right] + [(\boldsymbol{\Phi}\,\mathrm{vec}\,\mathbf{P} - \boldsymbol{\phi})'\boldsymbol{\lambda}].$$

The FOCs of the constrained estimate will, as before, be in differential form

$$-\frac{T}{2}\mathrm{tr}\left[\widetilde{\boldsymbol{\Omega}}_{\mathrm{v}}^{-1}(-2)\frac{(\mathbf{Y}' - \widetilde{\mathbf{P}}\mathbf{Z}')\mathbf{Z}}{T}\mathrm{d}\widetilde{\mathbf{P}}'\right] + \boldsymbol{\lambda}'\boldsymbol{\Phi}\,\mathrm{vec}\,\mathrm{d}\widetilde{\mathbf{P}} = 0$$

and using the fact that $\mathrm{tr}(\mathbf{H}\,\mathrm{d}\mathbf{A}') = (\mathrm{vec}\,\mathbf{H})'\,\mathrm{vec}\,\mathrm{d}\mathbf{A}$, we have

$$\{\mathrm{vec}[\widetilde{\boldsymbol{\Omega}}_{\mathrm{v}}^{-1}(\mathbf{Y}' - \widetilde{\mathbf{P}}\mathbf{Z}')\mathbf{Z}]\}'\,\mathrm{vec}\,\mathrm{d}\widetilde{\mathbf{P}} + \boldsymbol{\lambda}'\boldsymbol{\Phi}\,\mathrm{vec}\,\mathrm{d}\widetilde{\mathbf{P}} = 0$$

or

$$\mathrm{vec}[\widetilde{\boldsymbol{\Omega}}_{\mathrm{v}}^{-1}(\mathbf{Y}' - \widetilde{\mathbf{P}}\,\mathbf{Z}')\mathbf{Z}] + \boldsymbol{\Phi}'\boldsymbol{\lambda} = 0. \qquad (9.39)$$

so

$$\mathrm{vec}[\widetilde{\boldsymbol{\Omega}}_{\mathrm{v}}^{-1}\mathbf{Y}'\mathbf{Z}] + \boldsymbol{\Phi}'\boldsymbol{\lambda} = \mathrm{vec}[\widetilde{\boldsymbol{\Omega}}_{\mathrm{v}}^{-1}\widetilde{\mathbf{P}}(\mathbf{Z}'\mathbf{Z})]$$

and applying $\mathrm{vec}(\mathbf{ABC}) = (\mathbf{A} \otimes \mathbf{C}')\,\mathrm{vec}\,\mathbf{B}$

$$(\boldsymbol{\Omega}_{\mathrm{v}}^{-1} \otimes \mathbf{Z}'\mathbf{Z})\,\mathrm{vec}\,\widetilde{\mathbf{P}} = \boldsymbol{\Phi}'\boldsymbol{\lambda} + (\widetilde{\boldsymbol{\Omega}}_{\mathrm{v}}^{-1} \otimes \mathbf{I})\,\mathrm{vec}\,(\mathbf{Y}'\mathbf{Z}).$$

Solving for vec $\widetilde{\mathbf{P}}$ and substituting in the constraints (9.38) we have

$$\boldsymbol{\phi} = \boldsymbol{\Phi}\,\mathrm{vec}\,\widetilde{\mathbf{P}} = \boldsymbol{\Phi}[\boldsymbol{\Omega}_{\mathrm{v}} \otimes (\mathbf{Z}'\mathbf{Z})^{-1}]\boldsymbol{\Phi}'\boldsymbol{\lambda} + \boldsymbol{\Phi}\,\mathrm{vec}[\mathbf{Y}'\mathbf{Z}(\mathbf{Z}'\mathbf{Z})^{-1}]. \qquad (9.40)$$

Notice that the last term on the right-hand side $\mathbf{Y}'\mathbf{Z}(\mathbf{Z}'\mathbf{Z})^{-1}$ is the OLS estimate of $\mathbf{P}$, i.e. the unconstrained estimate $\hat{\mathbf{P}}$. Therefore solving for $\boldsymbol{\lambda}$

$$\boldsymbol{\lambda} = \{\boldsymbol{\Phi}[\widetilde{\boldsymbol{\Omega}}_{\mathrm{v}} \otimes (\mathbf{Z}'\mathbf{Z})^{-1}]\boldsymbol{\Phi}'\}^{-1}(\boldsymbol{\phi} - \boldsymbol{\Phi}\,\mathrm{vec}\,\hat{\mathbf{P}}) \qquad (9.41)$$

and from the LM test statistic formula (9.25), the LM test statistic in this case is

$$\mathrm{LM} = \boldsymbol{\lambda}'\{\boldsymbol{\Phi}[\widetilde{\boldsymbol{\Omega}}_{\mathrm{v}} \otimes (\mathbf{Z}'\mathbf{Z})^{-1}]\boldsymbol{\Phi}'\}\boldsymbol{\lambda} \qquad (9.42)$$

which substituting (9.41) becomes

$$\text{LM} = (\boldsymbol{\phi} - \boldsymbol{\Phi}\,\text{vec}\,\hat{\mathbf{P}})'\{\boldsymbol{\Phi}[\tilde{\boldsymbol{\Omega}}_{\text{v}} \otimes (\mathbf{Z}'\mathbf{Z})^{-1}]\boldsymbol{\Phi}'\}^{-1}(\boldsymbol{\phi} - \boldsymbol{\Phi}\,\text{vec}\,\hat{\mathbf{P}}). \tag{9.43}$$

From (9.40) we can write

$$\boldsymbol{\Phi}'\boldsymbol{\lambda} = (\hat{\boldsymbol{\Omega}}_{\text{v}}^{-1} \otimes \mathbf{Z}'\mathbf{Z})\,\text{vec}(\tilde{\mathbf{P}} - \hat{\mathbf{P}})$$

and substituting it into (9.42) yields

$$\text{LM} = [\text{vec}(\tilde{\mathbf{P}} - \hat{\mathbf{P}})'(\tilde{\boldsymbol{\Omega}}_{\text{v}}^{-1} \otimes \mathbf{Z}'\mathbf{Z})\,\text{vec}(\tilde{\mathbf{P}} - \hat{\mathbf{P}})]$$

and using fact that $\text{tr}(\mathbf{ABCD}) = (\text{vec}\,\mathbf{B})'(\mathbf{A} \otimes \mathbf{C}')\,\text{vec}\,\mathbf{D}'$, this becomes

$$\text{LM} = \text{tr}[\tilde{\boldsymbol{\Omega}}_{\text{v}}^{-1}(\tilde{\mathbf{P}} - \hat{\mathbf{P}})(\mathbf{Z}'\mathbf{Z})(\tilde{\mathbf{P}} - \hat{\mathbf{P}})'].$$

Substituting $\hat{\mathbf{P}} = \mathbf{Y}'\mathbf{Z}(\mathbf{Z}'\mathbf{Z})^{-1}$ and rearranging, the LM becomes

$$\begin{aligned}\text{LM} &= \text{tr}\{\tilde{\boldsymbol{\Omega}}_{\text{v}}^{-1}[(\mathbf{Y}' - \tilde{\mathbf{P}}\mathbf{Z}')(\mathbf{Y} - \mathbf{Z}\tilde{\mathbf{P}}') \\ &\quad - (\mathbf{Y}'\mathbf{Y} - \mathbf{Y}'\mathbf{Z}(\mathbf{Z}'\mathbf{Z})^{-1}(\mathbf{Z}'\mathbf{Y})]\} \\ &= T\,\text{tr}[\tilde{\boldsymbol{\Omega}}_{\text{v}}^{-1}(\tilde{\boldsymbol{\Omega}}_{\text{v}} - \hat{\boldsymbol{\Omega}}_{\text{v}})].\end{aligned} \tag{9.44}$$

Consider now the *Wald test criteria*. The Wald criterion (9.12) can be written now as

$$(\boldsymbol{\Phi}\,\text{vec}\,\hat{\mathbf{P}} - \boldsymbol{\phi})'\{\boldsymbol{\Phi}[\hat{\boldsymbol{\Omega}}_{\text{v}} \otimes (\mathbf{Z}'\mathbf{Z})^{-1}]\boldsymbol{\Phi}'\}^{-1}(\boldsymbol{\Phi}\,\text{vec}\,\hat{\mathbf{P}} - \boldsymbol{\phi}). \tag{9.45}$$

Notice that this is very similar to (9.43), the difference being the type of estimator used for $\boldsymbol{\Omega}_{\text{v}}$ ('$\hat{}$' rather than at '$\sim$').

Now consider maximizing the log likelihood function by the Cochrane–Orcutt method using the two sets of parameters $\boldsymbol{\Omega}_{\text{v}}$ and $\mathbf{P}$. We obtain a preliminary estimate of $\boldsymbol{\Omega}_{\text{v}}$ by applying the unconstrained OLS estimates of $\mathbf{P}$. We then maximize the likelihood function with respect to $\mathbf{P}$, for this value of $\boldsymbol{\Omega}_{\text{v}} = \hat{\boldsymbol{\Omega}}_{\text{v}}$. We next maximize the likelihood function with respect to $\boldsymbol{\Omega}_{\text{v}}$, keeping $\mathbf{P}$ constant, and so on. Take the first two stages of the process, i.e.

$$\min(\text{tr}\,\hat{\boldsymbol{\Omega}}_{\text{v}}^{-1}\mathbf{V}'\mathbf{V})$$

subject to

$$\boldsymbol{\Phi}\,\text{vec}\,\mathbf{P} = \boldsymbol{\phi}.$$

The corresponding Lagrangian is

$$\begin{aligned}\mathbf{C} &= -\tfrac{1}{2}\,\text{tr}(\hat{\boldsymbol{\Omega}}_{\text{v}}^{-1}\mathbf{V}'\mathbf{V}) + (\boldsymbol{\Phi}\,\text{vec}\,\mathbf{P} - \boldsymbol{\phi})'\boldsymbol{\lambda}^* \\ &= -\tfrac{1}{2}\sum_t \mathbf{v}_t\hat{\boldsymbol{\Omega}}_{\text{v}}^{-1}\mathbf{v}_t' + (\boldsymbol{\Phi}\,\text{vec}\,\mathbf{P} - \boldsymbol{\phi})'\boldsymbol{\lambda}^*\end{aligned}$$

$$= -\tfrac{1}{2}\sum_t (\mathbf{y}_t - \mathbf{z}_t\mathbf{P}')\hat{\mathbf{\Omega}}_{\mathrm{v}}^{-1}(\mathbf{y}_t - \mathbf{z}_t\mathbf{P}')' + (\mathbf{\Phi}\,\mathrm{vec}\,\mathbf{P} - \boldsymbol{\phi})'\boldsymbol{\lambda}^*.$$

The FOCs are given by

$$\begin{aligned} \mathrm{d}C &= \sum_t \mathbf{z}_t\,\mathrm{d}\mathbf{P}'\hat{\mathbf{\Omega}}_{\mathrm{v}}^{-1}(\mathbf{y}_t - \mathbf{z}_t\mathbf{P}') + \boldsymbol{\lambda}^{*\prime}\mathbf{\Phi}\,\mathrm{vec}\,\mathrm{d}\mathbf{P} \\ &= \mathrm{tr}[\mathbf{Z}\,\mathrm{d}\mathbf{P}'\hat{\mathbf{\Omega}}_{\mathrm{v}}^{-1}(\mathbf{Y}' - \mathbf{P}\mathbf{Z}')] + \boldsymbol{\lambda}^{*\prime}\mathbf{\Phi}\,\mathrm{vec}\,\mathrm{d}\mathbf{P} \\ &= \mathrm{tr}[\hat{\mathbf{\Omega}}_{\mathrm{v}}^{-1}(\mathbf{Y}' - \mathbf{P}\mathbf{Z}')\mathbf{Z}\,\mathrm{d}\mathbf{P}'] + \boldsymbol{\lambda}^{*\prime}\mathbf{\Phi}\,\mathrm{vec}\,\mathrm{d}\mathbf{P} \\ &= \mathrm{vec}[\hat{\mathbf{\Omega}}_{\mathrm{v}}^{-1}(\mathbf{Y}' - \mathbf{P}\mathbf{Z}')\mathbf{Z}]'\,\mathrm{vec}\,\mathrm{d}\mathbf{P} + \boldsymbol{\lambda}^{*\prime}\mathbf{\Phi}\,\mathrm{vec}\,\mathrm{d}\mathbf{P}. \end{aligned}$$

Therefore

$$\frac{\partial C}{\partial\,\mathrm{vec}\,\mathbf{P}} = \mathrm{vec}[\hat{\mathbf{\Omega}}_{\mathrm{v}}^{-1}(\mathbf{Y}' - \mathbf{P}^+\mathbf{Z}')\mathbf{Z}] + \mathbf{\Phi}'\boldsymbol{\lambda}^* = 0. \qquad (9.46)$$

This defines $\mathbf{P}^+$ as maximum of the LF at the second stage. This is equivalent to expression (9.39), but with $\hat{\mathbf{\Omega}}_{\mathrm{v}}^{-1}$ instead of $\tilde{\mathbf{\Omega}}_{\mathrm{v}}^{-1}$ and with $\mathbf{P}^+$ instead of $\tilde{\mathbf{P}}$.

By the same reasoning as for the LM test we can obtain an expression similar to (9.41) which in this case has the form

$$\boldsymbol{\phi} - \mathbf{\Phi}\,\mathrm{vec}\,\hat{\mathbf{P}} = \{\mathbf{\Phi}[\hat{\mathbf{\Omega}}_{\mathrm{v}} \otimes (\mathbf{Z}'\mathbf{Z})^{-1}]\mathbf{\Phi}'\}\boldsymbol{\lambda}^*$$

and substituting into (9.45) we obtain

$$\mathrm{W} = \boldsymbol{\lambda}^{*\prime}\{[\mathbf{\Phi}\hat{\mathbf{\Omega}}_{\mathrm{v}} \otimes (\mathbf{Z}'\mathbf{Z})^{-1}\mathbf{\Phi}']\}\boldsymbol{\lambda}^* \qquad (9.47)$$

from (9.46) in same way as before we obtain

$$\mathbf{\Phi}'\boldsymbol{\lambda}^* = [\mathbf{\Omega}_{\mathrm{v}}^{-1} \otimes (\mathbf{Z}'\mathbf{Z})\,\mathrm{vec}(\mathbf{P}^+ - \hat{\mathbf{P}})]$$

and substituting in (9.47) and doing some calculations as for the LM test we end up with

$$\mathrm{W} = T\,\mathrm{tr}[\hat{\mathbf{\Omega}}_{\mathrm{v}}^{-1}(\mathbf{\Omega}_{\mathrm{v}}^+ - \hat{\mathbf{\Omega}}_{\mathrm{v}})] \qquad (9.48)$$

where

$$\mathbf{\Omega}_{\mathrm{v}}^+ = \frac{(\mathbf{Y}' - \mathbf{P}^+\mathbf{Z}')(\mathbf{Y} - \mathbf{Z}\mathbf{P}^{+\prime})}{T}.$$

Finally, the *LR test criterion* can be written as (noticing that constant terms of both log likelihoods, constrained and unconstrained cancel)

$$T\log\det\tilde{\mathbf{\Omega}}_{\mathrm{v}} - T\log\det\hat{\mathbf{\Omega}}_{\mathrm{v}}. \qquad (9.49)$$

To prove the inequality we use expressions (9.44), (9.47) and (9.48) which are expressions of the three test statistics in terms of $\hat{\mathbf{\Omega}}_{\mathrm{v}}$, $\mathbf{\Omega}_{\mathrm{v}}^+$

and $\hat{\mathbf{\Omega}}_v$. We introduce $\mathbf{\Omega}_v^{-1/2}$ as a p.d. matrix such that $\mathbf{\Omega}_v^{-1/2}\mathbf{\Omega}_v^{-1/2} = \mathbf{\Omega}_v^{-1}$.

First let $\mathbf{L}$ be a matrix such at $\mathbf{LL}' = \mathbf{I}$ and such that it diagonalizes $\hat{\mathbf{\Omega}}_v$, i.e.

$$\mathbf{L}'\hat{\mathbf{\Omega}}_v\mathbf{L} = \mathbf{\Lambda},$$

or

$$\hat{\mathbf{\Omega}}_v = \mathbf{L\Lambda L}'$$

where $\mathbf{\Lambda}$ is a diagonal matrix.

Then define $\hat{\mathbf{\Omega}}_v^{1/2} = \mathbf{L\Lambda}^{1/2}\mathbf{L}'$ and $\hat{\mathbf{\Omega}}_v^{-1/2} = \mathbf{L\Lambda}^{-1/2}\mathbf{L}'$. Clearly $\hat{\mathbf{\Omega}}_v^{-1/2}$ is a symmetric matrix. We can define $\mathbf{D}$ by

$$\hat{\mathbf{\Omega}}_v^{-1/2}\tilde{\mathbf{\Omega}}_v\hat{\mathbf{\Omega}}_v^{-1/2} = \mathbf{I} + \mathbf{D}.$$

$\mathbf{D}$ is a symmetric matrix, and since

$$\tilde{\mathbf{\Omega}}_v - \hat{\mathbf{\Omega}}_v = (\tilde{\mathbf{P}} - \hat{\mathbf{P}})\frac{\mathbf{Z}'\mathbf{Z}}{T}(\tilde{\mathbf{P}} - \hat{\mathbf{P}})'$$

is non-n.d., $\mathbf{D} = \hat{\mathbf{\Omega}}_v^{-1/2}(\tilde{\mathbf{\Omega}}_v - \hat{\mathbf{\Omega}}_v)\hat{\mathbf{\Omega}}_v^{-1/2}$, so that D is non-n.d.

The same results are obtained by using $\mathbf{\Omega}_v^+$ instead of $\tilde{\mathbf{\Omega}}_v$ and so

$$\hat{\mathbf{\Omega}}_v^{-1/2}\mathbf{\Omega}_v^+\hat{\mathbf{\Omega}}^{-1/2} = \mathbf{I} + \mathbf{D}^+.$$

The fact that $\mathbf{D}$ and $\mathbf{D}^+$ are non-n.d. implies that all their roots are non-negative.

Now consider first the relationship between the Wald criterion (9.47) and the LR criterion (9.48).

From (9.49) the Wald test is

$$T\,\mathrm{tr}\,\hat{\mathbf{\Omega}}_v^{-1}(\mathbf{\Omega}_v^+ - \hat{\mathbf{\Omega}}_v) = T\,\mathrm{tr}\,\mathbf{D}^+ = T\sum\lambda_D^+$$

where λ_D^+ are the latent roots of $\mathbf{D}^+$.

The LR criterion (9.48) can be written as

$$\begin{aligned}\mathrm{leg}\det\tilde{\mathbf{\Omega}}_v - \log\det\hat{\mathbf{\Omega}}_v &= \log\det\tilde{\mathbf{\Omega}}_v\hat{\mathbf{\Omega}}_v^{-1}\\ &= \log\det(\mathbf{I} + \mathbf{D}) = \sum\log(1 + \lambda_D)\end{aligned}$$

where λ_D are the latent roots of $\mathbf{D}$.

Now, using the inequality $x > \log(1 + x)$ for $x > -1$, we obtain

$$T\sum\lambda_{\mathrm{D}}^{+} > T\sum\log(1+\lambda_{\mathrm{D}}^{+}) = T(\log\det\mathbf{\Omega}_{\mathrm{v}}^{+} - \log\det\hat{\mathbf{\Omega}}_{\mathrm{v}})$$

$$\geq T(\log\det\tilde{\mathbf{\Omega}}_{\mathrm{v}} - \log\det\hat{\mathbf{\Omega}}_{\mathrm{v}}).$$

The last inequality arises since the ML estimate minimizes $\log\det\mathbf{\Omega}_{\mathrm{v}}$.

Therefore

$$\mathrm{W} > \mathrm{LR}.$$

In order to prove LR > LM, we are going to use the fact that

$$\log(1+x) > \frac{x}{1+x}$$

which comes from

$$\int_0^x \frac{1}{1+z}\,\mathrm{d}z > \int_0^x \frac{1}{1+x}\,\mathrm{d}z, \quad \text{when } x > 0.$$

The LM criterion (9.44) can be written as

$$T\,\mathrm{tr}\,\tilde{\mathbf{\Omega}}_{\mathrm{v}}^{-1}(\tilde{\mathbf{\Omega}}_{\mathrm{v}} - \hat{\mathbf{\Omega}}_{\mathrm{v}}) = T\,\mathrm{tr}[(\hat{\mathbf{\Omega}}_{\mathrm{v}}^{-1}\tilde{\mathbf{\Omega}}_{\mathrm{v}})^{-1}(\hat{\mathbf{\Omega}}_{\mathrm{v}}^{-1}\tilde{\mathbf{\Omega}}_{\mathrm{v}})\hat{\mathbf{\Omega}}_{\mathrm{v}}^{-1}(\tilde{\mathbf{\Omega}}_{\mathrm{v}}^{-1} - \hat{\mathbf{\Omega}}_{\mathrm{v}}^{-1})]$$

$$= T\,\mathrm{tr}[(\mathbf{I}+\mathbf{D})^{-1}\mathbf{D}] = T\sum(1+\lambda_{\mathrm{D}})^{-1}\lambda_{\mathrm{D}}$$

$$< T\sum\log(1+\lambda_{\mathrm{D}}) = T(\log\det\tilde{\mathbf{\Omega}}_{\mathrm{v}} - \log\det\hat{\mathbf{\Omega}}_{\mathrm{v}}),$$

i.e.

$$\mathrm{LM} < \mathrm{LR}.$$

Hence we can say that in general

$$\mathrm{W} > \mathrm{LR} > \mathrm{LM}.$$

This inequality yields the possibility of a conflict among the three test procedures. Given a confidence limit, the probability of W being larger than that limit is greater than the corresponding probability of the LM. If the Wald test tells us to reject $\mathbf{H}_0$ while LM or LR tell us to accept it, the conflict cannot be solved without further information on the exact distribution of the criteria. In general we wish to use the most powerful test. The above inequality gives no information on power. The inequality order implies that for small samples letting L be the limit of confidence, if

$$\Pr(\mathrm{W} > L_{\mathrm{W}}) = p$$

and

$$\Pr(\mathrm{LR} > L_{\mathrm{LR}}) = p$$

then

$$L_{\mathrm{W}} > L_{\mathrm{LR}}$$

but says nothing about the power. Recent theoretical studies of second-order efficiency have shown that for a wide class of models for large enough samples LR is the most powerful. Some Monte Carlo studies of sample models have shown that this may not be true in sample sizes $T = 20, 50$. It is to be noted that the three criteria are often all biased upwards in the sense that the mean of the true distribution is above the mean of the asymptotic distribution, or more importantly for significance testing that the true upper 5 % limit is considerably above the corresponding asymptotic limit.

This type of result where conflict between test criteria arises (as well as experience in empirical research where we often encounter Wald test criteria which are double the corresponding LR test criteria) is not unknown. This only brings home the point that in practice asymptotic theory is a tenuous basis for economic decision making. Attempts to improve on this will, however, not be discussed here.

10

Methods of Numerical Optimization

Let us now consider the problem of maximizing the (log) likelihood function $L(\boldsymbol{\theta})$ where $\boldsymbol{\theta}$ is a $(p \times 1)$ vector of unknown parameters and $L(\cdot)$ is a continuously differentiable function. This requires solving the system of p equations from the FOCs

$$f_i(\boldsymbol{\theta}) = \frac{\partial L(\boldsymbol{\theta})}{\partial \boldsymbol{\theta}_i} = 0, \quad i = 1, \ldots, p \tag{10.1}$$

or, compactly

$$f(\boldsymbol{\theta}) = 0$$

where $f(\boldsymbol{\theta}) = [f_1(\boldsymbol{\theta}), \ldots, f_p(\boldsymbol{\theta})]'$.

Since $f(\boldsymbol{\theta})$ may be highly non-linear, the solution may often be obtained only by numerical methods.

In solving the likelihood equations $f(\boldsymbol{\theta}) = 0$ it is advisable first to 'concentrate' the likelihood function so as to reduce to the minimum possible the number of parameters to be estimated by numerical methods.

10.1 Concentrating the Likelihood Function

Let the p-dimensional parameter vector $\boldsymbol{\theta}$ be partitioned as

$$\boldsymbol{\theta} = (\boldsymbol{\theta}_1', \boldsymbol{\theta}_2')'$$

where $\boldsymbol{\theta}_1$ and $\boldsymbol{\theta}_2$ are respectively $(p_1 \times 1)$ and $(p_2 \times 1)$ subvectors, with $p_1 + p_2 = p$.

Suppose that we can find analytically the conditional maximum of $L(\boldsymbol{\theta}_1, \boldsymbol{\theta}_2)$ w.r.t. $\boldsymbol{\theta}_2$ holding $\boldsymbol{\theta}_1$ fixed. In other words, we treat $\boldsymbol{\theta}_1$ as fixed and we then maximize $L(\boldsymbol{\theta}_1, \boldsymbol{\theta}_2)$ w.r.t. $\boldsymbol{\theta}_2$. We assume that among the set of maximizers of the likelihood function w.r.t. $\boldsymbol{\theta}_2$, one of the set can be represented as a single valued function of $\boldsymbol{\theta}_1$ say $h(\boldsymbol{\theta}_1)$. This gives the concentrated likelihood function

$$L^*(\boldsymbol{\theta}_1) = L[\boldsymbol{\theta}_1, h(\boldsymbol{\theta}_1)] \tag{10.2}$$

where $h(\boldsymbol{\theta}_1)$ is a solution to the problem

$$\text{Max}_{\boldsymbol{\theta}_2} L(\boldsymbol{\theta}_1, \boldsymbol{\theta}_2) \text{ for } \boldsymbol{\theta}_1 \text{ fixed.}$$

Note that $L^*(\boldsymbol{\theta}_1)$ does not depend on the particular choice of $h(\boldsymbol{\theta}_1)$. Maximizing the concentrated likelihood function (10.1) w.r.t. $\boldsymbol{\theta}_1$ is then equivalent to maximizing the likelihood function $L(\boldsymbol{\theta})$. A simple proof by contradiction does not even require continuity in $L(\boldsymbol{\theta})$, but only the existence of some $h(\boldsymbol{\theta}_1)$ for each $\boldsymbol{\theta}_1$.

The concentrated likelihood function has all the properties of the original likelihood function. It is possible using the properties of partitioned inverse to show that the AVM of $\sqrt{T}(\tilde{\boldsymbol{\theta}}_1 - \bar{\boldsymbol{\theta}}_1)$ is equal to

$$\left[\text{plim}\left(-\frac{\partial^2 L^*}{\partial \boldsymbol{\theta}_1^2}\Big/T\right)\right]^{-1}$$

and that the test statistics of Chapter 9 can be derived from the concentrated likelihood function in the same way as they are derived from the original likelihood function.

Example 1: Consider the linear regression model

$$\mathbf{y} = \mathbf{X}\boldsymbol{\beta} + \mathbf{u}, \quad \mathbf{u} \sim \text{N}(0, \sigma^2 \mathbf{I}_T).$$

The log likelihood function is

$$L(\boldsymbol{\theta}) = -\frac{T}{2}\log 2\pi - \frac{T}{2}\log 2\sigma^2 - \frac{1}{2\sigma^2}(\mathbf{y} - \mathbf{X}\boldsymbol{\beta})'(\mathbf{y} - \mathbf{X}\boldsymbol{\beta}) \tag{10.3}$$

where $\boldsymbol{\theta} = (\boldsymbol{\beta}', \sigma^2)$. The FOC for a maximum w.r.t. σ^2 is

$$\frac{\partial L}{\partial \sigma^2} = -\frac{T}{2\tilde{\sigma}^2} + \frac{\mathbf{u}'\mathbf{u}}{2(\tilde{\sigma}^2)^2} = 0$$

from which we obtain

$$\tilde{\sigma}^2(\boldsymbol{\beta}) = \frac{\mathbf{u}'\mathbf{u}}{T}. \tag{10.4}$$

Substituting (10.4) into (10.3) gives the concentrated likelihood function

$$L^*(\boldsymbol{\beta}) = -\frac{T}{2}(\log 2\pi + 1) - \frac{T}{2}\log\frac{\mathbf{u}'\mathbf{u}}{T} \tag{10.5}$$

which can be maximized w.r.t. $\boldsymbol{\beta}$. Let $\tilde{\boldsymbol{\beta}}$ be the maximizer of the concentrated likelihood function. The ML estimator of $(\boldsymbol{\beta}', \sigma^2)'$ is therefore given by $[\tilde{\boldsymbol{\beta}}, \tilde{\sigma}^2(\tilde{\boldsymbol{\beta}})]'$.

10.2 Gradient Methods

In what follows $L(\boldsymbol{\theta})$ will denote the concentrated likelihood function assumed to be twice continuously differentiable.

A widely used class of methods of numerical optimization is based on an updating formula of the form

$$\boldsymbol{\theta}^{r+1} = \boldsymbol{\theta}^r + \lambda_r \mathbf{H}_r \mathbf{f}_r, \quad r = 0, 1, 2, \ldots$$

where $\boldsymbol{\theta}^r$ denotes the parameter estimate at the rth iteration, λ_r is a scalar number (called the step length), $\mathbf{H}_r$ is some approximation to (minus) the inverse of the Hessian matrix of the log likelihood function, i.e.

$$\mathbf{H}_r \simeq \left(-\frac{\partial^2 L}{\partial\boldsymbol{\theta}\partial\boldsymbol{\theta}'}\right)^{-1}_{\boldsymbol{\theta}^r} = \left(-\frac{\partial\mathbf{f}_r}{\partial\boldsymbol{\theta}}\right)^{-1}$$

and $\mathbf{f}_r = (\partial L/\partial\boldsymbol{\theta})_{\boldsymbol{\theta}^r}$ is the gradient vector of the likelihood function evaluated at $\boldsymbol{\theta}^r$. The vector $\mathbf{d}_r = \mathbf{H}_r\mathbf{f}_r$ represents the search direction and if $\tilde{\boldsymbol{\theta}}$ is the maximum of $L(\boldsymbol{\theta})$, then $\boldsymbol{\theta}^r \to \tilde{\boldsymbol{\theta}}$ clearly implies that $\lambda_r\mathbf{d}_r \to 0$. We want to ensure that at each step the value of the likelihood increases, i.e.

$$L(\boldsymbol{\theta}^{r+1}) > L(\boldsymbol{\theta}^r), \quad r = 0, 1, 2, \ldots$$

since this ensures stability of convergence to a maximum of the likelihood function. For this we consider a Taylor Series expansion of the likelihood function around $\boldsymbol{\theta}^r$

$$L(\boldsymbol{\theta}^{r+1}) = L(\boldsymbol{\theta}^r) + \mathbf{f}'_r\cdot(\boldsymbol{\theta}^{r+1} - \boldsymbol{\theta}^r) + O(\delta_r^2) \tag{10.6}$$

where

$$\delta_r = ||\boldsymbol{\theta}^{r+1} - \boldsymbol{\theta}^r||.$$

Substituting the update equation into (10.6) gives

$$L(\boldsymbol{\theta}^{r+1}) = L(\boldsymbol{\theta}^r) + \lambda_r \mathbf{f}'_r \mathbf{H}_r \mathbf{f}_r + O(\delta_r^2). \tag{10.7}$$

Thus if $\mathbf{H}_r$ is a p.d. matrix, $L(\boldsymbol{\theta}^{r+1}) - L(\boldsymbol{\theta}^r)$ will be positive of λ_r is chosen sufficiently small and positive so that the last term above is negligible compared with the penultimate term which is positive. The various methods in this class mainly differ in the choice of the matrix $\mathbf{H}_r$. Notice that if we are only interested in the asymptotic properties of the ML estimators, then the difference between $\boldsymbol{\theta}^r$ and the true maximum, $\widetilde{\boldsymbol{\theta}}$ is asymptotically negligible after the 1st iteration, if $\lambda_r = 1$, irrespective of the method employed, provided that $(\mathbf{H}_1 - \bar{\mathbf{H}})/T = o(1)$ asymptotically where $\bar{\mathbf{H}}$ is the Hessian at the true value $\bar{\boldsymbol{\theta}}$.

10.2.1 Newton–Raphson Method

Taking a Taylor Series expansion of the gradient vector $\mathbf{f}$ around $\boldsymbol{\theta}^r$ gives

$$\mathbf{f}(\widetilde{\boldsymbol{\theta}}) = 0 = \mathbf{f}_r + \left(\frac{\partial \mathbf{f}_r}{\partial \boldsymbol{\theta}}\right)(\widetilde{\boldsymbol{\theta}} - \boldsymbol{\theta}^r) + O(\delta_r^2) \tag{10.8}$$

where $\widetilde{\boldsymbol{\theta}}$ denotes the maximum of the likelihood function.

If $(\partial \mathbf{f}_r/\partial \boldsymbol{\theta})$ is a non-singular matrix we can solve for $\widetilde{\boldsymbol{\theta}}$ to obtain

$$\widetilde{\boldsymbol{\theta}} = \boldsymbol{\theta}^r - \left(\frac{\partial \mathbf{f}_r}{\partial \boldsymbol{\theta}}\right)^{-1} \mathbf{f}_r - O(\delta_r^2). \tag{10.9}$$

This suggests the following updating formula, which characterizes the Newton–Raphson method

$$\boldsymbol{\theta}^{r+1} = \boldsymbol{\theta}^r - \left(\frac{\partial \mathbf{f}_r}{\partial \boldsymbol{\theta}}\right)^{-1} \mathbf{f}_r. \tag{10.10}$$

Thus the Newton–Raphson method makes use of the Hessian of the likelihood function evaluated at $\boldsymbol{\theta}^r$, i.e.

$$\mathbf{H}_r = -\left(\frac{\partial \mathbf{f}_r}{\partial \boldsymbol{\theta}}\right)^{-1} = -\left(\frac{\partial^2 L}{\partial \boldsymbol{\theta} \partial \boldsymbol{\theta}'}\right)^{-1}_{\boldsymbol{\theta}^r}.$$

Furthermore the step length is a constant set equal to one.

Subtracting (10.9) from (10.10) gives

$$\boldsymbol{\theta}^{r+1} - \widetilde{\boldsymbol{\theta}} = O(||\boldsymbol{\theta}^r - \boldsymbol{\theta}||^2)$$

$$|\boldsymbol{\theta}^{r+1} - \widetilde{\boldsymbol{\theta}}| = O(||\boldsymbol{\theta}^r - \widetilde{\boldsymbol{\theta}}||^2), \tag{10.11}$$

i.e. convergence should be rapid once $\|\boldsymbol{\theta}^r - \tilde{\boldsymbol{\theta}}\|$ is small. Though attractive for its conceptual simplicity, this method suffers from several limitations:

(i) Each iteration is time consuming, particularly if the number of parameters in $\boldsymbol{\theta}$ is large since it involves the computation and inversion of the Hessian matrix of the likelihood function at each step.

(ii) The method may break down near a saddle point of the likelihood function where the Hessian matrix is close to singularity. Note that unless the iteration is started from a point in the set surounding the maximum where the Hessian matrix is n.d. throughout the set, for some r, $\boldsymbol{\theta}^r$ will cross the boundary of the set, $\mathbf{H}_r$ will be close to singularity, and $\boldsymbol{\theta}^{r+1} - \boldsymbol{\theta}^r$ will be large, and possibly such that $\boldsymbol{\theta}^{r+1}$ is far from the maximum.

(iii) The method may converge toward a minimum rather than a maximum if the Hessian matrix is p.d. rather than n.d. This problem may be serious in the early stages of the search for a maximum. It is for these reasons that we use an approximate Newton method in which $\mathbf{H}_r$ is not the inverse Hessian but a p.d. approximation to it.

10.2.2 Variable Metric Methods

In this class of methods the matrix $\mathbf{H}_r$ is chosen at each step by means of iterative formulae of the form

$$\mathbf{H}_r = \mathbf{H}_{r-1} + \alpha \mathbf{f}_{r-1}\mathbf{f}'_{r-1} + \beta \boldsymbol{\Delta}_{r-1}\boldsymbol{\Delta}'_{r-1} + \gamma(\mathbf{f}_{r-1}\boldsymbol{\Delta}'_{r-1}\boldsymbol{\Delta}_{r-1}\mathbf{f}'_{r-1}) \tag{10.12}$$

where

$$\boldsymbol{\Delta}_{r-1} = \boldsymbol{\theta}^r - \boldsymbol{\theta}^{r-1}.$$

The different methods (e.g. the algorithms devised by Davidson, Fletcher and Powell, and by Gill, Murray and Pitfield) differ in the choice of $\alpha\beta\gamma$. The aim of (10.6) is in any case twofold:

(i) It ensures that $\mathbf{H}_r$ is always a p.d. matrix.

(ii) Given a starting value of $\mathbf{H}_0$ for the iterations there is no need to compute 2nd derivative and to invert the Hessian matrix of the likelihood function at each step. $\mathbf{H}_0$ is usually chosen to be the unit matrix. As $r \to \infty$ the sequence of matrices $\{\mathbf{H}_r\}$ converges to (minus) the inverse of the Hessian of the likelihood function evaluated at the maximum $\tilde{\boldsymbol{\theta}}$.

The 1st derivatives of the likelihood function may be evaluated numerically by the 1st differences

$$\left(\frac{\partial L}{\partial \boldsymbol{\theta}_i}\right)_{\boldsymbol{\theta}^r} \simeq \frac{L(\boldsymbol{\theta}^r + \delta \mathbf{h}_i) - L(\boldsymbol{\theta}^r - \delta \mathbf{h}_i)}{2\delta}$$

where $\mathbf{h}_i$ is a unit vector with 1 in the ith position and zero elsewhere and δ is a sufficiently small number chosen by taking into account the risk of rounding errors. The step length λ_r is usually chosen at each iteration by means of a line search so as to maximise the value of the likelihood function in the direction $\mathbf{H}_r\mathbf{f}_r$. In other words, given $\boldsymbol{\theta}^r$ and $\mathbf{H}_r$, λ_r is chosen to solve

$$\text{Max}_\lambda L(\lambda) = L(\boldsymbol{\theta}^r + \lambda \mathbf{H}_r \mathbf{f}_r).$$

However a crude line search method may be used, designed only to ensure that L^r is increasing in r, since there is no great value in spending much time in such searches at an early stage in the iteration, and at a late stage it may not be necessary.

10.2.3 Gauss–Newton Method

The method exploits the properties of the likelihood function. Whereas minus the Hessian matrix of the likelihood function is not necessarily a p.d. matrix, its expectation (the information matrix) for $\boldsymbol{\theta} = \bar{\boldsymbol{\theta}}$ is a p.d. matrix for

$$\mathrm{E}\left(-\frac{\partial^2 L}{\partial \boldsymbol{\theta} \partial \boldsymbol{\theta}'}\right)_{\bar{\boldsymbol{\theta}}} = \mathrm{E}\left[\left(\frac{\partial L}{\partial \boldsymbol{\theta}}\right)\left(\frac{\partial L}{\partial \boldsymbol{\theta}'}\right)\right]_{\bar{\boldsymbol{\theta}}}. \tag{10.13}$$

If we start our iteration from a consistent estimate of $\bar{\boldsymbol{\theta}}$, then we can write

$$-\left[\frac{1}{T}\frac{\partial^2 L}{\partial \boldsymbol{\theta} \partial \boldsymbol{\theta}'}\right]_{\boldsymbol{\theta}^r} = \mathbf{V}_1 + \mathbf{V}_2$$

where $\mathbf{V}_2 = \mathrm{O}(1/\sqrt{T})$ and $\mathbf{V}_1$ is the p.d. matrix which corresponds to the right-hand side of equation (10.13).

This suggests using

$$\mathbf{H}_r = (\mathbf{V}_1)^{-1}$$

where $\mathbf{V}_1$ is evaluated at $\boldsymbol{\theta}^r$ which defines the Gauss–Newton iteration. The advantages of this method are that $\mathbf{V}_1$ is always p.d.

and usually has a simpler form and is easier to compute than the Hessian of the likelihood function.

10.3 Method of Alternating Maximization

Consider the likelihood function $L(\boldsymbol{\theta}_1, \boldsymbol{\theta}_2)$ and an initial set of parameter estimates say $(\boldsymbol{\theta}_1^r, \boldsymbol{\theta}_2^r)$. We may search for a maximum of the likelihood function by proceeding as follows:

We first choose $\boldsymbol{\theta}_2^{r+1}$ to solve

$$\text{Max}_{\boldsymbol{\theta}_2} L(\boldsymbol{\theta}_1^r, \boldsymbol{\theta}_2).$$

We then choose $\boldsymbol{\theta}_1^{r+1}$ to solve

$$\text{Max}_{\boldsymbol{\theta}_1} L(\boldsymbol{\theta}_1, \boldsymbol{\theta}_2^{r+1}).$$

Given the new set of parameter estimates, $(\boldsymbol{\theta}_1^{r+1}, \boldsymbol{\theta}_2^{r+1})$ we repeat the procedure to obtain $(\boldsymbol{\theta}_1^{r+2}, \boldsymbol{\theta}_2^{r+2})$ and so on until convergence. This method (often called the Cochrane–Orcutt iterative procedure) involves sets of successive maximizations w.r.t. one subset of parameters holding constant the value of all the others.

The procedure can be generalized by maximizing separately w.r.t. more than two sets of parameters. The case where each parameter is optimized separately is equivalent to the Gauss–Seidel method of solving systems of simultaneous equations.

Suppose that we write $\boldsymbol{\theta} = (\boldsymbol{\theta}_i^*, \boldsymbol{\theta}_i, \boldsymbol{\theta}_i^{**})$ where $\boldsymbol{\theta}_i^*$ are the set of parameters $\boldsymbol{\theta}_j$, $j < i$, and $\boldsymbol{\theta}_i^{**}$ are the set of parameters $\boldsymbol{\theta}_j$, $j > i$, and $\mathbf{f}_i(\boldsymbol{\theta}) = \mathbf{f}_i(\boldsymbol{\theta}_i^*, \boldsymbol{\theta}_i, \boldsymbol{\theta}_i^{**})$ for the ith equation in some set of equations. Then the iterative Gauss–Seidel procedure is to solve

$$\mathbf{f}_i(\boldsymbol{\theta}_i^{*r+1}, \boldsymbol{\theta}_i^{r+1}, \boldsymbol{\theta}_i^{**(r)}) = 0$$

for $\boldsymbol{\theta}_i^{(r+1)}$. This is done for $i = 1, \ldots, p$.

Clearly, (10.1) can be interpreted as the system of equations emerging from the FOCs for a maximum of the likelihood function. The advantages of this method are that it does not involve 2nd derivatives and may in some cases lead to relatively simple formulae. The method works very well for likelihood functions which have roughly circular contours. However, it is rather time-consuming if the likelihood function has contours of the form shown in Figure 10.1. In this case gradient methods are generally better since they approximate the likelihood contours by ellipses.

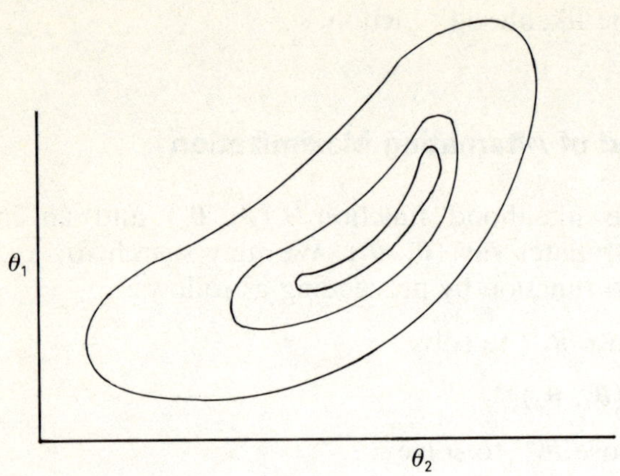

Figure 10.1

10.4 Conjugate Direction Methods

This class of method is based on a non-singular transformation of the parameter vector $\boldsymbol{\theta}$

$$\boldsymbol{\phi} = \mathbf{H}\boldsymbol{\theta}$$

subject to the likelihood function being approximated by a quadratic function

$$L(\boldsymbol{\theta}) \simeq (\boldsymbol{\phi} - \bar{\boldsymbol{\phi}})'\mathbf{D}(\boldsymbol{\phi} - \bar{\boldsymbol{\phi}})$$

where $\mathbf{D}$ is a positive diagonal matrix.

If the approximation is exact, i.e. the likelihood function is indeed quadratic, then we will get the maximum after a complete set of p minimizations w.r.t. the elements of $\boldsymbol{\phi}$.

A typical member of this class is Powell's method (1964). Let $\boldsymbol{\theta}^r = \mathbf{H}_r^{-1}\phi_r$, where $\mathbf{H}_r^{-1} = (\mathbf{h}_1^r, \ldots \mathbf{h}_p^r)$ is the set of search directions at the rth iteration.

A simplified version of the algorithm consists of the following three steps:

(i) Make a line search in each of the p current directions $(\mathbf{h}_1^r, \ldots \mathbf{h}_p^r)$, and a line search again in the direction of $\mathbf{h}_1^r$. This gives $\boldsymbol{\theta}_0^{r+1}$.

(ii) Define $\mathbf{h}_p^{r+1}$ proportional to $\boldsymbol{\theta}_0^{r+1} - \boldsymbol{\theta}_1^r$.

(iii) Construct a new set of search directions by retaining $\mathbf{h}_i^{r+1} = \mathbf{h}_{(i-1)}^r$, $i = 2, \ldots, p$.

The entire process is then iterated starting from (i). It can be shown that the set of directions generated in the case of a quadratic criterion function is $\mathbf{\Phi}$ conjugate after p iterations, i.e.

$$\mathbf{h}_1^{p\prime}\mathbf{\Phi}\mathbf{h}_j^p = 0$$

where $\mathbf{\Phi}$ is the Hessian matrix and

$$L(\boldsymbol{\theta}) = \tfrac{1}{2}(\boldsymbol{\theta} - \bar{\boldsymbol{\theta}})'\mathbf{\Phi}(\boldsymbol{\theta} - \bar{\boldsymbol{\theta}}).$$

In particular, the direction of total progress, $\boldsymbol{\theta}_0^{r+1} - \boldsymbol{\theta}_1^r$, is $\mathbf{\Phi}$ conjugate to all previous line search directions. After p iterations, a further p line search should give the maximum of the function. Powell recommends a more complex algorithm which when applied to a general non-quadratic function is less likely to lead to an $\mathbf{H}$ matrix which is close to singularity. In practice it has been found that convergence may be slow and uncertain when the number of parameters is over 20, and that the use of the Murray–Pitfield non-derivative optimization program included in the NAG library may be a preferable option.

10.5 General Conclusions

Although specialist optimization methods based on Newton–Raphson or Gauss–Newton methods have frequently been used in estimation programs based on optimizing suitable statistical criteria, there is little evidence that these are more efficient in terms of convergence time than the use of a suitable variable-metric algorithm such as the Murray–Pitfield. They are certainly more expensive in terms of the human investment in initially writing and debugging the computer program. The balance of advantage is very model-dependent, favouring the specialised program (assuming that this gives efficiency gains) for large and complex models which will be used intensively many times.

References and Bibliography

Chapter 1

Anderson, T. (1972). *The Statistical Analysis of Time Series*. Wiley, New York.

Cramer, H. (1946). *Mathematical Methods of Statistics*. Princeton University Press, Princeton, N.J.

Frydman, R. (1980). A Proof of the Consistency of Maximum Likelihood Estimators of Nonlinear Regression Models with Autocorrelated Errors, *Econometrica*, vol. 48, 853–60.

Fuller, W. A. (1976). *Introduction to Statistical Time Series*. Wiley, New York.

Hannan, E. (1970). *Multiple Time Series*. Wiley, New York.

Jennrich, R. I. (1969). Asymptotic Properties of Non-Linear Least Squares Estimators, *Ann. Math. Stat.*, vol. 40, 633–43.

Mann, H. B. and Wald, A. (1943a). On the Statistical Treatment of Stochastic Difference Equations, *Econometrica*, vol. 11, 173–220.

—— (1943b). On Stochastic Limit and Order Relationships, *Ann. Math. Stat.*, vol. 14, 217–77.

Rao, C. R. (1973). *Linear Statistical Inference and its Applications*. Wiley, New York.

Schonfeld, E. (1971). A Useful Central Limit Theorem for m-dependent Variables, *Metrika*, vol. 15, 116–28.

Chapter 2

Neudecker, H. and Magnus, J. R. (1979). The Commutation Matrix, *Ann. Stat.*, vol. 7, 381–94.

Rao, C. R. (1973). *Linear Statistical Inference and its Applications*. Wiley, New York.

Theil, H. (1971). *Principles of Econometrics*. Wiley, New York.

Chapter 3

Chow, G. C. (1974). Identification and Estimation in Econometric Systems - a Survey, *IEEE Transactions Auto. Cont.*, vol. 19, 119–34.

Fisher, F. M. (1966) *The Identification Problem in Econometrics*. McGraw Hill, New York.

Chapter 4

Cochrane, D. and Orcutt G. H. (1949). Application of Least Squares Regression to Relationships Containing Autocorrelated Error Terms, *J. Am. Stat. Ass.*, vol. 44, 32–61.

Cragg, J. G. (1982). Estimation and Testing in Time Series Regression Models with Heteroskedastic Distributions, *J. Econometr.*, vol. 20, 135–57.

Harvey, A. C. (1981). *Time Series Models*. Philip Allan, Deddington, Oxfordshire.

Magnus, J. R. (1978). Maximum Likelihood Estimation of the GLS Model with Unknown Parameters in the Disturbance Covariance Matrix, *J. Econometr.*, vol. 7, 281–312.

Theil, H. (1971). *Principles of Econometrics*. Wiley, New York.

Chapter 5

Brundy, J. and Jorgenson, D. W. (1971). Efficient Estimation of Simultaneous Equation Systems using Instrumental Variables, *R. Econ. Stat.*, vol. 53, 207–24.

Sargan, J. D. (1958). The Estimation of Economic Relationships using Instrumental Variables, *Econometrica*, vol. 26, 393–415.

—— (1959). The Estimation of Relationships with Autocorrelated Residuals by the Use of Instrumental Variables, *J. R. Stat. Soc.*, series B, vol. 21, 91–105.

Chapter 6

Cramer, H. (1946). *Mathematical Methods of Statistics.* Princeton University Press, Princeton, N.J.

Rothenberg, T. J. and Leenders C. T. (1964). Efficient Estimation of Simultaneous Equations Systems, *Econometrica*, vol. 32, 57–76.

Schmidt, P. (1976). *Econometrica*. Marcel Dekker, New York.

Zellner, A. and Theil, H. (1962). Three Stage Least Squares Simultaneous Estimation of Simultaneous Equations, *Econometrica*, vol. 30, 53–78.

Chapter 7

Berndt, E. R., Hall, B., Hall, R. E. and Hausman, J. A. (1974). Estimation and Inference in Non-Linear Structural Models, *Ann. Econ. Soc. Meas.*, vol. 3, 653–65.

Dhrymes, P. J. (1973). Restricted and Unrestricted Reduced Forms, *Econometrica*, vol. 41, 119–26.

Hausman, J. A. (1975). An Instrumental Variable Approach to Full Information Estimators for Linear and Certain Nonlinear Econometric Models. *Econometrica*, vol. 43, 728–38.

Hendry, D. F. (1976). The Structure of Simultaneous Equation Estimators, *J. Econometr.*, vol. 4, 51–68.

Hood, W. C. and Koopmans, T. C. (eds) (1953). *Studies in Econometric Methods*, Wiley, New York.

Sargan, J. D. (1961). The Maximum Likelihood Estimation of Economic Relationships with Autoregressive Residuals, *Econometrica*, vol. 29, 414–26.

Chapter 8

Hood, W. C. and Koopmans, T. C. (eds) (1953). *Studies in Econometric Methods*. Wiley, New York.

Sargan, J. D. (1958). The Estimation of Econometric Relationships using Instrumental Variables, *Econometrica*, vol. 26, 393–415.

—— (1959). The Estimation of Relationships with Autocorrelated Residuals by the Use of Instrumental Variables, *J. R. Stat. Soc.*, series B, vol. 21, 91–105.

—— (1980). Some Tests of Dynamic Specification for a Single Equation, *Econometrica*, vol. 48, 879–97.

Chapter 9

Berndt, E. R. and Savin, N. E. (1977). Conflict among Criteria for Testing Hypotheses in the Multivariate Regression Model, *Econometrica*, vol. 45. 1263–78.

Breusch, T. S.and Pagan, A. R. (1980). The Lagrange Multiplier Test and its Application to Model Specifications in Econometrics, *Rev. Econ. St.*, vol. 47, 239–53.

Sargan, J. D. (1980). Some Tests of Dynamic Specification for a Single Equation, *Econometrica*, vol. 48, 879–97.

Silvey, S. D. (1959). The Lagrange Multiplier Test, *Ann. Math. Stat.*, vol. 30, 389–407.

Wald, A. (1943). Tests of Statistical Hypotheses concerning Several Parameters when the Number of Observations is Large, *Trans. Am. Math. Soc.*, vol. 54, 426–82.

Chapter 10

Gill, P. E., Murray, W. and Pitfield, R. A. (1972). The Implementation of Two Revised Quasi Newton Algorithms for Unconstrained Optimisation, *Nat. Phys. Lab. Rep.*, NAC 11.

Goldfeld, E. M. and Quandt, R. E. (1972). *Non-Linear Methods in Econometrics*, North Holland, Amsterdam.

Powell, M. J. D. (1964). An Efficient Method of Finding the Minimum of a Function of Several Variables without Calculating Derivatives, *Comput. J.*, vol. 7, 155–62.

Index